Queerly Faithful: Queer People's Experience of Religion in Asylum

BY

CLAIRE FLETCHER

Oxford Brookes University, UK

emerald PUBLISHING

United Kingdom – North America – Japan – India – Malaysia – China

Emerald Publishing Limited
Emerald Publishing, Floor 5, Northspring, 21-23 Wellington Street, Leeds LS1 4DL.

First edition 2026

British Library Cataloguing in Publication Data
A catalog record for this book is available from the British Library

ISBN: 978-1-83797-491-7 (Print)
ISBN: 978-1-83797-488-7 (Online)
ISBN: 978-1-83797-490-0 (Epub)

INVESTOR IN PEOPLE

Queerly Faithful

This book is dedicated to the countless people who gave me their time, truth and trust. I feel immensely privileged that you shared with me your reflections, thoughts and stories. In solidarity now and always.

Contents

About the Author

Claire Fletcher is a Visiting Fellow at Oxford Brookes University and an Academic Consultant. She specialises in the UK asylum system and the experiences of LGBTQI+ people. She currently works as a policy manager specialising in asylum, with a focus on asylum support and safe housing for LGBTQI+ people seeking asylum and refugees. Claire has worked and volunteered at a range of different charities working with refugees and people seeking asylum that include Rainbow Migration, British Red Cross and the Refugee Council.

Acknowledgements

I would especially like to thank Professor Elena Fiddian-Qasmiyeh; it was a great privilege to have you as my primary supervisor during my PhD where the research presented in this book is from. Your willingness to guide, advise and support was endless, and I cannot ever express the depth of my gratitude.

Thank you also to Dr Tatiana Thieme, for your thoughtful comments and insight which pushed me to consider different angles. Thank you also to Dr Alex Powell, Dr Diego Garcia Rodriguez and Dr Carlo Giametta for reading earlier chapter drafts and making helpful suggestion to improve the chapters. Any errors or admissions in this work are mine alone.

To my wife Anna, and son Charlie, thank you for your endless support and help, which gave me the time and space to complete this book.

This work was supported by Economic Social Research Council who funded this research (grant number ES/J500185/1).

Introduction*

Religion is often positioned as a root cause of the persecution and displacement of LGBTQI+[1] people from their countries of origin (CoO) (Duffy Toft, 2012; Nawyn, 2006), creating a need for LGBTQI+ people to seek sanctuary in countries other than their own (Alessi et al., 2021). Further understanding is needed at the intersection of religion and sexuality in the context of claiming asylum, especially as religious beliefs and experiences are used against LGBTQI+ people within refugee status determination (RSD) to refuse protection (Danisi et al., 2021). Therefore, this book aims to provide a more nuanced interpretation of the role that religion plays in queer lives as a counter to the simplistic assumptions that religion is solely a persecutory and oppressive force in the lives of LGBTQI+ people.

In this book, I consider two key areas; the first explores the significance and complexity of religious experience in the lives of LGBTQI+ people seeking asylum, both within CoO and the UK. The second, using the UK as a case study, highlights the distinct barriers faced by LGBTQI+ people seeking protection and examines how intersecting social factors – using religious experience – have implications within the formal RSD process. By doing so, the intention is to show both the complex reasons why LGBTQI+ people continue to engage in religious communities, including homonegative[2] ones, and how this engagement can have negative impacts for claiming asylum on sexual orientation (SO) grounds.

* This chapter was developed using material from the thesis: Fletcher, Claire; (2024) Queerly Faithful: The experiences of religion for those seeking asylum in the UK. Doctoral thesis (Ph.D), UCL (University College London).

[1] Lesbian, gay, bisexual, trans, queer, intersex and the plus are used to indicate this list is not exhaustive and that there are a wide range of queer subjectivities which are not reflected within this acronym.

[2] Shidlo (1994) argues the term 'homophobia' refers more directly to an individual fear and/or disgust of LGBTQI+ people. Homonegativity was conceptualised to consider wider, negative attitudes towards LGBTQI+ people that were grounded in cultural and social norms (Herek, 1991, 2004). In this book, the terms homonegative or homonegativity should be understood to mean wider societal attitudes that

Queerly Faithful: Queer People's Experience of Religion in Asylum Seeking, 1–10

doi:10.1108/978-1-83797-488-720261002

For LGBTQI+ people, encounters with religious communities can intensify stigma, creating a fear of disclosure or risk of discrimination within the asylum system. At the same time, religious beliefs and religious communities can serve as significant sources of emotional support, practical assistance and community belonging. The dual role of religious communities is especially important given the limited and often fragmented avenues of support available to LGBTQI+ individuals navigating the UK asylum process. As an introduction to these tensions, I summarise one interlocutor's experiences. While her case is not unique, it serves to illustrate the tensions and conflicts that can emerge for LGBTQI+ people at the intersection of religious experiences, queer subjectivity and the UK asylum process.

I met Desire, a lesbian woman from West Africa, in 2020. Desire fled from her CoO after her husband discovered her in bed with another woman. After surviving a brutal attack by her husband, Desire was forced into hiding. Her husband made it known in her community that he would kill her if he found her again. Desire had no family to rely on, as she had previously been accused of 'lesbianism' at university, which had been reported to her family. Her father, a religious community leader, saw her as an 'abomination' and a 'sinner' and regularly beat her following this accusation. Desire had married her husband as a means of survival as the marriage not only hid her sexuality from her wider community but also provided an avenue of escape from the violence she experienced within her family home. However, after her husband's discovery of her sexuality, leaving her CoO was her only option as same-sex relationships are illegal in Desire's country and, therefore, she had no hope of protection from the state in the face of her husband's death threats.

Arriving in the UK with little money, Desire found shelter, accommodation and support within a Baptist church. She did not claim asylum, as she was completely unaware of her ability to claim based on her sexuality. Desire's previous experiences with 'religion' and religious communities in her CoO had contributed to her belief that her sexuality as a lesbian woman made her a 'sinner' and she had been rejected by God. She believed to maintain the support of the community it was necessary to hide her sexuality, saying: 'I couldn't come out and say that I'm a lesbian. I couldn't. Because it's an African church and I was so scared of what could happen'. Instead, Desire presented herself as a victim of domestic violence as the reason she had been forced to flee her CoO.

Part of the support she received from the community was advice and information about the asylum process in the UK, with one woman within the church congregation providing Desire with advice on how to claim. The church even helped Desire with the necessary funds to travel to Lunar House, the Asylum Intake Unit (AIU) in Croydon, London, to claim asylum. At her screening interview, Desire disclosed to the Home Office that her asylum claim was based on her SO. Desire thought that by claiming asylum, she would be offered protection, but instead she

---

attempt to condemn, devalue and marginalise the lives of LGBTQI+ people, for example, religious norms that frame LGBTQI+ people as sinful (Mayfield, 2001, Herny et al., 2026).

found herself handcuffed, detained and sent to Yarl's Wood Immigration Removals Centre (IRC). Desire was terrified and could not understand why she was being treated as a criminal.

Desire was only released from Yarl's Wood IRC with the intervention of a charity. Initially placed in asylum accommodation at a hostel, she was forced to share a room with numerous strangers. Subsequently, she was dispersed to a completely different part of the UK and moved into a shared house. In both these places, fearing the reaction and further violence from the other residents if they discovered she was a lesbian, Desire felt compelled to keep her sexuality a secret for her safety. While in asylum accommodation, she was repeatedly moved to different housing across the UK, constantly disrupting the limited support networks she managed to establish in each location.

During these displacements, Desire often relied on religious communities for material and emotional support, especially at times of extreme stress. However, on receiving her first refusal for her asylum claim, the Home Office had found her not to be a 'credible' lesbian. The refusal reasoning cited Desire's ongoing religious beliefs and involvement with religious communities since arriving in the UK, as one of the reasons for doubting the creditability of her asylum claim on the grounds of SO. The decision makers assumed that Desire's religious experiences, both in her CoO and in the UK, were purely homonegative. This refusal was the first of many, and Desire waited six years before it was finally accepted by the Home Office that she was a lesbian woman.

While seeking asylum, Desire moved between legal and illegal immigration statuses, during periods of irregularity Desire had her asylum support stopped. Her irregular immigration status prevented her from accessing any other form of statutory funds, leading to Desire becoming street homeless, sleeping in shop fronts and searching in bins for food to survive. The only support Desire could find was in informal spaces, such as religious communities. The inability to access any formal support exposed Desire to exploitation and harm and forced her to seek help from strangers, which resulted in experiences of exploitative working and a serious sexual assault.

Currently, there is a gap in academic knowledge on how social factors and experiences, such as informal support spaces, can have direct implications for LGBTQI+ people seeking protection. Dustin and Held (2021, p. 208) identified this gap and argue that it is important to consider the 'legal *and* the social experiences of SOGI (sexual orientation and gender identity) claimants, as they impact on each other'. In their research, they identified how religious experiences could create a barrier for SOGI claimants from making strong asylum claims. An example of this, seen in Desire's vignette above, is how seeking support within religious communities or maintaining religious beliefs can cast doubts on the authenticity of a person's stated SO. Dustin and Held argue that to ensure a just asylum system there is a greater need to understand exactly how and why social experience can negatively affect a person's asylum claim.

The Research

The genesis of this research started in 2018, when I began working in a third sector organisation that provided practical, legal, and emotional support to

LGBTQI+ people seeking asylum in the UK. Having volunteered at previous NGOs that provided a generalised service for people seeking asylum and refugees, I had regularly signposted people to religiously inspired organisations and communities for support. However, assisting LGBTQI+ people caused a reassessment of this, as LGBTQI+ people often wanted to avoid assistance from religious groups and organisations.

After reading numerous asylum refusal letters of people who had claimed on SO grounds, it was also apparent that for LGBTQI+ people who had stated a religious belief or maintained connections to religious communities, and disclosed this within their asylum claim, were met with suspicion by asylum decision makers. This could be seen within the reasons for refusals, with questions raised about the plausibility of why a 'genuine' LGBTQI+ person would continue to practice or believe in a religious tradition that held conservative and/or homonegative attitudes towards LGBTQI+ people.

However, in direct contrast to the assumptions in decision letters, I regularly had conversations with LGBTQI+ people whose religiosity remained deeply important to their sense of self. These discussions revealed how religious experiences at various stages of people's lives had both positive and negative influences. While previous religious encounters had led some people to actively reject any form of religiosity and religious spaces, others revealed different ways they remained engaged with religious communities, even ones that were homonegative.

These complex experiences demonstrate how a rejection of religion by LGBTQI+ people should not be assumed, even when, from the outside, it can seem to be at odds with their sexual and gender diversity. These evident tensions are at the core of the questions that led to the research, mainly: *How do those with queer subjectivities experience religion before, and after arrival into the UK to claim asylum? How does the legal asylum process intersect with the social experiences of queer people seeking asylum, and what is the place of religious experience within this?*

Religious experiences, regardless of individuals' motivation to engage with religion, can have negative implications for a person claiming asylum on SO grounds. Previous scholarship identifies that this is due to a presumption of the improbability of a 'queer religious subjectivity' (Giametta, 2014, p. 584), as historically, in Western liberal democracies, 'queer' and 'religion' have been positioned as 'uneasy bedfellows' (Scherer, 2017). As a result, people who identify as both queer and religious or maintain connections to religious communities are viewed as unbelievable by asylum decision makers, and this implausibility undermines a person's credibility within their asylum claim (Fiddian-Qasmiyeh, 2016). This positioning within the asylum decision making frameworks creates a tension for LGBTQI+ people whose religiosity remains important to them. Or for those who need support or wish to seek comfort within religious spaces and communities, especially within the context of hostile RSD processes.

In the UK context, this is particularly problematic in the face of rising destitution among asylum seeking and refugee communities (Ramachandran, 2024). A recent report by the All-Party Parliamentary Groups on Poverty and Migration revealed how even people seeking asylum and who have access to formal asylum support 'are living in deep poverty and many in destitution' (APPG Migration and Poverty, 2024, p. 9). Situations of destitution and poverty force people in the asylum process to become 'entirely reliant on the provision of emergency support by charities, religious groups and local communities' (*ibid*, p. 15). In this context, LGBTQI+ people are exposed to a heightened risk of becoming destitute due to the limited spaces in which they can seek support (Danisi et al., 2021). However, decision makers often ignore (maybe wilfully so) the influence social factors can have on a person's decision making and which social spaces they occupy. A common example relevant to this research is a person continuing to engage with a homonegative religious community as part of a destitution alleviation strategy (Wheeler, 2021).

Until recently, the consideration of how religious experiences featured in the context of LGBTQI+ people seeking asylum was relatively under explored in academic scholarship (cf: Giametta, 2014; Peumans, 2014). However, a small and burgeoning body of work considers the intersection of queer subjectivity and religiosity in the context of displacement (Peumans, 2018; Giametta, 2017; Dustin and Held, 2021; Fletcher, 2024; García Rodríguez, 2023, 2025; Greatrick, 2022).

This research confronts the preconception that religion and queer subject positions are incompatible. Although scholarship increasingly challenges the perceived incongruity of LGBTQI+ individuals seeking support in religious spaces (e.g. see Greatrick, 2022; Powell, 2024), this remains an understudied area. Crucially, gaps remain in how the Home Office's own policy frameworks force people seeking asylum to look elsewhere to sustain themselves within the system. Yet, seeking support in religious communities can often create a catch-22 situation for individuals, as this experience can create a variety of barriers which negatively impact credibility assessments by asylum decision makers. This type of stereotypical assumption by asylum decision makers ignores the wealth of support found within religious communities that is accessed by LGBTQI+ people, assumptions that position 'religion' as only an oppressive, controlling and punitive mechanism in the lives of LGBTQI+ people have led to a failure to consider the emancipatory potential of religion in the provision of support for LGBTQI+ people in the asylum system.

Book Structure

The central aim of this book is to provide an empirical intervention to challenge the preconceived notion prevalent in the asylum system in the UK that religious and queer subject positions are incompatible. The chapters in this book provide an illustration of how intrinsic religious experience can be for LGBTQI+ people who are often from countries where religion is highly influential and part of the very fabric of society.

Chapter 1 discusses the influence religious experiences can have on how LGBTQI+ people come to understand their sexual and gender diversity. The purpose of this chapter is to demonstrate the centrality of religious experience for many LGBTQI+ people in CoO contexts and to question presumptions about the ease with which religiosity can be dismissed, even for those who have experienced religiously inspired harm. The chapter demonstrates how religious experiences are not only complicit in negative constructions of sexually and gender diverse people, both in terms of a person's own self-understanding and more widely held societal beliefs about LGBTQI+ people. However, interlocutors in this research, also drew on religion for support in multifaceted ways in relation to their queer subjectivities. Interlocutors' narratives contest expectations of solely homonegative CoO religious experiences where the only option for establishing queer lives is to leave.

Chapter 2 shifts focus to the current UK context of seeking asylum on SO grounds. The aim of the chapter is to explore how the design of the current formal asylum support system presents specific obstacles for LGBTQI+ people, in terms of accessing support safely and increasing experiences of marginalisation and isolation. Additionally, due to gaps in formal support at particular junctures, LGBTQI+ people are forced to seek assistance in informal spaces, exposing them to an increased likelihood of maltreatment. In both contexts, LGBTQI+ people can feel compelled to hide their queer subjectivity, even though they are in a 'safe' country.

Chapter 3 turns to exploring reasons behind why LGBTQI+ people who arrive in the UK in search of safety avoid the formal asylum process and instead seek assistance within informal communities. The aim of this chapter is to bring attention to the social experiences of LGBTQI+ people who seek asylum in the UK, to increase understanding of the various complex reasons why individuals choose to keep their queer subjectivity hidden, even after arrival in a 'safe' country. This is particularly important as decision makers expect that LGBTQI+ people will live openly once they are in the UK. Chapter 4 attends to how social experiences appear within asylum decision making. The focus of the chapter demonstrates how social factors and experiences call into question the authenticity of asylum claims made on SO grounds and prevent people from being able to acquire expected objective evidence. By attending closely to these lived tensions, this book asks what is lost when religion is read only as evidence against queerness, rather than as part of how people endure experiences of displacement.

Chapters 5 and 6 switch focus from how religious experiences can become a liability for LGBTQI+ people by casting doubt on the authenticity of their SO, to how religious encounters can be a source of sustained support and healing. The final two chapters explore how religious experience can be part of the solution to redress the religiously inspired harms that LGBTQI+ people have faced. The focus of Chapter 5 is how interlocutors draw on religious experiences and encounters to move away from negative understandings of their own queer subjectivity. Evidence presented in chapter 5 illustrates the benefit of religiously literate responses to address previous incidents of harm that are grounded and motivated by religion.

Chapter 6 discusses the diversity of support found in both non- and queer affirming local faith communities (LFCs). While these spaces can provide sustained solidarity, especially considering the capacity issues in terms of the levels of support provided to LGBTQI+ people in the asylum system, support provided by LFCs can require complex negotiations for LGBTQI+ people to access. As a whole, this book provides empirical examples of how LGBTQI+ people who continue to engage with religious communities do so for a wide range of reasons and individual religiosity. In conclusion, it can be seen that religious experience for LGBTQI+ people is a source of both oppression *and* solidarity.

Methodological Considerations

The research presented in this book is grounded within a critical theoretical framework drawing particularly on two central tenets of critical theory: the problematisation of knowledge and a commitment to situating marginalised individuals and their experiences at the heart of the research inquiry (Swaminathan and Mulvihill, 2017). The data drawn on for this book is from my PhD research and stems from a series of narrative portraits of the experiences of 24 LGBTQI+ individuals who have encountered the asylum process in the UK. The narrative vignettes and quotations are based on 44 life history interviews that I conducted between 2020 and 2022. Life histories were chosen to centralise the voices of interlocutors, prioritising their telling of events and experiences that were significant to them, which allowed for the larger and more complex stories to emerge (Giametta, 2014).

In terms of the interlocutors who participated, 15 identified as cis-men and eight identified as cis-female, with one interlocutor identifying as non-binary. Thirteen people self-identified as gay, eight as lesbian and three as bisexual, although it should be noted that people could vary their terminology regarding their queer subjectivity throughout their narrative. All interlocutors were at various stages of the asylum process, from awaiting their initial asylum decisions through to being in the process of making further submissions to the Home Office for a fresh asylum claim.

The religious self-identity of the interlocutors was Catholic (5), Catholic and Anglican (1), Christian (3), Muslim (7), Pentecostal Christian (1), Muslim and Christian (2), 7th Day Adventist (1), Baptist (1), Jewish (1), no religious affiliation (2). Several interlocutors identified with more than one religious tradition or had converted to a different religious tradition by the time of our conversations. Individuals came from a wide range of geographical contexts, including Central America; South, Central, and West Asia; Central, East and West Africa. The aim of this book is not to provide a representative picture of 'the experience of religious LGBTQI+ people'. This does not exist; but by presenting a wide range of experiences, it is evident how complex the intersection of religious and queer subject positions can be, and how unrealistic a sole narrative trope of queer and religious incompatibility is.

Alongside the interviews with LGBTQI+ people, I conducted 34 semi-structured interviews with practitioners from NGOs, community groups and individual faith-based practitioners who were involved with a variety of responses to LGBTQI+ people in the UK asylum process. The term legal practitioner is used throughout the research to refer to individuals who have legal training and work in the legal profession in some capacity with LGBTQI+ people claiming asylum on SO grounds. Professions included solicitors, barristers and judges.

All interlocutors in this book are anonymous, while several individuals stated a preference to be named; it became clear in the analysis that the identification of even a minority of individuals would place other people who wished to remain anonymous at risk of having their identities discovered. Therefore, all interlocutors have been given a pseudonym to protect their identity. In addition, to ensure interlocutors' anonymity, it was necessary to give a broad geographical area rather than identify a person's CoO. This was also the case where locations were mentioned in the UK, and the names of specific organisations and community groups have not been used.

Key Terms

To imply that there are a set of behaviours, beliefs, identities or a set of principles which can be confined and defined within the term 'religion' is misleading. The conceptual definition of 'religion' has been heavily contested in academic scholarship and, as Asad (1993, p. 37) famously argued, 'there cannot be a universal definition of religion, not only because its constituent elements and relationships are historically specific, but because that definition is itself the historical product of discursive processes'.

It is not possible to employ 'religion' to define a firmly categorised and singular experience (Wilson and Mavelli, 2016). Any attempt to do so homogenises the sheer diversity of global religious experience, created through various and overlapping contextual, historical, geographical and discursive factors. Religions in all their guises remain constantly and ever evolving, with a fluidity that has denied attempts to develop rigid or fixed definitions and categorisations. For example, Saunders et al. (2016) argue that post-Reformation bias defines religion by sacred texts and core beliefs, but it is also a term which is used broadly in diverse methodologies and disciplines. They further argue that religion can also be used to capture intangible abstract concepts, such as emotions, feelings and motivations. Therefore, there is a need to understand religion as something which can 'both shape and be shaped by the human experience' (Saunders et al., 2016, p. 10). Religion is often used interchangeably with expressions such as 'faith', 'belief' and 'spirituality' (Lunn, 2009; Saunders et al., 2016; McGuire, 2008) and despite attempts by scholars to distinguish and develop specific definitions for these terms, definitions remain multiple and contested (Gozdziak and Shandy, 2002). In this book, when these terms appear, either through interlocutor usage or my own, they should be considered synonyms of 'religion'.

At the heart of the issue considering what religion 'is' and what 'it' encompasses, is, not only is there wide divergence within different religious traditions, but in any singular religious tradition, there is a 'significant variations of praxis.... or interpretations' (Macey and Carling, 2011, p. 6). McGuire's (2008, p. 6) research uncovered the variegated ways people practiced and believed, not only between different religious traditions, but she has demonstrated the degree of divergence within the same religious community. A key element in the consideration of how 'religion' is to be understood in the context of this research is the power that religious organisations can have to establish boundaries and exercise authority on approved practice within societies.

This is especially pertinent when thinking of the socialising force religious institutions can have in terms of accepted sexuality and gender norms in a society. As McGuire argues, religious organisations 'routinely try to shape such boundaries, exerting their authority to distinguish what they approve of as proper individual practice' (*ibid*), which encompasses the organisation of approved sexual relationships. Institutionalised religion is a powerful regulatory mechanism, especially in the creation of sexuality and gender social norms, and religious institutions will often seek to 'exclude certain bodies' from being seen in traditional and authorised religious spaces (Page and Yip, 2020, p. 12).

The conceptualisation of religion in this research is borrowed from the sociological understanding of 'lived religion' (Ammerman, 2016; McGuire, 2008; Wilcox, 2009; Hall, 1997). Drawing particularly on McGuire's research (2008, p. 17) who argues when exploring individual religiosity it 'rarely resembles the tidy, consistent, and theologically correct packages official religions promote.' McGuire used lived religion as a way of exploring the 'nonofficial' and hidden elements present in individual religiosity.

Lived religion helps us to understand the experiences of interlocutors in this research, as part of the conceptual aims of lived religion is a shift away from centring religious institutions and elites and instead brings attention to the experiences of marginalised groups, such as LGBTQI+ people (Ammerman, 2013, 2016).

The concept of lived religion enables a consideration of religious life outside of narrow doctrinal positions and teachings, produced and maintained by elites and institutions (Neitz, 2011). The conceptual broadening of the term lived religion can be used to understand how people who live in contexts which are heavily influenced by religious thought, teachings and beliefs can navigate conservative institutional religious dominance, even if their private beliefs and practices are at odds with dominant beliefs or their subjectivities falls outside of accepted religious norms (e.g. see Jeldtoft, 2011; McGuire, 2008; Zaman, 2022). Interlocutors' experiences in this research show both a development of personal and individual religious beliefs and practices, which have diverted away from the confines of their original religious traditions, without necessarily diminishing their religiosity.

Yet, as Ammerman argues, when considering lived religious practices, it is essential to understand the influence of institutional religion in a person's social world. Conceptualising lived religion as encompassing both individual beliefs and practices, as well as influences from institutional religious origins, enables an exploratory approach to understanding how religion may remain significant in a person's life, even when their queer subjectivity appears incompatible with their religious community's doctrine. This is found to be the case for interlocutors who reconstitute and redefine, or in some cases convert, their religiosity to counteract the (perceived) incompatibility of their religious and queer subject positions.

In terms of terminology, regarding sexual and gender diversity, I use both LGBTQI+ and queer subjectivity throughout the book to refer to sexually and gender diverse individuals. LGBTQI+ is regularly used in scholarship and was common terminology used by both interlocutors and practitioners as shorthand for sexually and gender diverse people. However, to avoid falling into essentialised understandings or categorisations of sexuality and gender where LGBTQI+ term is used, it should be taken to be read within the wider conceptualisation of queer subjectivity, which more broadly signifies a person who does not identify, or is not read by others, as fitting within heteronormative sexual and gender social norms.

The usage of queer subjectivity allows for the complexity within varied gender and sexual subject positions and avoids a replication of rigid identarian categories present in asylum decision making processes in the Global North.[3] Additionally, westernised understandings and conceptualisation of sexuality and gender have their origins in theoretical work deriving from academic institutions and activism in the Global North. Westernised categories of sexual and gender diversity, such as LGBTQI+, are geographically, socio-culturally and historically specific and do not allow for how queer subjectivities can change due to both temporal and geographical factors (Fajardo, 2008).

By using the term 'queer subjectivities' the intention is to allow for a fluid and flexible conceptualisation of sexual and gender diversity as understood and embodied in the lives of interlocutors. Interlocutors in this research often occupied contradictory positionalities and there are wide-ranging factors which contribute to the creation of one's sexual and gender subjectivity. Subjectivities are not only related to a person's constitution of self but are influenced by other factors, such as socio-cultural, historical and geographical contexts. Otu (2022, p. 79), who used 'queer subjectivities' in his ethnographic research exploring the lived experiences of sassos' in Ghana, argues through utilising 'queer subjectivities' there is the possibility for a consideration of subjectivity that sits at what he defines as 'vexed intersections'. For example, he argues, his interlocutors are at once colonial and anti-colonial, African and non-African, visible and invisible. While within a different context, interlocutors in this research often found themselves at 'vexed intersections.'

On a final note, I have deliberately only considered SO asylum claims throughout the book; this is because none of the interlocutors I had conversations with had sought asylum on the grounds of gender identity. This is certainly an area for further inquiry, but the experiences of trans people should not be homogenised with the experiences of those claiming on SO grounds. Previous scholarship has identified the problem of how trans experiences are often conflated within the umbrella of LGBTQI+ asylum experience (van Der Pijl et al., 2018, p. 9). While there can be overlaps, particularly the heteronormative framings of asylum polices that places those with trans subjectivities at an increased risk of harm, people with trans subjectivities face unique barriers and experiences which are deserving of independent critical scholarly attention (for examples of this scholarship, see Avgeri, 2021; Balaguera, 2023; DasGupta, 2019).

---

[3] The terms 'Global North' and 'Global South' will be used throughout this research. These terms will not be used to delineate a particular geography, more to allude to the power and relational dynamic between countries. The understanding, which I have taken from Brown et al (2010, pp. 1567–1579), conceptualises the Global South as 'a relational term that emphasises a diversity of uneven and unequal geopolitical power relations, both historically and in the contemporary period.

Chapter 1

Religious Experiences and the Conceptualisation of Queer Selfhoods*

Within Western liberal democratic states, 'religion' is often positioned as 'inherently and intrinsically at the forefront of antiqueer world-making' (Puar, 2013, p. 205). This oppositional framing of queer and religious subject positions is reflected within asylum decision making in Western liberal democratic states (Danisi et al., 2021) and results in suspicion towards LGBTQI+ people who embrace religiosity (Khan, 2020). As Puar (2007, p. 13) has argued, 'queer secularity' is the normative expectation for LGBTQI+ people, which demands the transgression of 'religious norms that are understood to otherwise bind that subject to an especially egregious interdictory religious frame'. Consequently, decision makers view queer and religious subject positions as incompatible, and encounters with 'religion' and/or religious communities often have negative implications for a person claiming asylum on SO grounds, as stereotypical tropes imagine that LGBTQI+ people will 'free' themselves of religion as soon as they arrive in countries of asylum (Page and Yip, 2020).

Many LGBTQI+ people, who leave their CoO in search of safety do not simply abandon their religious beliefs. Their faith often remains important as they cross borders and rebuild their lives in new countries and communities. Assumptions of religious abandonment completely disregard the fact that LGBTQI+ people who seek asylum often come from countries where religion plays an integral role in everyday life. Considering people who have sought asylum in the UK, at the time of writing, the top five countries where people claiming asylum on SO grounds

* This chapter was developed using material from the thesis: Fletcher, Claire; (2024) Queerly Faithful: The experiences of religion for those seeking asylum in the UK. Doctoral thesis (Ph.D), UCL (University College London).

Queerly Faithful: Queer People's Experience of Religion in Asylum Seeking, 11–41

doi:10.1108/978-1-83797-488-720261003

came from were Pakistan, Bangladesh, Nigeria, India and Uganda (Home Office, 2024). Population data from each of these countries identified religion as 'very important' to the majority of the population (Templeton, 2010–2019). Of course, this is not an exact predictor of individual religiosity, but it provides a blunt illustration of how religion has a significant place in the societies where LGBTQI+ people who claim asylum come from.

Offering a challenge to the simplistic assumptions within RSDs of queer and religious incompatibility, the vignettes of interlocutors' lives, presented in this chapter, show how religious experiences are intertwined in both positive and negative occurrences for interlocutors in their CoO. Narratives highlight how situations that force people to flee cannot be neatly packaged into narratives of either religious oppression of LGBTQI+ people or a homogenised homophobic environment that makes queer lives impossible. Experiences presented here show how binary narrative tropes of oppression to freedom erase the experiences of living in the in-betweenness of rights. These erasures ensure that 'refugee spectres ...are absent in the accounts that emphasise oppression in the "sending country" and freedom and opportunities in the "receiving country"' (Shakhsari, 2014, p. 1008). Oppositional narrative tropes discount the day-to-day encounters and complexities in which LGBTQI+ people can build and sustain lives in predominantly homonegative environments. As Page and Yip (2020, p. 4) argue, 'to truly understand the complexity of the place of religion in queer people's lives we must listen to adherents on their own terms'.

The purpose of the narratives presented in this chapter is to reflect the different ways religious experiences are woven into how LGBTQI+ people come to understand themselves and can shape negative self-understandings of queer subjectivity. Therefore, the chapter moves to explore how religious encounters play a central role, not only in punitive measures that target those who transgress sexuality and gender social norms, but how they can provide a route for those who publicly transgress these norms to remain within CoO contexts. Furthermore, religious beliefs were drawn on by interlocutors in times of distress, as were religious communities and leaders.

The last part of this chapter explores family and community relationships. Persecution of LGBTQI+ people is often caused by those closest to them, rather than more widely recognised forms of persecution perpetrated by the state and state actors. Narratives illustrate the complex negotiations individuals undertake to navigate their lives and achieve the ability to live queerly in ways that are aimed at remaining within their CoO. Far from motivated by a sole desire to leave, interlocutors worked hard to remain in their CoO and preserve important relationships with family and community. Danisi et al. (2021, p. 142) argue that

> it can be years before a specific incident, or intersecting factors converge and create a situation where remaining in their CoO is no longer safe.

Overall, this chapter builds knowledge of the multifaceted ways people build queer lives in their CoO and provides examples of the intersecting factors which can force them to leave. To do this, there is a need to pay attention to the complexity of experiences, – both positive and negative – within queer lives.

Normative Violence and Precarious Subjectivities

Norms and normative discourse are used to police people, particularly regarding expressions and embodiments of gender and sexuality. Norms are employed within societies to discourage certain behaviour and justify punishment for those who deviate from them (Young et al., 2015). Visible non-conformity can result in discrimination, violence and even death. Norms create what Butler has described as 'normative violence', causing non-normativity to become visible outside mainstream social norms and results in the marginalisation of those who are perceived to transgress these social norms (Butler, 1999).

The definition of 'normative violence' utilised in this chapter is not a concept that explains a type of violence[1] that is normative, but instead describes how norms themselves can be violent and complicit in sanctioning violence towards certain people (Dhawan, 2013). Normative violence is an important consideration as it can and is used to incite and enable actual violence. Essentially, 'normative violence' is a way of conceptualising a violence that erases, is complicit in and provides impunity to the aggression and persecution of those whose subjectivities fall outside of social norms. By considering norms in this way, it makes it possible to bring 'this violence into view' (Butler, 1999, p. xix). Additionally, normative violence is useful to understand how interlocutors come to view their subjectivity as 'other' and outside of social norms, as discursive formations used about sexuality inform individuals in the deepest of ways and influence how people react to normative sexuality in their own context (Donnan and Magowan, 2012). These discursive framings of normative sexuality and gender influence individuals' behaviours and external presentations of self, especially when living in homonegative contexts.

Butler's theorising on the creation of a 'legible personhood' is useful in considering how interlocutors' employed a variety of strategies to establish and retain a legibility vis-à-vis socially acceptable normative behaviour, or at least the guise of it, allowing them to remain in CoOs (Butler, 1999, 2004a). Normative legibility is deeply linked to survivability; in the context of the experiences detailed in this chapter, it is seen how the establishment and maintenance of a legible personhood is directly linked to a person's ability to safely remain in their CoO, although it remains conditional and precarious (Buxton and Ritholtz, 2026). Disruptions of legibility often have dire consequences, and illegibility can

[1]The definition of violence in this chapter is drawn from feminist scholarship, which moved conceptualisations of violence beyond considerations of a sanctioned, legal state violence. For example, Sarat (2018) developed a concept of violence that encompasses group pattern violence, structural violence, representational and symbolic violence and epistemic violence, with further feminist scholarship conceptualised violence that is racialised and gendered.

result in social exclusion, abandonment by family and friends, acts of violence and even death.

Furthermore, norms are complicit in qualifying who is human and, therefore, who has access to a life that is liveable (Butler, 2004b, 2016). Butler argues, by positioning certain subjectivities in this way assigns a value to the life we deem necessary, while those who challenge societal norms are subjected to stigmatisation and punishment. Norms are complicit in the creation of apathy towards a certain type of violence, which in turn leads to immunity to the harm metered out against bodies that are not considered normatively human. Part of creating this apathy towards certain people is framing them as 'symbols of evil' and, therefore, in their death, there is not only an absence of grief but also of accountability (Butler, 2004a). This is particularly relevant in terms of the persecution metered out by family or communities against LGBTQI+ people. Apathy created by social norms results in negligible consequences to violence against LGBTQI+ people; this immunity against violence committed against those who transgress sexuality and gender norms by both state and non-state actors creates persecutory environments for LGBTQI+ people, even in the absence of official state sanctions, such as laws criminalising or discriminating against LGBTQI+ people.

Drawing on religious experience provides an example of how intersecting factors create and subject LGBTQI+ people to an 'unliveable life'. The narrative excerpts presented below demonstrate how those who visibly transgress sexuality and gender norms must often choose between remaining in their social context facing isolation at the margins of society, at the risk of violence, imprisonment and death or, if possible, finding ways to leave. However, what is also evident in the narratives is that flight often comes after years of living queer lives in their CoO and narratives challenges that leaving their CoO is always the desired goal for LGBTQI+ people who live in homonegative contexts (Giametta, 2016).

Religious Experience in Understandings of Queer Subjectivity

Religion is framed as 'one of the strongest socialising determinants to explain the rejection of homosexuality' (Janssen and Scheepers, 2019, p. 1924). Narratives revealed how religious teachings, beliefs and experiences played a crucial part in how interlocutors understood themselves as queer subjects, and as 'other' or undesirable within their social contexts (Alessi et al., 2021). Through their experiences, it can be seen how 'religion' in various guises is often deeply entwined in the lives of people who eventually seek asylum in the UK. Therefore, simplistic assumptions of religious rejection and abandonment by asylum decision makers are unrealistic and show insufficient understanding of the importance religion can play for people who seek asylum on SO grounds.

Non-affirming religious settings and teaching can be central in influencing the development of homophobic attitudes and stigma for individuals who grow up in homonegative religious environments. For those with queer subjectivities, who remain in these contexts, this can foster and sustain an internalised homophobia (Barnes and Meyer, 2012). Interlocutors who lived in CoO communities where there was a societal awareness and commentary on LGBTQI+ people remarked how their notions about queerness were often influenced by religiously inspired teachings, beliefs, religious discourse and religious parables. Negative discourse and derogatory terms[2] most often used within narratives, when discussing how queer subjectivity was referenced to within their CoO, were: 'evil', 'an abomination', 'people of Lut', 'a sin', 'sinners' and 'having demons'. Forms of religious teaching and preaching within religious communities on sexual and gender diversity outside of heteronormative social norms also contributed to interlocutors' understandings that queerness was deviant, prohibited and undesirable. A theological concept that had one of the most significant impacts on interlocutors was the idea that sexuality or gender transgressions would lead to 'eternal damnation' and risk a person's ability of achieving eternal salvation.

Normative violence is used as a tool to suppress those whose subjectivities deviate from heteronormative sexuality and gender norms. This was apparent in how interlocutors, even before having any realisation of their own queer subjectivity, had preconceived ideas of queerness and the extent to which it was excluded and derided in their social and cultural environments. Butler's conceptualisation of 'normative violence' is useful here as it helps us to understand how queer subjectivity comes to be understood by interlocutors as negative and deviant and as something that should be feared and hidden.

Bunkechukwu, a gay man who grew up in West Africa in a strict Roman Catholic family, spoke fondly of his time spent as a child with his parents and siblings. His father, a catechist in their family's church, regularly gave sermons, led liturgy and mass and conducted marriage classes for couples before they took the sacrament of matrimony. By the time he was a teenager, Bunkechukwu said he was heavily involved in his family's church and belonged to two religious organisations. He preached the doctrine of the church to the wider community, which included homophobic rhetoric and condemnation of LGBTQI+ people, saying:

> I'm also part of people who inform the congregation that homosexuality is an abomination, it is a sin of Sodom and Gomorrah and is not acceptable in the Catholic Church.

His whole life, growing up, was framed around the church and religious activities, and talking about his parents' expectation for him, he said they wanted him to grow up to become a 'catholic extremist'.

Family life centred around the community church and Bunkechukwu recalled:

---

[2]In their narratives, people spoke of individuals who were targeted by people within their social contexts because they were assumed to be LGBTQI+, however, there is no possibility of confirming the person themselves identified as LGBTQI+.

> My daily activity has always been just church, home, church, home...When I was growing, sexuality is something, especially coming from an African perspective, you would never want to talk about, and you believe it's normal because of the way you were taught. This is illegal, this is an abomination. God never, never accepted it.

Even as young child, Bunkechukwu understood that he would not be accepted as a gay man and that discovery could lead to familial rejection, reflecting the pervasiveness of homonegativity in his social context.

In Bunkechukwu's excerpt above, it is seen how queer subjectivity was framed as sinful and prohibited by God, with his quote referencing religious stories and parables to warn against engaging in same-sex sex or relationships. *Sodom and Gomorrah* and *City of Lut* were common religious parables cited by interlocutors when discussing their early understandings of queer subjectivities. Additionally, Qur'anic or biblical stories interlocutors internalised led to some interlocutors interpreting their queer subjectivity, as not only making them an abomination in the eyes of God, but that their queer subjectivity would lead to repercussions for their whole community. For example, Jamilah, a Lesbian from northern Africa, recollected an earthquake in her hometown, saying:

> I'm sleeping alone, and this is when I'm having my 'me time'. That was when I was like fifteen, and this was when I realised, 'oh my god, I'm lesbian'. There's no kidding about it; I know now that I'm lesbian. And you know what happened? Same year, we had an earthquake. I was like, 'shit, I haven't even been with a woman, and we had a bloody earthquake!' I remember like running towards our building, there were people coming down the stairs because of the earthquake....... the lights, the chandeliers and everything were broken. It was a powerful earthquake... In my head, I was like, 'shit, I'm doomed'.

This example shows how interlocutors could interpret negative events that were inflicted on the wider community, as a direct consequence of their deviations away from religiously sanctioned sexuality norms. Jamilah believed her same sex desires resulted in a punishment from Allah because of the sexual thoughts she was having about other women.

Due to their religious beliefs and the religious teachings on LGBTQI+ people, many interlocutors spoke of the emotional turmoil they felt on experiencing same-sex attraction. Religious beliefs created negative feelings towards sexuality that strayed from heteronormative expressions. Interlocutors used words such as 'evil' or 'sick' when reflecting on how they viewed themselves in the recognition of their own queer subjectivity. Bunkechukwu, for example remembered:

> I feel like, God this is evil. As far as I'm concerned, it's evil. I kept being concerned about homosexuality, there is nobody I can even confide to. I could not even tell my mum, not even my brother or my sisters. I was growing up. I was so scared.

This awareness of their difference for interlocutors living in homonegative contexts created an underlying fear. As Bunkechukwu's quotation above demonstrates, his understanding of how derided queer subjectivity was in his CoO meant he was aware that he could not even rely on his own family to keep him safe.

Religiously inspired framings of queer subjectivity as deviant and abhorrent meant interlocutors knew the potential severity of the consequence if their queer subjectivity was discovered. Monodou, a gay man from a Muslim family in West Africa, who was brought up in a strict religious household within a community that openly condemned LGBTQI+ people, described the consequence in his CoO's if he was outed as a gay man.

> If you are caught you are definitely going to be in trouble, very big one, but you can feel in your body what you want, you can't show it. It all has to be secret within. You have gay people in (location removed), but they can't show themselves because of the stigma and the trauma they're going to go through when they identify themselves in the society. Obviously when I was in (location removed) if I said, 'I like guys in my compound', I wouldn't see the sun that very night because I know I'd be killed, because it's going to be something like, you're going to bring shame to the family. The moment you tell your parents, that kind of stuff you'd be gone.

Monodou's excerpts provide an example of the levels of fear people can have within homonegative contexts and demonstrate how it can often be family members who can provide the biggest threat. Many interlocutors referred to how they felt isolated both within their immediate family and wider communities when they realised their sexuality transgressed heteronormative social norms because of the associated risks. Interlocutors commonly referred to how LGBTQI+ people face stigmatisation, abandonment, extreme forms of violence and, in the worse cases, disappeared or were killed by family and community members.

Monodou's excerpt also illustrates how individuals are keenly aware of the need to conceal any evidence of their queer subjectivity. His reference to keeping his queer subjectivity as a 'secret within' was mirrored in other narratives. People commonly referred to the necessity of keeping queer subjectivity internal, ensuring body movements, dress and actions displayed no external signs that their internal selves deviated from the sexuality and gender norms of their CoO. This is because apparent displays of sexuality and gender that are inconsistent with social norms make non-conforming individuals a 'hyper-visible' (Mohammed et al., 2018). As Epprecht (2012) has argued, outward visibility of transgressions can compel the wider community to pay explicit attention, which in homonegative contexts put LGBTQI+ people at risk (Epprecht, 2012).

However, preventing this visibility of non-conformity was something that could not always be managed by interlocutors, especially if they were unaware of their difference. Garrett, a Catholic gay man from Central America, remembers being badly bullied at school by other boys who used to throw stones at him and call him names. They would say 'You are gay, fuck you, gay'. Garrett said, at the time, he did not understand why he was being targeted by the other children. It was not until, at the age of 12, he was filmed while working for an international organisation. On watching the video back, Garrett recalls:

> Garrett: When, I watched the video about me, I watched a woman. My attitude, my everything.
>
> CF: You thought you were feminine?
>
> Garrett: Yes. When I was watching the video, I'm going to sit alone. And when I watched the video, I cried, and I said, 'I don't want to see a woman, I don't like it'. When I watched what happened with me. And I understood, for that reason, the other boys wanted to fight with me, and told me, 'Fuck you, gay', for that reason people hated me.

Garrett's outward embodiment transgressed social gender norms of masculinity, which led to violent targeting by his peers. As he got older, he deliberately set out to change his appearance, working out regularly in the gym to build a muscular physique to ensure he matched social expectations of masculinity. This physical change prevented him from being targeted, as his outward appearance now conformed with his CoO gender norms. External embodiments that were deemed to transgress social gender norms appeared throughout other interlocutors' narratives and interlocutors referenced facing societal disproval because of the way they moved their bodies, spoke or dressed, with transgressions contributing to creating persecutory environments in their CoO.

It was not only concerns about family and society interlocutors referenced when they started to become aware of their sexuality. Jamilah, who was brought up in a strict Muslim household, said she was taught by her parents that 'homosexuality' was a sin from an early age. When she started to acknowledge her attraction towards women in her teenage years, even though her sexuality remained a secret, she still suffered internal feelings of shame, viewing herself as a 'sinner'. While she did not act on her sexuality until her 30s, Jamilah said the very fact that she thought about other women in a sexual way, or even that she allowed herself to consider what this might mean, made her a sinner, which opened her up to punishment from Allah. Jamilah tried to internally justify her feelings that she was having towards women and initially rejected that she was experiencing same-sex attraction, saying:

> When I look at them (women), and I'm like, 'no no no, I'm not!' I'm just admiring them like you admire a nice painting, or a beautiful scenery, because I'm not a sinner! I always felt guilty and then. I think as a child, it's a challenge, you know, because sometimes you're curious, I mean I know a hundred percent I'm lesbian, but maybe as a child, you might wonder, you might have these thoughts, and it's not fair to say that even if you have that thought, even if you're curious about something, that means you're a sinner.

Jamilah's introspection shows how her religious upbringing created internal struggles. Religious experiences not only had implications on interpersonal relationships and external modifications of behaviours but also had inferences on interlocutors' internal thoughts and feelings, even though these could not be scrutinised by the external world. Jamilah's excerpt is an example of how interlocutors often self-policed their own queer subjectivity. Self-moderation in relation to deviating from religiously inspired sexuality and gender norms is more potent in individuals when there is a 'recognition of an omnipotent, omniscient, and omnipresent divine power (e.g. God) who is discursively constructed as the origin and guardian of…heteronormative norms and values' by the person (Yip, 2015, p. 122).

Interlocutors considered themselves 'abominations' or 'sinners' and often considered afflictions as punishment by God/Allah because of their transgressions from heteronormative norms. As Farid, a gay Muslim man from the Middle East, stated:

> God is watching me, and he doesn't like it. I was having these feelings of guilt. But religiously I was feeling, 'Maybe I am sick, and God doesn't like me because I am doing this'. So, I was always asking God for forgiveness, 'You help me to change this. I want to overcome this'.

Interlocutors believed their religious deity provided the ultimate judgement as to whether they had lived good lives, which increased internal feelings of guilt and anxiety about their queer subjectivity. For them, the importance of living pious lives in accordance with God's wishes was not only related to their mortal existence but tied to their religious beliefs regarding a 'final judgement' by God on their death. Interlocutors, who believed in an ultimate judgement, were not only concerned about the ramifications of their queer subjectivity in their present life but also its implications it would have in death. Transgressions of accepted religiously prescribed sexuality and gender norms were equated to a person's inability to achieve eternal salvation, which led people to fear they would be subjected to 'eternal damnation' or 'hell'.

A belief in the omniscience of the divine power caused interlocutors' severe distress, as while people spoke of modifying behaviour to hide queerness from family and community, those who conceived their deity as omniscient believed it was an impossibility to hide internal feelings from a divine knowing. The sentiments expressed by interlocutors above speak to a religious experience as also a lived interpersonal relationship with God, one that is set apart from institutional and community practice and beliefs. This part of interlocutors' religious experience is important in understanding the complexity and long-standing impact that religiously inspired harm can have, even after people have left CoO contexts (for further discussion, see Chapter 5).

It was not only negative emotions that interlocutors reported regarding their queer subjectivities. For example, Bunkechukwu said that throughout his childhood he could not have imagined the possibility that his life's path would not fit within the heteronormative ideal (Berlant and Warner, 1998). As a child and into his teenage years, he fully expected in adulthood he would marry a woman and have children, and initially he was confused when, at the age of 12, he became aware his feelings did not match his only understanding of romantic/sexual relationships, explaining:

> I remember when I am being sent on an errand to go and get something for my mum or my dad. I discovered a place where some, we call them 'XX'[3] (young men). These are people, street boys, they don't have homes. But basically, after their daily work, they come to a particular canal that has a flowing water. They come there to shower, and I just saw them, and I like going there to look at them when they're taking their wash. I feel happy about it, but that was how I started understanding.

While in his quotation, Bunkechukwu fears what his enjoyment of male nudity means, he also refers to being 'happy' watching the young men washing. For Bunkechukwu, realisation of his queer subjectivity was not only framed negatively, and this memory holds also happy emotions. Joyful experiences regarding queer subjectivity in CoOs were not out of the ordinary for many interlocutors. Njema, a lesbian woman from Central Africa, in her narrative, spoke of a girlfriend she had when her father sent her to university far away from her family as punishment for catching her with a woman. Recalling this time, she said, 'Anyway at the end I met R as I said, and I don't regret it. It was good. Honestly, it was amazing. It was the best'.

However, expressing positive emotions regarding queer subjectivity in RSD interviews when claiming asylum on SO grounds directly contradicts the expectations of decision makers. In the UK, the assessment of asylum claims on sexual orientation have heavily influenced by the *Difference, Stigma, Shame, Harm* model, commonly referred to as DSSH (Powell, 2026). The influence of the DSSH model in the UK has led decision makers to expect SO claimants to recount feelings of shame regarding sexual difference, resulting from the societal stigmatisation of LGBTQI+ people. As Powell, argues the issue with DSSH model is it

[3]This term was removed as it is geographically specific and, therefore, could identify the interlocutor.

has contributed to a 'fixed conception of sexual diversity' that is expected to be present within SO claimants narratives. Happy recollections or positive emotions call into question the credibility of their sexual orientation and increase the likelihood the claim is refused Åberg (2023). Fixed expectations have led to a suspicion of certain emotion, this has led to decision makers assuming an impossibility of positive experiences for those who seek asylum on SO grounds and who come from contexts where homonegativity is commonplace (Walker-Said, 2022). This is because a person's internal narratives (joyful experiences) do not match external factors (homonegative geographical contexts) in the eyes of decision makers.

Silence was another key theme to emerge within interlocutors' narratives at the intersection of religious experience and queer subjectivity. Interlocutors referred to how silence and an invisibility regarding LGBTQI+ people that existed throughout their childhood and teenage years caused confusion when they started to develop subjectivities that felt outside of heteronormative sexuality and gender norms. The absence of any frames of reference to understand or place their subjectivity caused interlocutors distress and anguish on the realisation their own subjectivity deviated away from heteronormative norms. As Butler (2004a) argues,

> The public sphere is constituted in part by what cannot be said and what cannot be shown. The limits of the sayable, the limits of what can appear, circumscribe the domain in which political speech operates and certain kinds of subjects appear viable actors. (p. xvii)

Silence is achieved through the allocation of stigma, and religious institutions are drawn upon by a variety of actors, such as state authorities or community leaders, to stigmatise and silence the public emergence of subjectivities deemed undesirable. Monolithic religions over the centuries have been used to bolster the societal authority of heteronormativity and patriarchy (Shah, 2020). Social institutions – such as religious institutions – promote presumptions towards heterocisnormativity that creates a bounded environment (although not uncontested) which removes the possibilities of different forms of embodiment (Lee et al., 2018). For people to be able to see themselves within their societies, individuals need to have recognisable identities within a peer group, or at least within one's wider social network (Bornstein, 1994).

The very existence of any form of diversity outside heteronormative expressions of sexuality and gender was often not alluded to at all within family, religious or educational contexts. As Imran, a gay Muslim man from South Asia, described, 'growing up, it was just normal. Everybody lives the same, you don't even know something's wrong'. The unspeakability about queer subjectivities led to confusion and concern for people on the realisation that they were experiencing same-sex attraction. Jamilah explained one of the main difficulties for her in her CoO context was the belief that other queer people did not exist, saying:

> The whole realisation, 'Oh, shit, I like girls'. So that was really amplified in my head at the time, and there was no one to support. I think that the idea that there was no one to talk to, and maybe

> if there was someone I talked to, that person would have said, 'Well, there are people like you'. I think that I really needed to hear, but I thought I was on my own in that degree, there was no other lesbian girls.

Growing up in contexts where there is an absence of the visible difference regarding sexual and gender diversity within social contexts meant interlocutors had no social reflection of their internal selves. As a result, they had no reference point to locate what same-sex attraction meant, and caused them to feel isolated, believing their experience to be exceptional and abnormal. For interlocutors, who were aware of the existence or other LGBTQI+ people, even though they were referred to negatively, they at least had some form of reflection of their own experiences within the wider society.

Here, the concept of normative violence can be used, but in a way that differs from the previous section which illustrated how the negative framing of queer subjectivity becomes a form of discursive injury that is internalised. As with Jamilah's recollection above, discursive silence can be complicit in normative violence as violence is inflicted upon those who cannot recognise their own subjectivity reflected in the experience of others. Discursive silence on certain subjectivities ensures that some bodies are refused humanity and 'their dehumanization occurs first, at this level' (Butler, 2004b, p. 25). Jamilah's excerpt is a real-life reflection of this argument, as the absence of an image of self in her social world led her to assume the uniqueness of her position, which in turn caused her to feel isolated within her social environment. The pervasive absence of queer subjectivities in interlocutors' social contexts led to feelings of dislocation, leading individuals to believe their queer subjectivities to be invalid (to echo Butler).

Silence surrounding queer subjectivity, not only manifested in interlocutors experiencing feelings of difference growing up. For some interlocutors only became aware that their sexuality did not fit neatly within heteronormative they boundaries through a chance encounter.

Musa, a Christian gay man from West Africa, remembers 'When I was coming up, I never knew how to describe the word "gay", until that day when I had sex with my friend'. Musa grew up in a rural community; because of his family's financial circumstances, he was unable to attend university. Instead, he trained to be an excavator and followed his family's expectations and married. On qualifying as an excavator, it was standard practice to work on site, living away from home for months at a time. While living on site, Musa said he developed a close friendship with one of his male colleagues. One day his friend asked if he could stay with Musa in his accommodation, as he had family visiting. Musa said, it was while his friend was staying with him that he confessed to Musa he was gay. Musa recalled:

> Allowing him to sleep in my place, for the first time in my life to hear about the word 'gay', he told me that he's a gay. He don't like women. He likes making love with men. I was shocked, I was shocked that night to hear that he's a gay. He asked me if I could

> make love with him. I said no, I can't make love with you. That night it was confusing for me, I've never heard about this thing in my life. But we slept together, we wake up in the morning, but I was not happy with him....That same night, talking between us that he will come back and sleep in my place because his brother and his wife are still staying. During that night, he woke up again and said, 'you are my best friend, no one in this community knows who I am. The only person I explained myself to is you, this is who I am. This is my sexuality, there is no way I can change it, there's no way I can go back, I love being a gay'. So, he explained a lot to me. I was carefully listening to him as a friend, so he asked me to make love with him that night. So, no option for me, I make love with him, obviously it was different making love with a man, and different, after making love with him I feel ashamed, because I realised I like it.

The silence in Musa's social world on the existence to any alternatives to heteronormative relationships meant that he was oblivious to the different forms sexual relations could take until this encounter with his friend.

How Musa recalls the moment he came to understand his sexuality transgressed sexual and gender norms of his CoO did not happen through a gradual realisation of difference, often expected in RSD interviews (Berg and Millbank, 2009). In Musa's own words, he describes his sexuality as, 'before being a gay, I was married'. At no point in his narrative does Musa articulate feelings that he was aware of a 'difference' growing up or recount an emotional journey towards a realisation of sexual difference. Again, in RSD processes in the UK it is assumed claimants will produce narratives that tell of a gradual awakening that their sexuality departs from normative expressions of sexuality in their social context. This is explicitly linked to the framework established under DSSH that SO claimants will provide narratives of difference (Powell, 2026). Musa's CoO experience directly challenge this assumption that people with non-normative sexualities will feel different within CoO. Furthermore, Musa did not view any contention between his same-sex encounter in relation to his religious beliefs. When he began an actual relationship with this friend in his CoO context, he justified that while in his CoO disapproval of same-sex relationships was found within institutionalised religious teachings, he viewed religion as a personal relationship between the person and God, not one governed by institutional religious doctrine which was created by people.

If interlocutors lived in contexts of silence in terms of sexual and gender diversity, discovery of the existence of other LGBTQI+ people and being able to name their experience was often accompanied by positive feelings. Mainly as interlocutors realised their experiences were not exceptional. Hazelle, a bisexual woman from Central Africa, first heard about same-sex attraction in a biology lesson at school, at 15 years of age, through the question of a classmate. In the excerpt below, she describes her recollection of this moment.

> It's like having puzzle pieces falling into place. It's like, OKAY, what I'm feeling now is being a lesbian or being gay, then at the same time you feel like you can't live openly, so it made me really worried and scared. I was relieved knowing there are people who can be the same as me because I've not grown up or seen anybody who would tell me, 'I'm attracted to ladies. I'm attracted to women', or things like that. I got home that night, I was like, 'Wow!'

Hazelle's quotation is a good illustration of this relief and accompanied happiness on discovery that what they are feeling can be named and is not unique. These emotions can be attributed to a person's individual need to identify with others and is one of the driving forces of culture (Bornstein, 1994). As Bornstein argues, there is nowhere more pertinent for individuals to recognise themselves within others than in the areas of gender and sexuality norms. Having a recognisable and accepted form of identity in one's social context not only provides protection from normative violence, but the ability to recognise your internal subjectivities in others provides reassurance that your identity is within acceptable expressions of human experience. Interlocutors who became aware that their subjectivity fell outside of social acceptability, said that evidence of the existence of other LGBTQI+ people did provide a form of reassurance.

While it was more common for individuals to struggle with their queer subjectivity based on conservative and theologically grounded understandings of gender and sexuality, and the implications of embodying and living it within their CoO contexts, this was certainly not the case for all interlocutors. A minority of individuals did not frame their queer subjectivity, negatively despite growing up within religious environments that considered LGBTQI+ people as deviant and socially undesirable. For example, Saafir, a bisexual Muslim man from West Africa, who endured a religious exorcism in his family's mosque on their discovery of his sexuality, said:

> When they take me to the mosque, they started praying for me. Gave me a lot of advice. I told them that, because I don't know what to respond to them, I thought it was normal. That's who I am. That's my sexuality. I'm doing my thing. You do your thing. I'm saying the wrong thing. They tie my hands and tie my legs. Started praying for me that they want to remove an evil something and they want to remove it from my body, and I say, 'No, I'm okay. There's nothing wrong with me'.

Interlocutors who articulated religious beliefs that did not frame queer subjectivity as something that would bring divine disapproval, had separated their personal religious beliefs and relationship with God from wider religious norms of their families and communities. These interlocutors viewed that the intolerance towards LGBTQI+ people was an external problem, and one that had been created by religiously inspired heteronormative sexuality and gender social norms of their geographical, cultural and social context. Interlocutors viewed the positioning of queer subjectivities within religious belief systems as something deviant, had been created by people in power for personal motivations, such as financial or political gain.

Religious Experiences of Transgressions and 'cures'

Religious beliefs and teachings are implicated in punishing those who transgress sexuality and gender social norms and are complicit in upholding and authenticating the privileged societal status of heteronormativity (Yip, 2015) and heteropatriarchy (Muthien, 2007). Religious experiences appeared in narratives, regarding disciplinary and rehabilitative approaches towards LGBTQI+ people who transgressed sexuality and gender norms. Religious rituals aimed at curing transgressions were defined by interlocutors as exorcisms, deliverances and cleansings, and while having different names within narrators' accounts, all were performed with the purpose of removing and preventing the person's queer behaviour or embodiment re-emerging. Hazelle described the purpose of cleansings in her CoO as, 'they believe they're going to clean you from it, and you will go back to normal, you will be straight, like straight-straight' (heterosexual).

Nofoto, a non-binary queer person from Southern Africa who was brought up in a traditionalist household, which she defined as a belief in both the power of a person's ancestors and Christianity, found her life became difficult when her first girlfriend's sexuality became visible in their local community. As a result, Nofoto also came under scrutiny as her gender presentation was not in line with social norms and ideals of femininity. Nofoto remembered how she was repeatedly admonished by her mother for her shortcomings in expected displays and embodiments of femininity, and her mother continually criticised her clothing choice, hair style and an absence of makeup.

On the discovery of the relationship, Nofoto's mother attributed Nofoto's involvement in a same-sex relationship to be the result of a demonic possession. To 'cure' Nofoto, her mother sought the help of their community church and its leader to provide a 'cleansing ritual' for her. Nofoto's reflection of this time is particularly powerful and an example of the numerous intersecting factors that can create experiences of persecution for LGBTQI+ people. She said:

> She was African,[4] so we got on, you know. We used to go out, do things together but, unfortunately, our relationship was affected because the two of us, we were raped. For her, they killed her because she lived in (location removed), so unfortunately, she passed on. I have seen girls who were caught in-between. It's either,

[4]In our conversation, I asked Nofoto what she meant by her description of her girlfriend as 'African'. Nofoto said she was referring to the fact that she was a 'Black African like her' and explained the situation for Black Africans, in terms of being obviously LGBTQI+, especially within townships was contradictory to the experiences of differently racialised people.

> you show yourself, that you are a lesbian, or you become what is accepted within the community. Most of the time, they were living both lives, but they would not make their sexuality visible, in order for them to be able to continue in the community. Those who were rebellious they would be raped, and they were killed. If your parents are good enough, they will take you to church for you to go through the spiritual cleansing, deliverance. They'll make you drink all of these herbs and concoctions. You have to scream, say that you are going through the process of being delivered. If you didn't get the chance to go through the process of being delivered, then they will use a tyre, put it on top of you and you are gone. They will set you alight. Either you go through the process of cleansing, or they will use the tyre and set it alight, they'll rape you and cut your genitals and then they will dump you in the little streams. In (location removed), we have these little streams, so they will go and dump your body there. That's what happened to my partner. They cut her genital parts, and they went and threw her in the stream in (location removed). Yes, so the people who were very, very disobedient, because you saw some women, they would try, they wanted to come out because they wanted the community to accept that there are people who are different, they would never survive.

Nofoto's excerpt above outlines the consequences for women in her community who transgressed and resisted sexuality and gender norms. Nofoto's references to 'sort of' and 'caught in-between' are indications of how queer subjectivity had to be negotiated and kept invisible or be contained within certain bounds to ensure queerness could remain unacknowledged by the wider community, such as accepted outward embodiments of gender or at heterosexual marriage. There is often tolerance in many societies, seen as largely homonegative, where a certain degree of same sex activity is accepted if it is not made publicly visible (Boellstorff, 2005).

However, public flouting of religious norms of sexuality and gender is seen in a variety of different geographical contexts as unacceptable. For example, Bonthuys and Erlank's (2012, p. 273) undertook research in South Africa on the views of a Muslim population regarding same-sex civil unions. They concluded that because civil unions had become publicly acknowledged, the wider community were unable to ignore the transgression from Islamic religious norms. Previously, 'forbidden sexual relationship' could be ignored and remain unacknowledged if same-sex relationships happened discreetly. Positive shifts, in terms of the legal rights of sexually and gender diversity people can have unintended consequences of actually making those with queer subjectivities less safe. This form of public debates can draw attention or force conservative groups to condemn previously ignored sexual and gender diversity (Otu, 2022). Interlocutor narratives revealed how individuals understood the necessity of maintaining boundaries between public and private behaviour, as active or visible resistance to sexuality and gender norms could lead to extreme and public violence against the transgressor, as demonstrated in the case of Nofoto's girlfriend.

Contrastingly to the fate of her partner, Nofoto was 'cleansed' of her sins by the religious leader and, therefore, was given a path to remain within her community. The higher socio-economic status of her family offered Nofoto a degree of protection not afforded by her partner. Nofoto attributes her survival to having 'good enough' parents who could financially afford to pay for the route through the church which allowed Nofoto to publicly and visibly atone for her transgression. By undergoing a religious 'cleansing' by a respected religious leader, this public act ensured she was accepted back into her community, having been washed clean of her sins. Nofoto, in her retelling of the religious cleansing, demonstrated her awareness of the need to provide an outward expression to 'prove' the effectiveness of the ritual, even though she did not herself believe that the religious cleansing would 'cure' her. Performative expressions, such as screaming, provided external evidence to the community that the ritual was working. It was clear in Nofoto's narrative that she was very aware her complicity in the ritual ensured she escaped the same fatal retribution that was metred out against her girlfriend.

Nofoto said she was also required to get married to a man chosen by the religious leader and change her outward embodiment, dressing femininely and changing her personal grooming habits in terms of her hair styles and wearing makeup. The combination of her religious performativity of divesting herself of 'demons' and committing to, and performing, expected heteronormative sexuality and gender norms ensured Nofoto could safely remain in her community. Nofoto's vignette is an example of the need to take an intersectional approach to assess experiences of persecution (Dustin and Held, 2018) and shows the multi-faceted forms of persecution that can be experienced by LGBTQI+ people who need to seek asylum. Nofoto's partner's persecution involved gendered, racialised and socio-economic elements that all contributed to the violence against her, but Nofoto was able to avoid the same outcome, both because of the socio-economic status and her willingness to comply and perform heteronormative social norms.

Religious 'cures' were not only used for public transgressions. Yetunde, a Muslim lesbian woman from West Africa, explained how she was caught kissing her girlfriend at boarding school. This incident led to her expulsion and the school informing her mother about her indiscretion. As a result of the incident, her mother took her to an Imam to seek guidance and a 'cure' for Yetunde's offence. Yetunde, recalling the incident, said:

> So, she (her mother) took me to him, and he prayed for me… It was just me staying in the mosque and then when it's time to pray, everyone gathers to pray for me, and they were giving me some things to drink, which was absolutely shit. All the prayers were always focused on me. I think at that moment while the man prayed for me, she (her mother) thought maybe okay, maybe the prayers had worked or something, maybe there are parts of me that has left me, and she didn't really pay much attention to me. She just said that's it, that's gone.

Unlike Nofoto, Yetunde's same sex behaviour was not made public within the community, as Yetunde's school wanted the incident to remain hidden for reputational reasons. Seeking a 'cure' for Yetunde's behaviour, her mother took her to an Imam located in another part of the country, to ensure the episode remained a secret from Yetunde's father and the family's wider community. On conclusion of the ritual, Yetunde's mother believed Yetunde's queer subjectivity was 'cured' and, as the incident had remained a secret, there was no need to speak of it further and life could return to normal.

Excerpts above highlight how the intersection of in/visibility and queer subjectivity can have implications for the persecution people can face in CoO contexts. Narrative excerpts above illustrate how religious institutions are drawn on to play a performative role, such as cleansings or rituals, to provide a justification for a person's transgressions. Religious beliefs were implicated in an explanation and excuse for the existence of queer subjectivity, such as a 'demonic possession' or an 'evil spirit', which placed the transgression outside of the person's ability to control or be responsible for. Therefore, institutional religion is not only complicit in policing sexuality and gender norms but can also ensure those who deviate are given a route back to reintegration into communities; however, this is usually in exchange for heteronormative compliance. While interlocutors' narratives showed such rituals were often performative, as in Nofoto's example, in Yetunde's case, this could be interpreted differently. The actions of Yetunde's mother seeking the help of an Imam in secret, is suggestive of a genuine belief in the ability of religious intervention to provide a 'cure' for deviations from heteronormativity, which was the case for several interlocutors. In both Yetunde's and Nofoto's cases, while they experienced the religious cleansings as harmful, it was not intention of their family members to inflict harm but to save and protect them.

Interlocutors independently sought religious leaders and communities to 'cure' queer subjectivity. Garrett described his experience of seeking religious support in an attempt to stop his attractions towards other men. He believed occupying a religious space for religious contemplation would help prevent these attractions. While he kept his sexuality hidden when interacting with other members of the church and its priest, within the community, he met another man also struggling with his sexuality. Garrett said they started a non-sexual, but romantic relationship and their bond and romantic attachment developed due to their mutual discovery of each other's sexuality. The couple abstained from any sexual activity by joint agreement, as they were both attending church in the hope of changing their sexuality. The comfort of finally finding another he could relate to and share thoughts and concerns with was a great relief to Garrett.

Their connection ended when the priest discovered their relationship, and while Garrett identified as a gay man, his partner identified as bisexual. Due to this, the priest accused Garrett of seducing his partner away from having a 'normal' relationship with a woman, which highlights a hierarchical notion of sexuality (Rubin, 1984), which interestingly can also be seen in RSD where bisexuality is often ignored, due to the possibility a person can have a 'normal' heterosexual relationship (Rehaag, 2009). Garrett said:

> He called me into the office, and he told me, 'I don't like gay people here. If you don't change, get out of here'. 'Your Dad is the Devil, not God'.

Despite the priest's reaction to him, Garrett remained a member of the church community for six years, with a continuing hope he could change. Garrett drew strength from the religious teachings, space and prayers to prevent his same-sex feelings and he said he actively spoke to God to help him change, a habit that started at the age of six. He became visibly upset during our conversation and started to shake and cry when speaking of trying to change his sexuality, displaying both physical and emotional anguish.

> Garrett: I remember always, I spoke with God. 'Change this within me, I don't like it'. Every day. Every day.
>
> CF: Every day?
>
> Garrett: Every day. When I was six years old, seven, eight, 28, every day. Every day.

As part of this hope, he began a six-year relationship with a woman within the community and, even though he liked her, he failed to experience a sexual connection. The relationship with his girlfriend finally ended, and while Garrett did not start a relationship with another woman, he did not pursue a sexual relationship with a man for over 12 years.

> Garrett: I liked men but didn't have sex with men. I stayed with the church; I never had sex with men.
>
> CF: And why did you not have sex with men?
>
> Garrett: I thought it was bad. In the Bible it's so bad that you can't do it.

This example shows that Garrett, due to his religious beliefs, struggled to accept his same-sex feelings and his religiosity prevented him from actively pursuing a relationship for many years after he realised he was gay. His feelings of transgression were long lasting, and at the time of our conversation, it was clear his faith still caused him to view himself negatively because of his sexuality, even though he had a long-term boyfriend.

Bunkechukwu also actively sought support from his priest, but in contrast to Garrett, he was open regarding his sexuality and that he was searching for help to 'cure' himself. On hearing Bunkechukwu confession of his sexuality, the priest made him sit for hours at the back of the church before he would speak with him. Not only because the sin he had committed was seen as the worst type of sin, but as a form of penance and public acknowledgement of his sins. Bunkechukwu remembers:

> I waited for a long hour and after the confession, so he came and said, 'Look you need to do this', and gave me prayers and I need to be coming to the mass, morning masses for about one month or so because of my sin, it's horrible. After that I need to report, again come to him and he's going to pray and then the feelings may go. I did everything and, in the end, I came back, he prayed and said, 'Don't do it again'.

For Bunkechukwu, it became obvious to him that religious intervention would not prevent his same-sex attraction. Instead, he chose to move away from his family and community to prevent public scrutiny. However, in both Garrett's and Bunkechukwu's cases, religious experience was drawn on as a source of strength, even within homonegative contexts, and, for Garrett at least, his religious experiences did provide a form of comfort.

Religious Experiences Within Family and Community

When people are from geographical contexts where religion plays a significant socio-cultural role, it is especially important to consider the intersection of the family and religion in building an understanding of the experiences of LGBTQI+ people seeking safety (Fensham, 2021). Religion can play a central role in terms of people's experiences of socialisation within families, as family and religious institutions often intersect to establish heteronormativity as the 'normal' and 'natural' way of organising society (Sullivan, 2003, p. 119). In terms of relationships, in many parts of the world, there are few options for people to form other types of socially accepted relationships outside of these heterosexual formations (Altman and Symons, 2016). Fensham (2021, p. 1113) argues:

> Because religion and family relationships are often deeply intertwined and socio-culturally enforced for religiously involved people, it is critical to consider the role of both family relationships and religion in the experience of LGBTQI refugees and migrants.

Exploring the intersection of family and religion provides important insights into the variety of ways this convergence can create persecutory environments and untenability for individuals in their CoOs. Persecution is often framed in terms of public and private notions of violence (Millbank, 2009), yet the violence experienced by interlocutors in this research often blurred this distinction. The intersection of family is important in understandings of how people navigate their social environment in their CoO and their motivations to undertake certain actions, such as heteronormative accommodations, for example heterosexual marriage or having children. This is also of relevance in relation to RSD processes as 'accommodations of heteronormative expectations are frequently interpreted as counterevidence' of queer subjectivity (Walker-Said, 2022, p. 119). This is despite evidence that heteronormative strategies are regularly used by those seeking asylum on SO grounds (Giametta, 2017). Compliance with sexuality and gender norms are commonly framed within heterosexual imaginings, and interlocutors were very aware of the heterosexist and hetero-patriarchal norms of their communities in terms of expected bodily performances, emotional and sexual attachments. Religious institutions were portrayed as a strong influence in the promotion and perpetuation of heteronormative dominance within family and community settings.

Interlocutors' participation and adherence to religious beliefs were presumed and expected by immediate and extended family and within wider community. Bunkechukwu, for example when talking about where he spent his time as a child, said 'if it wasn't home, it was church'. Religious experiences in early life were highly prevalent, and all interlocutors spent their childhood in households where religion was important to at least one parent, but most often both, and religious faith was adhered to by extended family members and community. All interlocutors grew up in geographical contexts where there was an expectation that a person would adhere to a religious faith.

Childhood experiences were punctuated with everyday religious ritual and prayer with religious social norms dictating daily life. Hazelle, explained her early childhood experiences:

> Going to church was not a choice, you had to go to church. So, from a young age, I went to kindergarten that was close to the church. The kindergarten was part of the church so from a really young age, I'm talking about 6 years old, I was church based. Our school was church based. We had to go to church.

Hazelle's narrative is a good illustration of the expectations of religious adherence within, not only the confines of the family, but also how religion heavily influenced other areas of life, such as education. Seen in the opening of this chapter, all interlocutors came from countries where religion was cited as highly important to much of the population (Templeton, 2010–2019). As Jamilah explains:

> We are not individuals who came out and said, 'Okay, I'm going to read about all the religions in the world, and then I'm deciding what I want to be'. This is not how it happens. It happens that you grow up in a certain household that believes in something, and this is how you believe.

Jamilah's quotation is an example of the automatic assumption of religious beliefs and adherence.

As discussed earlier, construction of self-hood were influenced by religious experiences, often articulated through a repetition of family traditions, religious teachings and rituals that solidified religious social norms on sexuality and gender. Examples include family prayer rituals, religious festivals and the expectation that individuals will adhere to religiously sanctioned behaviours in both appearance and dress. Farid, a gay man from the Middle East, who grew up in a Muslim household, explained:

> I remember in my family for my sister and in the bigger family of uncles and aunties, all the girls had the hijab before the age of 9, just to practice with, it always seems funny for me. Like, my dad encouraging me that, 'You can do your prayers and practice with me, you're 15 now', The age that boys are expected to start doing the prayers and that sort of thing. Telling us the stories about good things and bad things to do, and practices like when you go to do *wudu* how you should wash yourself.

Farid articulates an acute awareness of accepted gender norms, and ideas of what 'good' behaviour and 'good' subjectivities are within his social context (Rubin, 1984). Interlocutors reported early modelling of religious social norms, with social roles often organised through a rigid dichotomy of expected male/female behaviour and embodiment within the framework of heteronormativity. As seen in Garrett's example earlier, those who did not conform to socially accepted notions of masculinity and femininity were punished, either within the family system or wider community.

The family was a key site where interlocutors began to understand that their queer subjectivity was at odds with the sexuality and gender norms of their social context, again through religious framings. As Bunkechukwu recalls:

> My father would preach against it. We usually have this morning prayer and evening prayer when we want to go to bed. We read some verses of the scripture, and I remember several times he would preach against homosexuality, that it's a sin, it's an abomination. I can remember one time when he said I don't want to see any of you being homosexual. Because if I get to know, I'm going to disown you.

Negative framings of LGBTQI+ people were often grounded in religious teachings, with the rightness of heteronormativity promoted in the same way. Religious practices within the family reinforced interlocutors' understandings that sexuality that transgressed outside the boundaries of heteronormativity was 'sinful' and 'an abomination'. Farid's quote below is a demonstration of not only the promotion of heteronormativity as the accepted and desired relationship formation but also the consequences of deviating from it:

> If you are Muslim, like it says in the Qur'an, a relationship should be between a man and a woman. It's never mentioned between the same sex anywhere in the Qur'an. You've been wanting to have a relationship with the same sex, it's like something very, very forbidden. Even if you are killed by somebody, God is going to reward that person for killing you because you disobeyed God.... They say a marriage should be between a man and a woman, not between the same sex. It's something people believe in; you can't change people's view about that because they have seen it in the Qur'an. If

> it is something you have seen in the Qur'an that's what they believe in, they say it's the word of God, that word can never be changed.

The experiences of interlocutors set out in this chapter, illustrate how the institution of the family is utilised as a vehicle to reinforce religious teachings and helps to mobilise heteronormative compliance. Farid's quotation also speaks directly to how states, while not explicitly involved in the persecution of LGBTQI+ people, such as through criminalising laws, can implicitly condone the demonisation of LGBTQI+ people merely through inaction. This can lead to the violent policing of LGBTQI+ people by non-state actors, such as family members or communities. This is seen in Emenike's example below:

> I was really, really unfortunate. I was beaten very, very well. It was the police. The crowd were beating me. So, initially, they thought probably I was a criminal or something, so they came around, 'What is going on here?' So, they told them that, 'Oh, he was caught having sex with a man'. So, police were like, 'Oh, you carry on and deal with it'. So, they left. I was tortured and beaten even-, I was really, really messed about. You know, really, really screwed up. Some people were using a stick to poke through my backside to teach me some lessons.

As seen in Emenike's example, state authorities provided no protection, and state authorities, such as the police, do not seek to redress violence and injustices meted out against LGBTQI+ people (Walker-Said, 2022).

Commonly, interlocutors spoke of coming under increased pressure to conform to family and societal norms of marriage. As Luibhéid, (2014, p. 124) has argued, that while practices and ideologies vary greatly in different socio-cultural contexts, 'Male– female marriages have been promoted as the desired sexual norm in virtually all societies'. This was replicated within the narratives, and interlocutors indicated a limited ability for autonomous decision making within their familial and community structures regarding decision surrounding marriage (Altman and Symons, 2016). On reaching the socially acceptable age to marry, which varied considerably depending on geographical context, cultural norms and socio-economic status, the pressure to marry increased and non-conformity of marriage expectations intensified family and community scrutiny. Musa describes the pressure he came under after the death of his father.

> Musa: Growing up in a family of religion or too much control, there's no way you can say no, you can't say no. There was no option for me to get out of the marriage. My intention was not to get married, because I was still finding a better way for me to live and to support my mum.
>
> CF: What would have happened if you had said no?

> Musa: Especially the Muslim home, if you defy your parents, they said 'okay, we want you to be like this', and you say no, automatically they will shun you. They will kick you out of the home.

As in Musa's quotation above, people often complied with family expectations to maintain relationships with their family and continue to be able to access support structures provided within the family environment, such as financial support.

Family obligation was a common theme when the topic of marriage was referred to within interlocuters narrative. While in her CoO, Hazelle was in a secret relationship with another woman, but Hazelle was forced to end the relationship when her family arranged for her to marry the son of a family friend. Explaining the obligation she felt towards her family, she said:

> So, it's like you have to die to self.... I was so not into guys at the beginning.... But I had to learn to love him, if that makes sense? I had to be there because of my family. I had to be there not to disappoint them. I had to be there for their pride. Yes, I just had to be there for them. The pride of my family was top priority. I sacrificed myself in a way, and even if I could find a way out, what could I have done? I didn't have much choice.

Hazelle's feelings of duty towards her family were her key motivation in her agreement to marry. Her quotation indicates how, if she had refused, it would not only have impacted her relationship with her family, but the standing of her family within the wider community. Other interlocutors referred to how marriage was key to protecting the honour and reputation of the family. Dinesh, a practitioner who worked with people who identified as queer Muslims, explained:

> For a lot of LGBTQI+ Muslim people, especially women, it's very difficult because this whole idea of *'izzat'*, which means honour, family honour and shame, is quite big in the community.

The protection of their family's reputation and honour was often mentioned by individuals within explanations of why they agreed to their family's wishes, even though they contradicted their own desires.

Tied to the pressure of marriage was the expectation of interlocutors to have children. Heteronormative reproduction was raised regularly by interlocutors, and this burden was experienced by all interlocutors regardless of their gender. Umaru, a gay man from West Africa, explains:

> Man, and man, even when you are together, you cannot give birth to a child. So, it's like you are just wasting your time. You cannot waste your time. Sometimes it's even commented 'Well the Bible said, go into the world and multiply'. When you are in the world, you have to find a wife. You need to settle down and have children.

Umaru's quotation is an illustration of the emphasis on the importance of procreation, which again was supported by religious framings. As seen in Umaru's quotation, religious teachings were used to support heterosexual family arrangements. Habib (2012, p. 12) argues that the gender binarisms promoted within Orthodox Islamic religious doctrine mean that not only are deviations away from the gender binary seen as undesirable but as a direct contradiction from the 'Creator's intention due to social constructions that geared towards progeny'.

The assumed naturalness of gender norms that are uncritically applied in societies can result in the violent policing of those who do not comply (Butler, 1999). This awareness of the violent potential for non-conformity was evident when individual spoke about their experiences with family and communities. There was significant variations and individual nuances in experience of punishments metered out by family towards those who transgressed heteronormative expectations. Negative experiences resulting from deviations ranged from verbal and physical abuse to incidences of rape, torture and mob violence. Jamilah describes her own experiences with her family:

> I was beaten to have manners because no man would marry a woman who was ill-mannered. My dad forced me to wear a veil because a veil would indicate that I'm a good woman, or a good lady, or a female, at the time so that means a man would be interested in marrying me. So, it was horrible. It was horrible that wherever I looked, it made me feel as if, 'Okay, what's the point?' you know? I think when I was around 15 that's why I wanted to jump out of the window. In my mind, later, it felt as if it was all because I was angry about being forced to wear a veil. It wasn't that. I think the bigger explanation was, 'Okay, so what's next for me?' you know? .... I was 21, maybe? I was still getting beaten horribly, especially when she (her mother) would get a suitor to see me, and I would say no to marriage. So, basically, I would go to work, and this is I think where my mental state was like, I would go to work, I was a very respectful person at work, but then the minute I stepped in the house, the whole argument about getting married, and then she would beat me.

Jamilah's experiences are an example of the violent consequences of refusing to conform to family expectations and an example of the types of persecution LGBTQI+ individuals often face in the private sphere. Jamilah, due to her self-described 'different' appearance compared to normative feminine embodiment in her CoO, was subjected to rumours and speculation about her sexuality. Jamilah's non-conformity to gendered expectations not only meant she was subjected to violence within her home, but in her community, with the abuse eventually leading to a brutal sexual attack.

Sexual and gender-based violence (SGBV) against those who commit gender and sexual norm violations were common occurrences within interlocutors' narratives. SGBV violence experienced by interlocutors included, corrective rape to 'cure' same-sex tendencies, marital rape, rape and SGBV as a form of punishment (McKnight et al., 2024). Njema was discovered by her father on two occasions with a female partner. After the first incident, Njema's father forced her to travel with him to one of the villages to take part in a traditional ritual to 'cure' her from her deviant behaviour. Nejema was sent away from the family home to a university on the other side of the country as a punishment, as Njema said this was because her father feared she would bring shame on the family. At university, Njema met her second girlfriend with whom she had a long-term relationship. Towards the end of her studies, the couple were caught kissing by a member of her girlfriend's family. The incident was reported back to her father and on returning home from university Njema's father locked her in a room in the family home with a man who her father had arranged to subject her to corrective rape to 'cure' her. Njema recalled, 'He became so upset and he locked me inside a room with a man. I was nearly raped, if not for my mum'.

While female interlocutors spoke more frequently of familial and community policing that ended in SGBV, male interlocutors also reported being victims of sexual violence. Interlocutors, believed they were victims of this violence due to their deviation from the hegemonic form of masculinity, as they embodied behaviours that were coded as feminine, within their social context (Connell, 2020). Two male interlocutors within this research sustained long-term child sexual abuse by male perpetrators, which they attributed to their effeminate appearance. There were also repeated references in interlocutors narratives as how men who appeared to embody gender norms, associated within their community as feminine, would become targets for familial and community violence (Otu, 2022).

In interlocutors' narratives, as in Jamilah's quotation above, individuals often referred to the despair they felt about the impossibility of a non-heteronormative future within their CoO (Edelman, 2004). Hazelle recalled her girlfriend's desire to run away together in their CoO to be able to continue their relationship and avoid heterosexual marriages. Hazelle spoke of the impossibility of financial survival away from their families in their CoO as a 'hopeless dream' as in her CoO it was extremely difficult for women to live alone Women who did so faced social stigmatisation and those who lived without the support of the family, especially male family members, were at a greater risk of violence.

In many geographic contexts, aside from making women more vulnerable to violence, women are unable to rent property or work without the permission of a male family member. A primary gendered difference in the narratives was that male interlocutors were afforded greater mobility and freedom to independently live and travel outside of familial spaces. Female interlocutors in particular spoke of how they would not be safe if they were to leave their family home. Jamilah explained:

> It's not as if I can just grab some of my stuff and leave the house and go disappear somewhere in (location removed). It's not going to happen. They'll find you or you're going to be in a worse situation. Someone is going to, you know, abuse you or kill you or rape

> you because they know you left to your family. So, if you've left your family, you're fair game.

Refusals in asylum decision making in SO asylum claims are often refused, as asylum decision makers claimants' ability to internally relocate away from persecution within their CoO. As seen in Jamilah's example, decision reasoning along these lines ignores intersectional factors of persecution, such as gender, as the ability to internally relocate in CoO for women is often an impossibility.

Undercurrents regarding the violent consequences of non-conformity to sexuality and gender social norms led to heightened levels of anxiety when interlocutors reached the age of which heterosexual relationships and/or marriage was expected. Interlocutors referred to fears that their queerness would be discovered because of questions and speculations regarding their unmarried status. This potential meant interlocuters increased their vigilance to keep queer subjectivity internalised and hidden. As part of this, strategies outward expressions of heteronormativity were important for keeping their self-hood as unremarkable and invisible ensuring no questions were raised as to whether their subjectivity was compliant with social norms. Abdul, a gay man from West Africa, spoke of his reasons for engaging in a heterosexual relationship:

> What I'm trying to say, if I continued to engage in a relationship, the wider community and my other family members would not know much about my sexuality…. But inside me by then it's not me. Inside me it was not me. But I just had to, to keep the family and community mute about my sexuality.

Heterosexual marriage and relationship were a common strategy to reduce family and community speculation surrounding individuals' sexuality (Giametta, 2017). Farid said he started a relationship with a girl when he was at university due to the constant questioning of peers and family as to why he did not have a girlfriend. Some interlocutors reported that the strategy of perusing heterosexual relationships had significant, negative impact on their well-being. Desire, who married to escape the violence she experienced within her family and to stop rumours about her sexuality, faced further violence within her marriage. She struggled with the repeated sexual demands of her husband, saying:

> Having sex with me, I always tried to refuse, giving an excuse. But because of our culture in (location removed) you can't say no to your husband no matter what. He can have his fucks anyway so he's basically always having his way with me, but he would rape me. Even when I conceived my second child this was during when he raped me.

These extracts depict how heterosexual relationships were utilised to ensure interlocutors could distance themselves from speculation regarding their queer subjectivity, yet these strategies did not necessarily protect interlocutors from harm.

Family members were both complicit in strategies to keep interlocutors' queer subjectivity hidden in homonegative contexts and could also be the main perpetrators in the incidence of persecution. Male family members were referenced more frequently as directly involved in violence and abuse of LGBTQI+ family members, with female family members more likely to provide protective roles in hiding or aiding the escape for LGBTQI+ people who were discovered and threatened with harm. For example, Emenike, a gay man from West Africa, was aided by his eldest sister to escape his CoO after he was discovered by a group of men in his community having sex with his boyfriend. Emenike's father was a high standing member of the community, and when Emenike was caught, his father demanded he was handed over for him to punish personally. Emenike explained:

> Eventually, my dad got involved because he was well known as a parishioner, so he told the villagers to leave me, that he is going to take care of things. So, out of respect, they left me for him to take care of. Meanwhile, I was bleeding all over my body, so he took me back home. That is where the trauma and torture, started. I was physically kept in isolation because my dad now perceived me as an embarrassment to our culture, an embarrassment to our tradition, an embarrassment to the family. It was crazy. There was no type of name I wasn't called. There was no emotional kind of trauma that I didn't go through. There was no amount of maltreatment, emotional maltreatment, he didn't place on me. In fact, at this point, he said that he felt that I had a gay spirit in me, and he was to get rid of it.

Emenike's oldest sister defended him within the family, as the oldest sibling Emenike said his sister commanded a degree of respect and was, therefore, allowed to bring him water and care for him. Emenike remained a prisoner in his own home, but his sister planned and organised his escape. It was only through her help that Emenike was able to travel to Libya, from where he eventually managed to reach Europe.

Family members also challenged the religious beliefs of other people within the family unit, who viewed LGBTQI+ people as sinful and deviant. Rafael explained how his mother who, in her 90s and a staunch Catholic, defended him and challenged homophobic comments made by his brother when he found out he was gay, saying:

> My older brother, he's 73, he's more conservative than my mum. I remember, well, he knows now about me, and he said 'Mum, do you know that Rafael is gay?' No. He just used the other word, a bad word. 'Do you know that he is a faggot?' My mum says, 'Faggot? What faggot?' My brother said, 'He's gay'. My brother said, 'This is a sin, no? How is it possible you are not sad?'

Rafael said his mother responded:

> 'Okay, you are perfect? No. I accept you, the way you are'. He said, 'But I am not gay, mum'. 'Yes, but you're stupid, yes. I accept you, what is the problem?' So, he was very upset. My brother never talked about this topic again.

The reactions and actions of family members directly impacted how possible it was LGBTQI+ people to remain in their CoO. Saafir remembers starting primary school and how he was drawn to the other boys, although he was not aware that this was an early sign of his queer subjectivity. Saafir said he was especially enamoured with one boy, and he eventually touched him inappropriately; this led to his family becoming aware of the possibility his sexuality deviated from the heteronormative norm. After this incident, his brothers would ensure he was not left alone outside of the family home and accompanied him everywhere:

> Saafir: When the bells rang for the lunch, they really want to come to my class and took you out to eat. Because they were guiding me seriously. They didn't want me to play with the usual friends so that they won't know what's really happened. They were just covering me.
>
> CF: Why would they do that?
>
> Saafir: Because they didn't want my sexuality to be exposed.

From this incident onwards, Saafir's family policed his behaviour, not only for his protection, but also for their own, as deviations from gender and sexuality norms not only had implications for Saafir's safety, but for his family's as well. Saafir, in our conversation, referred to other LGBTQI+ people he knew about who, 'don't behave seriously'. The result of their behaviour meant they were nearly killed, and their family exiled from the community.

Community, in relation to risks that could jeopardise the safety of LGBTQI+ people, were regularly spoken about by interlocutors in reference to actions taken by member of their family towards them because of their queer subjectivity. Individuals described how close-knit social ties meant they were often well known within the wider community, and this was linked to pressures, real or perceived, to conform to sexuality and gender norms. Yetunde's narrative is an example of the significant impacts exposure of queer subjectivity can have on immediate family.

Yetunde, had begun a secret relationship with a woman during her year of national service. Undertaking national service meant Yetunde could move to a different part of her country and it gave her a justification for living alone, away from the scrutiny of her family. The freedom of living independently provided her with more privacy, which allowed her to become involved in a same-sex relationship without fear of her family finding out. On completion of her national service, Yetunde moved to the UK to complete her master's degree. Unfortunately, during her time in the UK, Yetunde girlfriend died due to a long-term illness. After her death, Yetunde's partner's family cleared her girlfriend's home and discovered her diary, with the entries revealing the couple's relationship and Yetunde's identity. While still in the UK, Yetunde started to receive death threats from her partner's family. However, the perpetrators also began to target Yetunde's family back in her CoO. This led to her family disowning her and cutting her off from all family ties. She explained:

> They feel like it's an abomination, it's a sin to have something to do with someone who is the same sex as you. So, the religion, even the culture played a huge part in why they reacted that way. And people would see them as 'their child is lesbian', for them they think it is not a good reputation. So maybe they don't want to spoil their reputation in the environment, in the streets. People would just see your family as committing a very huge sin. No one is going to want to interact with you anymore.

Yetunde believed her family's rejection of her was to ensure they were not implicated with the stigma of her queer subjectivity in their community.

Fear of retribution by others within their social context was commonly referred to, as those with queer subjectivities were seen as a source of community shame. Musa recalled how the entire community was involved in his cleansing ritual, this was because his same-sex activity was viewed as tainting the whole community with sin. Therefore, the entire community needed to be absolved from and cleansed from his 'sin'. Violent actions towards individuals are not just an individual punishment, such as punishments for violation of religious norms, but harmful actions inflicted on LGBTQI+ people can often be part of a collective form of community cleansing.

Concluding Remarks

The aim of this chapter was to portray the diversity of experiences in CoO of LGBTQI+ people that need to seek refuge in the UK. Interlocutors' experiences demonstrate the centrality of religious framings in self-understandings of queer subjectivity. Non-affirming religious teachings resulted in many interlocutors developing an internalised queerphobia, resulting in their understanding of their queer subjectivity as a problem, and a deficiency in themselves.

Vignettes presented in this chapter provide insight of how self-understanding of subjectivity is intimately entangled with expectations and approval from the family and wider community which is also influenced by religious norms. However, just as attitudes towards queer subjectivities were influenced by religious beliefs and teachings, so too were the 'remedies' that interlocutors evoked in search of a 'cure' or comfort regarding their queerness. While religious beliefs and practices can create negative perceptions of queer subjectivities, religious encounters in CoO contexts are also sought out for comfort and redemption. Considering liberal narrative tropes prevalent in the global North about the inevitability of flight for those with queer subjectivities (El-Tayeb, 2012), interlocutors' narratives above challenge this and demonstrate the efforts some interlocutors exerted to 'cure' their queer subjectivity to remain in their CoO.

Religious experience was not only implicated in seeking a 'cure' for individual transgressions or deviations from sexuality and gender norms but also in cures for family and communities as a whole. Related to families and communities, this chapter challenges the idea that certain geographical contexts are homogenously homophobic. In the narratives presented, it can be seen how friends and family were involved survival strategies for those with queer subjectivities living within homonegative contexts, which were often essential to help interlocutors escape from unsafe situations when their queer subjectivities were discovered. In conclusion, it can be seen how growing up in geographical contexts where religious observance is highly prevalent within society, it is hardly surprising that all individuals would not wish to divest themselves of religious beliefs on immediately reaching the UK, regardless of any homonegativity that might be present within their religious beliefs and traditions.

Chapter 2

Hostility and Harm: Structural Failures in UK Asylum Support for LGBTQI+ People*

Globally, we are facing a political climate of rising anti-migrant and anti-LGBTQI+ hostility. The upsurge of far-right politics has seen an increased focus on immigration policies, and in a range of geographic contexts, a regression of gains made regarding the legal rights for LGBTQI+ people. Retrogressions have ranged from the removal of laws and policies aimed at protecting the rights of sexually and gender diverse people, to deliberate criminalisation and state persecution, with religious freedoms often used as a justification for these rollbacks (Kaleidscope Trust, 2025). Because of this shift, LGBTQI+ people displaced from their CoO find themselves sitting at the 'intersection of a double backlash, against migration on the one hand and against the rights of queer and trans people on the other' (Buxton and Ritholtz, 2026, p. 7).

At the time of writing, 66 countries, globally, criminalise same-sex sex between consenting adults, and in 12 countries, it is possible to receive the death penalty (Human Dignity Trust, 2026). In other Countries, while no criminal sanctions exist, LGBTQI+ people are still persecuted and discriminated against because they transgress cultural and religious sexuality and gender norms. In this instance, LGBTQI+ people can experience exclusion from access to housing, employment and healthcare, which make sustaining a livelihood incredibly challenging (Badgett, 2020). The global backlash towards LGBTQI+ people means it is increasingly likely there will be an escalation in the number of people forced to find safety in countries other than their own. At the time of writing, the total of refugees globally currently stands at 123.3 million (UNHCR, 2025), while there

* This chapter was developed using material from the thesis: Fletcher, Claire; (2024) Queerly Faithful: The experiences of religion for those seeking asylum in the UK. Doctoral thesis (Ph.D), UCL (University College London).

Queerly Faithful: Queer People's Experience of Religion in Asylum Seeking, 43–58

doi:10.1108/978-1-83797-488-720261004

is no reliable data on the numbers of LGBTQI+ refugees globally, estimates have assumed five per cent of refugees identify as LGBTQI+ (Shaw and Verghese, 2022; Tang and Dempster, 2024).

In the UK, LGBTQI+ people seeking asylum have been targeted, by right-wing politicians and media outlets proclaiming 'record numbers' of people claiming on sexual orientation (SO) grounds are 'pretending to be gay' (Davis, 2024). People who claim on SO grounds are accused of making 'bogus' and 'fake' asylum claims. Suella Braverman, a previous Conservative Home Secretary, accused SO claimants of 'gaming' the system, a fact the Home Office was later forced to retract as there was no evidence to substantiate the claim (Alwakeel and Bychawski, 2023). Compared to overall asylum numbers, people claiming asylum on SO grounds are only a small proportion of claimants. Recent statistics released by the Home Office on SO asylum claims showed that in 2023, 2 per cent (1,377) of asylum claims included SO as part of the basis of claim (Home Office, 2024).[1]

Socio-legal scholarship has considered the issues within the legal asylum process in the UK (for examples see: Danisi et al., 2021; Dustin and Held, 2021). However, there remains a gap regarding how statutory asylum support and the provision of asylum accommodation within the asylum support framework creates unique barriers for LGBTQI+ people seeking asylum. This chapter argues that these policies increase the vulnerability of LGBTQI+ people, which have been further exacerbated by recent policy changes.

While new forms of asylum accommodation have reshaped the environments in which people seeking asylum live, the risks created by these spaces for LGBTQI+ people are intensified by longstanding features of the asylum system. These include low levels of financial support, the over-riding principle of 'no choice' in accommodation provision and the dispersal policy, aimed at preventing people seeking asylum living in concentrated areas. Together, these structural conditions limit LGBTQI+ individuals' ability to avoid unsafe living situations and gain access to supportive networks. This not only exposes people to an increased risk of harm but the social factors that are created by the statutory asylum support framework create barriers for LGBTQI+ people fairly accessing the RSD process.

Before moving onto consider the formal asylum system, it is important to briefly reflect on the factors which have led to the recent policy changes. The current UK context mirrors the global political shifts in a sharp rise in anti-migrant and anti-LGBTQI+ sentiment, fuelled by the far-right politicians and media. Anti-migrant sentiment has risen sharply, driven in part by the relatively new and very visible phenomenon of migrants crossing the English Channel via small boats.

---

[1]It should be noted that these figures are not an accurate reflection of the total number of LGBTQI+ people in the asylum system with queer subjectivities as asylum claims are only recorded if SO is part of the grounds of the asylum application (Alessi et al., 2025). Home Office's data collection is routinely criticised as of a poor standard, and a previous report by the Independent Chief Inspector of Borders and Immigration (ICIBI) labelled data collection by the Home Office as 'inexcusably awful' (ICIBI, 2022, p. 2).

Before 2020, small boat arrivals were low, totalling only 10,608 between 2018 and 2020. Since 2021, there has been a marked increase and 2022 saw the highest arrival numbers at 45,774. At the time of writing, recent statistics showed that by the year ending September 2025, 45,659 people had arrived by small boats (Home Office, 2025a). In relation to small boat arrivals, politicians have used dehumanising labels such as 'swarms', 'invasion' and 'terrorists' to position people seeking safety as a threat to 'legitimate' citizens (Squire, 2009; Smellie, 2023). The use of securitisation and criminalisation framings have long been utilised to justify increasing border controls and restricting entry and protection to those seeking safety. Securitisation logics are used in conjunction with dichotomous understandings of those who 'deserve' or 'legitimately' seek asylum versus 'illegal migrants' who threaten the safety and security of the UK (Mayblin, 2017, p. 3).

Recently, this rhetoric has been drawn on to pave the way for rapid immigration legislation, justified by an urgent need to 'bring back control' to Britain's borders. Stanley (2025, p. 8) argues, state violence is often 'professionally performed and is justified as means to an end for solving a "problem" that the maintenance of state violence relies upon. To do this, Stanley contents that institutions needs to 'consistently assert a legitimatizing framework'. This can be seen in political debates related to immigration and asylum regimes, which have focused on the 'problem' of 'illegal migration' which can only be solved by a significant reduction in the rights afforded to people seeking asylum and increased border controls and enforcement. The creation of this 'problem' is reflected in political slogans used by consecutive Prime Ministers: Boris Johnson's (2019–2022) 'Taking back control of our borders', Rishi Sunak's (2022–2024) 'Stop the Boats', Keir Starmer's (2024–2025) 'Smash the Gangs' and now Home Secretary Shabana Mahood's 'Restore Order and Control' (2025).

The previous Conservative government initiated a raft of hostile immigration reforms, and argued reforms were warranted to fix the UK's 'broken' asylum system. In the past five years, the Nationality and Borders Act 2022 (NABA 2022), the Illegal Migration Act 2023 (IMA 2023) and the Safety of Rwanda (Immigration and Asylum) Act 2024 all reached Royal Assent. This rapid cycle of new immigration legislation has continued under Labour, who came to power in July 2024. While initially attempting to temper debates surrounding immigration, the government has since abandoned this due to growing levels of political popularity of Reform, one of the UK's far-right political parties. New legislative measures under the Border Security, Asylum, and Immigration Act (2025) and the Home Secretary, Shabana Mahmood's Restoring Order and Control: A statement on the government's asylum and returns policy in November 2025, bring further punitive changes to the asylum system and limits the rights of those who seek safety.

Another 'problem' that has come to the political fore are the high levels of spending on statutory asylum support, levels of government spending have further inflamed debates on asylum. Increased spending has been driven by the large numbers of people who have had to be housed in temporary asylum accommodation, termed as 'contingency' accommodation. While hotels have previously played a role in housing people seeking asylum, in 2020, the use of hotels rapidly increased, and between 2014 and 2023, the number of people in statutory asylum accommodation jumped from 28,300 to 119,000, representing a 320 per cent increase (Jorgensen, 2025).

The numbers of people in the asylum process being accommodated in asylum accommodation, particularly contingency hotels, are regularly linked by politicians and the media to the number of people arriving on small boats. Yet, the increase supported by the state has been created by several factors. These include the Home Office's own mismanagement of asylum caseload (NAO, 2025a), the frequent introduction of new legislative measures brought in by successive governments, especially new inadmissibility procedures (Lenegan, 2024) and the number of small boat arrivals. This combination of factors created a huge build-up of asylum cases, which at its peak reached 134,000 in June 2023 (Kirk-Wade, 2026). While overall numbers have since reduced to 47,700 in December 2025 the overall asylum caseload is still very high and, at the time of writing stood at 224,742 cases, with 32 per cent of asylum applicants having waited over 36 months for their case to be resolved (Home Office, 2026a).

This backlog of asylum cases caused by the Home Office's own poor management is the central cause of spiralling asylum support costs (Gower, 2023). A report by the National Audit Office detailed how the Home Office's original predicted total spend on asylum support contracts (2019–2029) has jumped from the original estimate of £4.5 billion to £15.3 billion (NAO, 2025b). At the time of the report, the then Prime Minister, Keir Starmer criticised the cost of hotel accommodation as 'eye-wateringly expensive', with the previous Home Secretary Yvette Cooper singling out asylum accommodation as an "appalling waste of taxpayers' money' (House of Commons Home Affairs Committee, 2024, Q36). This level of spending placed the government under huge political and public pressure to end hotel use to house people in the asylum system, with Chancellor Rachel Reeves pledging to stop using hotels by 2029 in the June 2025 spending review (Francis and Fenwick, 2025).

Despite this pledge, the cost associated with housing people seeking asylum remains politically toxic. Government spending on asylum support is used by far-right politicians to drive anti-migrant agendas. Historically, asylum housing is sourced in areas already experiencing high levels of poverty and social deprivation because of the affordability of housing (Casey, 2016; Hynes, 2011). The current cost-of-living crisis in the UK has further fuelled tensions, and in the summers of 2024 and 2025, anti-migrant protests erupted around the country, often taking place outside of hotels housing people seeking asylum. One of the worst incidents occurred outside a Holiday Inn Express near Rotherham in August 2024. The hotel, housing approximately 200 people seeking asylum, was set alight and had windows smashed by rioters, with protesters heard chanting 'get them out' and 'we want our country back' (Fox, 2024).

A policy introduced by the previous Conservative government in an attempt to reduce the costs of asylum support was the use of large sites; typically, ex-military of defence sites, such as Napier barracks in Kent and Weathersfield in Essex. Large sites were not only introduced as a cost saving measure but as a deterrent, with Robert Jenrick, serving as the Minister for Immigration at that time, stating 'we need to suffuse our entire system with deterrence, and this must include how we house illegal migrants'(Gower, 2023, p. 19). Large sites are heavily criticised, dubbed as 'quasi-prison' and 'quasi-detention' spaces, with organisations who work with people in the asylum system argue that this policy direction of housing people seeking asylum blurs the distinction between accommodation and detention (Cartwright, 2023).

The policy direction of utilising large sites to accommodate people in the asylum process was abandoned by the previous Conservative government due to heavy criticism of the use of such sites and their spiralling costs (Home Affairs Committee, 2025). However, the Labour government has revived this policy direction, in response to rising hostile attention from the far-right focusing on the government's use of hotels, in an attempt to reduce future costs and as a deterrence measure (Fenwick, 2025). Two new sites have been identified to house people seeking asylum, with Crowborough army training camp in East Sussex already operational and open. Cameron Barracks in Inverness currently, facing delays in opening due to ongoing disputes over licensing requirements (Eardley and Davies, 2025).

Queer Precarity in the Asylum Support System

The focus on asylum support provision is due to the UK's welfare state having long been framed by politicians as a pull factor for people seeking asylum, despite evidence to the contrary (Mayblin et al., 2020). Indeed, the Home Office's own analysis confirms that people who flee their CoO are rarely aware of legislation, policies and immigration guidance in the countries they seek sanctuary in (Walsh and Sumption, 2024). Despite this, support provided to people seeking asylum and refugees is often drawn into political debates and can be seen most recently in this statement by Shabana Mahood.

> While some are genuine refugees, others are economic migrants, seeking to take advantage of the asylum system. Even amongst those who are genuine refugees, economic incentives are at play. Instead of stopping at the first safe country even genuine refugees are searching for the most attractive place to seek refuge, many now 'asylum shop' their way across the continent, in search of the most attractive place to seek refuge (Home Office, 2025b).

By establishing a binary between 'economic migrants' and 'genuine' refugees, this rhetoric is brought into play within UK politics to justify punitive measures towards people seeking asylum, such as restricting access to public funds. States have ideologically positioned immigration, and particularly those seeking asylum, as a threat to public goods, and this has resulted in public resentment towards states' providing support for people in the asylum system, however deficient this support may be. As Mayblin and James (2018) have argued because of public attitudes, there is no incentive for states to adequately provide for people in the asylum system.

Mayblin (2017) argues that state populations have come to expect that the treatment of people seeking asylum is less than the standard afforded to citizens until their 'deservedness' is proven. This is grounded within colonial histories and current neo-colonial projects that see Western liberal democracies continually permitted to degrade and dehumanised people within the asylum process. The logics of colonialism designate a different worth and value to a variety of human bodies, which are used to rationalise differing treatment (Mayblin, 2017). Common in Western liberal democracies is the myth that harsh and punitive legislation towards migrants will prevent people from moving, and therefore, draconian policies and treatment of people seeking asylum are accepted by state citizens (Stanley, 2025).

Despite Mahmood's labelling asylum support as a 'generous package of state-funded support', destitution is rife among people seeking asylum and refugees (Home Office, 2025b). The formal asylum support system is consistently criticised as vastly inadequate to meet the needs of those in the asylum system (Human Rights Watch, 2023), and in reality, asylum support has, for a long time, fallen woefully short in terms of meeting even basic need (Joint Committee on Human Rights, 2007). The decades of constant restrictions on access to public funds have resulted in people in the asylum system liable to become destitute at any stage of their claim (Mayblin and James, 2018). The government's deliberate use of forcing people into destitution while seeking asylum as part of wider policy measures to create a hostile environment has led to the government of being accused of using 'destitution as a weapon of immigration control' (Wheeler, 2024, p. 5). The main aim of these policy measures is an attempt to create a deterrent for others attempting to seek asylum in the UK (Allsopp et al., 2014; Mayblin et al., 2020; Randall, 2015).

Policymaking over the past five years has escalated the problems for people seeking safety, especially in terms of social exclusion, homelessness, destitution and discrimination. Widespread destitution seen in asylum seeking and refugee communities is rapidly increasing year-on-year (British Red Cross and UNHCR, 2022; Ramachandran, 2024; NACCOM, 2023). Human Rights Watch has criticised the UK's asylum support system as 'plagued by serious deficiencies, in violation of people's human rights to housing, food, education, health, and social security'. Academics have utilised the term 'slow violence' to conceptualise how hostile asylum policymaking has affected people's everyday lives while in the asylum systems Mayblin, 2019. Entrenched poverty for people in the UK asylum system creates sustained and significant deterioration of physical and mental wellbeing, subjecting them to a form of 'slow death' (Mayblin et al., 2020; Darling, 2022).

Policy and service provision geared towards migrants (including those seeking asylum) remains 'organized around the premise that migrants are heterosexuals (or on their way to becoming so) and queers are citizens (even though second-class ones)' (Luibhéid, 2008a, p. 169). For LGBTQI+ people, this creates an added burden as they must navigate a system which is underpinned and governed by heteronormative[2] assumptions (Wimark, 2021).

Financial Support

Until recently, regulation 5 of the Asylum Seekers (Reception Conditions) Regulations 2005[3] levied a duty on the government to provide asylum support for people seeking asylum who were destitute.[4] In the Restoring Order and Control, policy statement the government announced its intention to revoke this duty. This came into force on the 2 June 2026, and the Home Office now has a discretionary power to provide asylum support under the Immigration and Asylum Act 1999 (IAA 1999). The government has announced further changes to the asylum support system, but at the time of writing these changes were being consulted on. Currently, asylum support is provided under the IAA 1999 which established a separate system of support that excluded those subjected to immigration control from the UK's main welfare system. Asylum support rates are currently £49.18 per person, per week if accommodation is self-catered or £8.68 per week if accommodation is provided on a full board basis. Asylum support rates are less than the rate offered under Universal Credit, which means the asylum support rate is 50 per cent below the poverty line in the UK (APPG Migration and Poverty, 2024).

The main forms of asylum support are: section 98, which is temporary support provided while the support application are considered. Section 95 is the main form of asylum support for those who have an active asylum claim, with section 4 support provided to individuals in limited circumstance when their asylum claim has been refused or if they have made further submission to the Home Office

---

[2]The conceptualisation of heteronormativity utilised in the context of this research is: 'the institutions, structures of understanding practical orientations that make heterosexuality seem not only coherent – that is, organized as a sexuality – but also privileged. Its coherence is always provisional, and its privilege can take several (sometimes contradictory) forms: unmarked, as the basic idiom of the personal and the social; or marked as a natural state; or projected as an ideal or moral accomplishment. It consists less of norms that could be summarized as a body of doctrine than of a sense of rightness produced in contradictory manifestations – often unconscious, immanent to practice or to institutions' (Berlant and Warner, 1998; see also Warner, 1993).

[3]*The Asylum Seekers (Reception Conditions) Regulations* 2005, SI 2005/7. Available at: https://www.legislation.gov.uk/uksi/2005/7/contents/made.

[4]Under the IAA, 1999, a person is considered destitute if, at the time of the application or with 14 days: they do not have adequate accommodation or any means of obtaining it (whether or not their other essential living needs are met) or have adequate accommodation or the means of obtaining it but cannot meet their other essential living *Immigration and Asylum Act 1999, 95 (c)*. Available at https://www.legislation.gov.uk/ukpga/2012/7/contents/ [Accessed 8 August 2025].

for a fresh claim. Asylum support applications are complicated, and third sector organisation have been found to spend a large portion of their time helping people access asylum support (Mayblin and James, 2018). If an asylum support application is refused, specialist support from a third sector organisation is often essential (Hutton and Lukes, 2024).

Asylum support is removed from people seeking asylum if they do not have an active asylum claim. If a person's asylum claim is refused, asylum support is terminated after 21 days while people who receive a positive decision on their claim have 42 days before their asylum support is terminated. For those who have no outstanding asylum claim, section 4 support can be accessed in very limited circumstances, such as agreeing to voluntarily return to their CoO, a barrier to returning to their CoO that is recognised by the Secretary of State for the Home Department or establishing they have a significant mental or physical health need.[5] Additionally, if a person can gather fresh evidence to make further submissions to the Home Office for a fresh claim and this is accepted, they are also able to apply for section 4 support.

Organisations working with people in the asylum system are seeing increasing numbers of people falling between the cracks when their initial asylum claim is refused, despite having a right of appeal, leading to asylum claimants losing statutory support. A common example is when an unrepresented person receives a refusal on their initial claim from the Home Office and have a right of appeal, because of a shortage in available legal advice in the UK, they are either unaware or do not understand how to submit their asylum appeal paperwork (NACCOM, 2023). This leads to people with valid asylum claims failing out of the system. Currently, the UK is experiencing a major shortfall in legal aid practitioner to advise people in the asylum system. Whole areas of the UK are legal advice deserts, which is adding to the issues already present due to insufficient provision of support (Wilding, 2021). Recently published statistics show only 57 per cent people seeking asylum in England and Wales have access to legal representation (Wilding, 2024).

If a person has no legal leave to remain in the UK, they are often referred to as having 'no recourse to public funds' or 'NRPF', simply put, this means people are ineligible to access welfare benefits and social housing (McKinney et al., 2025). People who are NRPF are vulnerable to exploitation, which is directly created by their ineligibility to access any form of statutory support (Gardner and Patel, 2021). In these circumstances, the only option open to people is to seek support through informal networks and communities, however, this form of support is precarious, unreliable and unpredictable (NACCOM, 2023).

The inadequacies in asylum support place LGBTQI+ people at further risk. Queer scholarship has demonstrated how queer migrants can find themselves marginalised, both as ethnic minorities in the destination society and as sexual minorities within the diaspora communities (Mole, 2021). Often, LGBTQI+ people choose to avoid diaspora and religious communities altogether, as they can be hostile and unwelcoming (Alessi et al., 2020). Limitations in support

[5]Immigration and Asylum Act 1999 under reg 3(2) of Section 4(2).

for LGBTQI+ people mean they are more likely to be exposed to experiences of poverty and destitution, which in turn raises the probability that they will encounter, discrimination and violence while seeking asylum and these experiences are discussed more widely in Chapter 3.

Asylum Accommodation

Asylum accommodation is identified as a key source of harm to LGBTQI+ people seeking asylum by both the interlocutors and practitioners in this research. These findings are replicated in research conducted by organisations who work closely with LGBTQI+ people in the asylum system (LGBT Health Wellbeing, 2023; Balogun and Williams, 2024; McKnight et al., 2024). Mainstream asylum accommodation is organised around the assumption of heteronormativity, which leaves LGBTQI+ people with insufficient safe housing provision (Fletcher, 2024b; Danisi et al., 2021; Wimark, 2021). Dustin and Held (2021) argue that because of the heteronormative arrangements of asylum accommodation spaces, LGBTQI+ people feel 'out of place' even without any adverse events having taken place because of their anxiety about their non-normative sexuality being discovered.

Currently, the Home Office must provide accommodation for destitute people in the asylum process. Asylum housing is currently outsourced by the Home Office to private housing contractors through the Asylum and Support Services Contracts. The management of asylum accommodation by both the Home Office and the private contractors has been heavily criticised because of the absence of adequate safeguarding frameworks to protect people in asylum accommodation. The Home Office has been criticised for poor management and oversight of the private contractors. (Home Affairs Committee, 2025). Asylum accommodation itself is routinely criticised as substandard, overcrowded and provides residents with limited access to services, especially healthcare and an insufficient provision of nutritious food (Townsend, 2023; Human Rights Watch, 2023).

There are three main types of accommodation currently in use, initial, dispersal and contingency. Initial accommodation is provided, often on a full board basis in a hotel or hostel. In initial accommodation, people can be expected to share a room with up to 10 strangers and initial accommodation is particularly unsafe for LGBTQI+ people (Townsend, 2023). Once destitution is proven, people are moved into dispersal accommodation, which includes smaller shared houses in the community, hotels, larger houses of multiple occupation and ex-military of defence sites.

Interlocutors, living in mainstream asylum accommodation, regularly reported how living in asylum accommodation caused them to live in a constant state of anxiety and fear (Fletcher, 2024b). Fears were often linked to other residents finding out they were LGBTQI+ and the consequence of this. For example, Bunkechwu recalling the other residents in the asylum hotel he was staying in, said:

> A lot of them are so violent, the fact that they are new to the country, hasn't deprived them of their religious mentality. I felt they could still attack me, and say they are working for their prophet

> Mohammed to kill the evil one. Not if they get to know you, irrespective, because some of them are-, I mean the way they do things, they say, 'I don't mind dying, as long as I'm working for Mohammed, let me kill him because he is gay', you know.

Practitioners working with LGBTQI+ people in the asylum system reported how mainstream accommodation spaces forced people to hide their sexuality. Kierian a Support Manager working in LGBTQI+ organisation said:

> Asylum seeker housing is an issue, often they're sharing the house with people, from the very country they've had to flee, the faith they've had to flee, or just people that are generally hostile, or they have to go back into the closet.

Interlocutors were often made to live with other residents from their CoO or religious communities, who they had experienced persecution from. The presumed religiosity of other residents was often mentioned by interlocutor as to why they assumed other residents would be queerphobic. For example, Jasur a gay man from Central Asia, in his interviewed, referred to how he was scared to live in the accommodation as he had to share the accommodation with people he perceived to be Muslim. It should be noted he had no evidence that the people he feared held negative views towards LGBTQI+ people (Fletcher, 2024b).

Other research has identified how conflicting religious beliefs can be a source of tension in accommodation spaces, and LGBTQI+ people can experience pressure from other residents to conform to the religious practices. If conformity is resisted, this can result in hostility (Balogun and Williams, 2024). For example, Farid, who lived in a shared house, described how he found it difficult to inhabit a space where Islamic religious customs and rituals were practiced because of his CoO experiences, The other residents in his put accommodation pressure on Farid to follow to their religious customs, particularly around prayer and the prohibition on certain types of food. In his CoO, he had suffered with severe mental health problems due to his realisation thar he was gay, as queerness was framed in his CoO as a sickness, and '*haram*' (forbidden). Farid said the reminders of Islamic faith and practices in his accommodation caused him anxiety, and due to the religiosity of his housemates, he did not feel safe or secure in the house.

LGBTQI + people living in asylum accommodation reported not being able to live openly regarding their queer subjectivity. This prevented them from being able to have other LGBTQI+ people visit or engage in LGBTQI+ organisations and communities (Fletcher, 2024b). Micro Rainbow, an organisation that supports LGBTQI+ people seeking asylum and refugees, argues it is important for LGBTQI+ people to be housed in larger cities due to the increased prevalence of LGBTQI+ support in urban Micro Rainbow, 2025. Asylum accommodation is often located in rural areas where LGBTQI+ communities do not have a visible presence.

If LGBTQI+ people are dispersed to areas where there is no or limited support, this can impact their ability to gather the evidence they need for their asylum claims (Danisi et al, 2021). A report by the African Rainbow Family, a charity supporting

LGBTQI+ people in the asylum process, found 56 per cent of their respondents had no access to LGBTQI+ support groups or had LGBTQI+ resources available in their accommodation (Balogun and Williams, 2024). Low levels of financial support prohibit people from travelling far to access specialist support. Interlocutors also raised the curiosity and questioning from other residents, stating this scrutiny prevented them from attending LGBTQI+ community events or organisations, especially in large-scale accommodations where people often congregated in communal areas or at the entrance to the accommodation.

As will be discussed further in Chapter 4, it is often expected that those claiming on the grounds of SOGI will have supporting evidence from LGBTQI+ organisations and members of the LGBTQI+ community. Danisi et al. (2021) highlighted how asylum accommodation located in rural locations provided a particular challenge to SO in relation to credibility, as an absence of engagement with LGBTQI+ organisations damaged the credibility of SO claimants. As asylum accommodation is provided on a 'no-choice' basis, requests to be relocated to be close to LGBTQI+ communities will often be denied, especially if there is no compelling emotional or medical evidence to support relocation.

As stated above, the high number of people in the asylum system has led to an increased and reliance on 'contingency accommodation' due to a shortage of stock of dispersal accommodation. Contingency accommodation is most often feared as it is often provided in large hotels or large ex-military sites. Rainbow Migration (2023) reported LGBTQI+ people found all communal places daunting and unsafe, especially large dining areas and communal spaces. This often led to people foregoing their meals, which, due to low levels of financial, support they are unable to replace.

Interlocutors accommodated in hotels reported a significant deterioration in their mental wellbeing, which they directly attributed to living in asylum hotels. High prevalence of self-harm and suicide ideation among LGBTQI+ people in asylum accommodation is replicated in other research (LGBT Health and Wellbeing, 2025). Jasur spoke of attempting to take his own life while living in an asylum hotel. saying:

> All night nobody sleeping because of rooms you don't have Wi-Fi. Everybody going out of hotel, and everybody with Wi-Fi there talking all night, and somebody smoking every 40 minutes, 30 minutes, fire alarm working. You know, two weeks I am not sleeping like this, two weeks. My brother not talking to me, sister not talking to me. I made a lot of stress for that, and two weeks I am not sleeping. I go to near to beach, and there have a big bridge. I stayed there, and I start killing myself, and jumping from that bridge. Around two o'clock, three o'clock night, morning, one couple see me, and helping me, touched me, and hugged me.

Other interlocutors spoke of how hotel accommodation caused them to become increasingly depressed and anxious, caused by living with so many people from their CoO or religious communities. Mental health concerns were not only raised by interlocutors in references to their own wellbeing but also in terms of the mental health of other residents. Bunkechwu said:

> I was just scared, because some of them are very, very violent, even the way they act in the hotel, you know, they are violent. Sometimes the police have come several times to handcuff some of them, you know, when they get drunk, a lot of those acts are attributed to their depression.

As in Bunkechwu excerpt, LGBTQI+ people also feared they would be targets for those seeking an outlet for pent up feelings caused by post-traumatic stress and trauma of fleeing conflict, Interlocutors said, other residents viewed them as acceptable targets because their queer subjectivity as they viewed them as violators of cultural or religious social norms.

Asylum Support Policy

The overriding principle of how asylum accommodation is allocated is on a 'no choice basis' (Home Office, 2026b), with the allocation of asylum accommodation organised through the dispersal policy under the IAA 1999.[6] The dispersal policy was introduced as an attempt to alleviate the housing pressures of accommodating people in the asylum system from the South East of the UK and establish an equitable distribution of asylum housing throughout the UK (Hynes, 2011). In simple terms, the dispersal policy means people in the asylum system have no choice in where they live, and it has been described as 'a violent imposition' on those living in mainstream asylum accommodation (Darling, 2022, p. 3).

The dispersal policy has proved to cause a deterioration in people's mental wellbeing in the broader asylum seeking community, mainly as dispersal severs people from existing support networks. However, the implications of dispersal for LGBTQI+ people can have significantly more adverse effects. While people seeking asylum can often rely on CoO and religious communities to provide them with support (Mallett and Hagen-Zanker, 2018), for LGBTQI+ people they tend to rely more on personal relationships or social networks than more traditional forms of support (Bell and Hansen, 2009). If dispersed away from these support networks, it can be more difficult for LGBTQI+ people to re-establish safe forms of support.

Interlocutors housed in asylum accommodation were often moved frequently, at short notice and often far away from their previous accommodation. These sudden relocations caused great distress for people; Emenike recalls his feelings on being dispersed away from the town he had grown accustomed, to different city on a day's notice, saying:

> Oh my God, it was the worst day. It was the worst, you know, because I was thinking, 'Oh my God, I've already settled in, I've met friends.' They just moved me out of there to (location removed) where I don't know nobody.

[6]The policy of dispersal was introduced by the Immigration and Asylum Act 1999.

Desire was moved on numerous occasions with little warning to different locations throughout the UK, which she found traumatising both in terms of being sent to an unfamiliar place and the fear of having to live with different people. She said:

> I was being moved around (location removed) from one shared accommodation, to another, to another. I was moved to, like, four different ones.... In the accommodation they provided for us I have to hide. We share the bathroom, and we share the toilet. But I'm scared that in the kitchen I could be poisoned due to my sexuality.

For LGBTQI+ people, the dispersal policy exposes them to 'the ordeal of having to "come-out" as LGBT+ or conceal their identity in their next location' often on multiple occasions (LGBT Wellbeing, 2023, p. 6).

The 'no choice' basis on which asylum accommodation is offered also has negative implications unique to LGBTQI+ people. Assigning accommodation to asylum claimants is governed by the Allocation of asylum accommodation policy (AoAAP) (Home Office, 2026b). Despite the safeguarding risks LGBTQI+ people face in a range of asylum accommodation, there are insufficient provisions within the guidelines to protect LGBTQI+ people from harm. Under the AoAAP, it is possible to request a particular type of accommodation related to individual need, including needs related to their physical and mental health or if there is a need to be in a certain location. However, requests for specific accommodation are considered only in 'exceptional circumstances' and on a case-by-case basis, which would include a serious risk to health, safety and security (Fletcher, 2024b).

To evidence this need, individuals are regularly required to produce objective evidence to 'prove' they have an 'exceptional' need that must be accommodated by the Home Office, and medical evidence is often requested in relation to proving exceptional circumstances and that the current accommodation is unsuitable. Micro Rainbow, an NGO that supports LGBTQI+ people in the asylum process and runs safe LGBTQI housing, submitted evidence to the Home Office Select Committee on asylum accommodation, which stated:

> Medical evidence is often requested by the Home Office, through Migrant Help, or housing providers to support the need for a different type of accommodation, such as self-contained or a relocation to different accommodation. However, the requirement or request of medical evidence is wholly unsuitable in the case of LGBTQI+ individuals, as identifying as LGBTQI+ is not a medical condition. (Fletcher, 2024b)

As stated in the quote above, requests for medical evidence are inappropriate in relation to proving a safeguarding risk an LGBTQI+ person faces in mainstream asylum accommodation.

LGBTQI+ people who live openly or are discovered to be LGBTQI+ by other residents can be victims of discrimination, abuse, harm and violence, including incidents of sexual assault and rape (McKnight et al., 2024). Organisations have reported safeguarding incidents generally have increased with the reintroduction of the policy of room-sharing of unrelated adults in asylum accommodation under Operation Maximisation in June 2023 (McKnight et al., 2024). This policy had previously been phased out during the Covid-19 pandemic but was brought back to try to reduce the costs of asylum support (NAO, 2025b, p. 9). There is wide-ranging evidence of how room-sharing significantly impacts the wellbeing and safety of LGBTQI+ people (Fletcher, 2024b; Law Center NI, Migration Justice Project, and Rainbow Refugees NI, 2024; McKnight et al., 2024; LGBT Health and Wellbeing, 2023). The Guardian newspaper reported that:

> A trans man who had been brutally beaten and raped in his home country was placed by the Home Office in dormitory accommodation. He woke up to find some of the men he was sharing the space with were stripping off his clothes. (Taylor, 2023)

Micro Rainbow (2025, p. 4) reported how one of their beneficiaries was forced to share a room with a man who told him 'gay people should die'. Despite the risks to LGBTQI+ people, the AoAAP has been updated to make it harder for people to obtain self-contained and single room accommodation. The AoAAP has consistently been updated by the Home Office enforcing stricter guidance on who would be considered to fall outside of room-sharing requirements (Fletcher, 2024b).

Safeguarding in asylum accommodation is governed by asylum support contracts safeguarding framework[7] which has been found to be ineffectual in protecting LGBTQI+ people due to delays in resolving safeguard incidents and a lack of transparency and clear routes for individuals and organisations to escalate safeguarding incidents (Home Affairs Committee, 2025). An ICIBI report found 'no evidence of prioritisation on the basis of vulnerability and, as the Home Office did not collect data on vulnerabilities, there was no mechanism for it to be able to prioritise on this basis in adult casework' (ICIBI, 2024, p. 8).

Dinesh, a practitioner supporting LGBTQI+ people, reported poor responses and long waiting times for private contractors of the Home Office to resolve accommodation issues He said:

> I've come across people being housed with people from the same cultural background or religious background, and that can be very conflicting. One of our members, I had to spend evenings with him because the house he was living in there was a lot of other Muslim men from different places, and they had found out that he was claiming asylum on the basis of his sexuality, so they didn't want to be in the same room as him, and they were constantly making him feel bad. So that was horrible for him. I remember him having to stay away from this house until they rehoused him somewhere else.

---

[7]https://www.gov.uk/government/publications/asylum-support-contracts-safeguarding-framework/asylum-support-contracts-safeguarding-framework.

Poor safeguarding is caused not only by inadequate policies and processes but also by insufficient staff training. African Rainbow Family found that 87.04 per cent of their respondents thought asylum 'accommodation staff were not adequately trained to understand and address the unique challenges faced by LGBTIQ + people' (Balogun and Williams, 2024, p. 12). The same report also found, LGBTQI+ people faced hostility and discrimination from accommodation staff.

Practitioners in this research, who worked closely with LGBTQI+ people, regularly referred to the insufficient training of accommodation staff to adequately respond to complaints brought by LGBTQI+ residents. Residents who raised complaints about other people they are living with are often required to remain in the same accommodation until alternative accommodation is located. This can be in cases even when individuals have been victims of violence and sexual violence (Rainbow Migration, 2023).

Safeguarding issues are compounded by delay in responses to complaints made to Migrant Help[8] and LGBTQI+ residents face significant delays or inaction by the private housing providers or the Home Office to adequately respond to threats and harassment made towards them (*ibid*). While a minority of interlocutors reported feeling safe in their formal asylum housing, these individuals were accommodated in smaller accommodation, such as shared houses in large urban cities.

As a consequence of how the formal asylum accommodation system is managed, interlocutors' narratives showed how some LGBTQI+ people deliberately avoided the formal asylum support system. The three common factors routinely raised by interlocutors, underpinning their reluctance to access asylum support, included: an unwillingness to move from current geographical because the move would separate people from established social networks, previous negative incidents in mainstream asylum accommodation, or a real, or perceived, fear of homophobic harassment, abuse or violence from other people seeking asylum. The rejection of the formal asylum support consequently results in people becoming reliant on financial, material and housing support from CoO communities or religious communities, which is discussed in the next chapter.

Concluding Remarks

Interlocutors' experiences outlined in this chapter draw attention to how social experience caused by inadequacies in asylum support provision can create issues for a person in terms of their asylum claim. This is because, for LGBTQI+ people, the way the formal asylum support is organised often causes them to hide their queer subjectivties. While the UK context is a hostile context for anyone seeking asylum, the analysis in this chapter illustrates how current asylum support policy making creates unique barriers and risks for LGBTQI+ people.

This is particularly apparent in mainstream accommodation spaces, where both other residents and inadequate policymaking expose LGBTQI+ people to

---

[8]Migrant Help is the charity which manages complaints for the Home Office, under the Advice, Issue Reporting and Eligibility Contract (AIRE).

further discrimination, abuse and violence. Policies that frame the provision of asylum support, fail to attend to the heightened risks LGBTQI+ people face. Safeguarding frameworks need to set out clear and transparent escalation routes to allow LGBTQI+ people to raise the issues they face. Dispersal policies move LGBTQI+ people away from established support networks, and those moved to rural locations are cut off from LGBTQI+ organisations and communities. Access to LGBTQI+ support is not only important in terms of a person's wellbeing, but evidence of social experience with LGBTQI+ communities and organisations is expected to be presented as part of a person's claim for asylum on SO grounds.

In addition, the gaps in any form of statutory support for those who do not have an active asylum claim disproportionally impact LGBTQI+ people as there are very few specialist charities and organisations that support LGBTQI+ people seeking asylum. LGBTQI+ people seeking asylum can fear mainstream support and generalised refugee organisations due to the potential presence of people from CoO. Furthermore, insufficient formal asylum support and a shortage of capcity in specialist organisations to support LGBTQI+ people in the asylum process often means LGBTQI+ people have to rely on informal forms of support. This again, can have implications for their safety and their ability to live openly as LGBTQI+, which, again, is expected by asylum decision makers. Informal support contexs in the UK are considered in greater detail in the next chapter.

Chapter 3

Seeking Sanctuary: Religious Experiences Seeking Asylum in the UK*

For people claiming asylum on sexual orientation (SO) grounds, decision makers expect that on arriving in the UK, people will live openly and visibly about their sexuality. Evidently, 'out' queerness is anticipated by decision makers to be embodied and performed 'loud and proud' which Akin has coined a 'rainbow splash' (Akin, 2017, p. 463). People claiming asylum on SO grounds are expected to be able to demonstrate visible and active engagement with LGBTQI+ communities and organisations, or social activities such as attending Pride, socialising in gay bars and clubs and have evidence of same-sex partners (Dustin and Held, 2018). Visibility expectations stand in stark contrast to the ability of many LGBTQI+ people to live openly (or want to) while seeking asylum. These requirements are grounded in stereotypical and westernised assumptions of LGBTQI+ lives that conform to neoliberal and homonationalist narratives of sexual citizenship, based in visibility politics, consumption and an identity in the public sphere, (Duggan, 2003). This type of queerness replicates middle class, white, gay male experience, ignores the wide range of global queer subjectivities and embodiments (Manalansan, 2006).

This area of enquiry is important as not living visibly regarding your sexual orientation can increase the likelihood of having an asylum claim refused (the specifics of which are discussed in Chapter 4), but this increases further if a person claiming on SO grounds continues to engage with homonegative religious communities. This is because stereotypical expectations in decision making assume LGBTQI+ people can easily sever ties with religious communities and disassociate from past religious beliefs (Page and Yip, 2020). This chapter

* This chapter was developed using material from the thesis: Fletcher, Claire; (2024) Queerly Faithful: The experiences of religion for those seeking asylum in the UK. Doctoral thesis (Ph.D), UCL (University College London).

Queerly Faithful: Queer People's Experience of Religion in Asylum Seeking, 59–75

doi:10.1108/978-1-83797-488-720261005

demonstrates that, for a wide variety of reasons, this assumption is unrealistic and unjustly punitive towards LGBTQI+ people who draw on religious communities as part of livelihood strategies (Fletcher, 2016). Currently, the process of claiming asylum in the UK is not designed to take into account, or wilfully ignores, the realities of a person's everyday life resulting in queer realities being 'barely understood' and 'subjected to much ignorant assumption' (Ryan-Flood and Munt, 2021). As Danisi et al. (2021, p. 174) identify, the difficulties experienced by sexual orientation and gender identity (SOGI) claimants often start well before the evaluation of their asylum request and have clear implications for the submission of an asylum application on SOGI grounds.

The structural factors and policy failures, which prevent people from living openly, were identified in Chapter 2. In this chapter, the lens of religious experience is used as a mean to developing further understanding of how the informal spaces people navigate while seeking asylum can create the need to conceal their queer subjectivity. This concealment is often part of survival strategies people undertake while navigating the asylum process. However, these strategies of invisibility can have negative implications within the asylum claim itself. The research presented in this chapter contributes to the underexplored area of how social experiences can have negative impacts on a person's legal asylum claim (Dustin and Held, 2021). Lived experiences documented in this chapter show how decision makers' expectations in the RSD process are often unrealistic and fail to account for the layered and intersecting marginalisation of LGBTQI+ people in countries of asylum.

The hostile policy making and the gaps that exist in the formal asylum support system create the necessity for people attempt to mitigate gaps in support within informal spaces, such as religious communities for survival. Consequently, LGBTQI+ people often have to continue to conceal their queer subjectivities and[1] align themselves with majoritarian identities, namely, heterosexuality, to ensure safety. It is not only failures in state policy making that force people to seek support informally, but the hostile political climate towards migrants more generally often means people fear state immigration authorities. This fear can lead to the avoidance of formal routes to protection. In this context, religious communities offer places of comfort, familiarity and belonging, even when belonging in countries of asylum is fragile and conditional (Allen, 2010; Fletcher, 2016).

This chapter is influenced by the concept of 'strategic invisibility' which is used to help to highlight the range of strategies people employ to ensure or attempt to access support. The concept of strategic invisibility is used as an agentic strategy individuals can draw on, which, importantly, prevents (re)stigmatisation and a repetition of harm (Ham and Gerard, 2014). Strategic invisibility has previously been used to explore the resources and strategies people under situations of

[1]It should be noted that the focus of this chapter mainly explores only the negative experiences of religious experience; this should not be taken to reinforce essentialist understandings of the incompatibility of religious and queer subjectivities and the positive experiences with religion will be discussed in detail in Chapters 5 and 6.

precarity and duress employ (Bjarnesen and Turner, 2020). In doing so, this chapter brings attention to the complex reasons why individuals continue to engage with homonegative religious communities, even though these choices can have negative consequences in terms of claiming asylum on SO grounds. Interlocutors' experiences highlight the key junctures where people claiming on SO grounds face increased vulnerabilities. This chapter provides detailed empirical examples in the hope to provide greater understanding of how social factors and experiences lead to the need of LGBTQI+ people to conceal their sexual orientation or engage in actions which appear contradictory to their asylum claim. Common junctions where social experiences impact LGBTQI+ people's decision making are the wish to avoid the formal system, shortage of formal support, the desire for emotional support and friendships and on receiving a negative decision in their asylum claim.

Religious Refuge: Arrival

Trauma, fear of authorities and insufficient awareness of the asylum process in the UK were all given as reasons as to why interlocutors delayed formally claiming asylum. This is supported in other scholarship focusing on SO asylum claims (Ferreira, 2023; Danisi et al., 2021). Social experiences and factors were often central to the reasons why a person would not claim asylum immediately on reaching a 'safe' country. Delays can create problems within an asylum application, as the Home Office expects that people who are genuinely in need of protection will claim asylum as soon as possible, either at a port of entry or in-country at the AIU.

A need to find help on reaching the UK, after fleeing their CoO, often in traumatic and/or sudden circumstances, emerged repeatedly for interlocutors. On arriving in new countries in search of safety, religious communities are often the first places people seek support, especially if flight from CoO is spontaneous and unplanned (Nawyn, 2006). Other motivations as to why religious communities are sought out relate to strong religious affiliations to a particular religious tradition. Due to these ties these religious communities can provide a sense of familiarity for new arrivals (Snyder, 2011b) as religious communities can foster feelings of belonging in new cities for migrants (Baker, 2016).

This was the case for Desire, who left her CoO suddenly when her husband discovered her with another woman. Desire said that while she knew she had to leave her CoO to save herself, she had no awareness that claiming asylum based on her sexual orientation was even a possibility. She said, 'the only thing I know, about asylum is just that it's based on people running from political problems, or countries that are under famine'. Desire had chosen the UK only because she already had a visa for entry from a previous trip. Interlocutors often cited insufficient awareness of the ability to claim on SO grounds. Commonly, refugee protection is assumed to be only for people fleeing war or political persecution.

Desire, on reaching the UK, headed to an address given to her by a friend, but on arriving at the house no one was living there by the name of her friend's contact. With no other option, Desire checked herself into a bed and breakfast, but the little money Desire had soon ran out, and she was asked to leave. Walking the streets, Desire said she saw a Baptist Church; when she entered she saw the church's congregation was mainly people from different parts of Africa. Desire said the church felt familiar and safe and she felt able to approach the church members and ask for support and a place to stay. In many parts of the world where there is limited or no welfare provision by states, religious communities are often key sites of support, which is why religious communities are often sought out by people seeking asylum (Cammett and MacLean, 2011).

People who arrive in the UK are met with inadequate privacy at ports of entry, which prevents people from feeling comfortable to disclose sensitive information, such as sexual orientation. As seen in Chapter 1, people who are seeking safety are often from geographical contexts where there is a silence or stigma towards LGBTQI+ people and people have worked hard to keep their queer subjectivity hidden due to high levels of homonegativity in CoO contexts. Helen, a legal practitioner, experienced in working with people claiming asylum on SO grounds spoke of the difficulties people had disclosing their sexual orientation to immigration officials:

> Now if you are a claimant who is claiming based on their sexuality or gender orientation, you are not likely to be in a position to come out to a complete stranger in a detention centre or in an airport holding cell to say I can't go back because of my sexual orientation because, possibly, you have not said that to anybody in the past, let alone somebody who is about to detain you and remove you from the UK. It is a situation that takes no account of people's cultural background or their own reactions because of what they have faced within the culture of the country of origin and within the UK.

Seen in this quotation is the absence of consideration by immigration authorities that many people come from geographical contexts where a cultural taboo exists, not only regarding sexual and gender diversity, but also in discussing topics of sexuality more generally (Tamale, 2011). This can prevent or make it difficult for people to disclose sexual orientation as soon as they reach country of asylum and can again cause late disclosure of sexual orientation.

Helen refers to how fears of being detained are another factor as to why people choose to avoid claiming asylum altogether (Lewis, 2023). Interlocutors who claimed asylum at either a port of entry or an AIU referred to fearing they would be detained on telling an immigration officer that they wanted to claim asylum. People fear detention itself, and were scared of what would happen to them if other detainees found out they were LGBTQI+ or that being detained would result in their removal back to their CoO.

The violence of the detention estate and the risks it poses to LGBTQI+ people is well-evidenced, and research shows how LGBTQI+ people face hostile encounters from both other detainees and staff (Singer, 2021). Even after release, the experience of being detained can have significant long-term impacts on an individual's mental well-being and there is evidence detention leads to re-traumatisation (Danisi et al., 2021). Desire, for example, was detained when she initially approached the Home Office to claim asylum:

> Getting to Croydon, I told them the truth of my lesbianism, what had transpired. But instead of them putting me into proper emergency accommodation, they took me to detention. From the Croydon office, they handcuffed me into the vehicle, the fear of what was going on, I couldn't even say, 'Why you handcuffing me?' I was just lost. That, why did I come in the first instance? It's better that I should have died. Now that I needed them to support me, to help me to be on my feet and to be free to be who I am, rather, they arrested me.

The experience of being detained in Yarl's IRC was extremely traumatic and Desire became visibly distressed when re-calling her time in Yarl's Wood. In terms of making an asylum claim, it should also be noted that detention can create additional barriers for LGBTQI+ people to collate the necessary evidence to 'prove' their sexual orientation (Harvey, 2023; Bachmann, 2016). Due to a fear of detention people choose to remain hidden in countries where they sought safety, finding other ways of living without formal assistance, such as seeking support within informal communities for work and accommodation (Alessi et al., 2025).

Interlocutors who had experienced traumatic events before leaving CoO or during their journey to the UK were more likely to delay claiming asylum. Jamilah, who had suffered a serious sexual assault by three perpetrators shortly before her arrival in the UK, explained how even simple tasks were beyond her, let alone the ability to engage effectively with the hostile asylum process. As Jamilah recounts below:

> I arrived here.... That release of emotion happened but then, I was not me anymore. I was a mess, I was not thinking of anything, in a sense that I just wanted to be inside the house. I just wanted to sleep if I can. I was a totally different person. Honestly, I can't tell you how many months or weeks I stayed in that state, like, it's very hazy in my mind, vague, what happened. I had no existence, basically. I remember once I went out to go to the shop, but I failed, I came back midway, I didn't want to talk to people.

Because of traumatic events, it can often take long periods for individuals to heal. As in Jamilah's case above, even the completion of daily tasks felt insurmountable. Alessi and Kahn (2018) have described the process of expecting people to claim asylum in short timeframes as a form of institutional violence, which has psychological consequences. As García Rodríguez (2023, p. 533) summarises claiming asylum requires 'early disclosure of traumatic experiences, short timelines for submitting a refugee claim, and premature coming-out processes are all ways through which the asylum machine negatively impacts the mental health of LGBTQ claimants'. Other research has found trauma, and not wanting to 'come out' leads individuals to seek refugee protection through other grounds of claim as a means of preventing the need to retell and relive traumatic experiences (Dudhia, 2023; UKLGIG, 2018).

Fear of authorities, such as border force, police and government officials, was another common reason interlocutors avoided seeking asylum when arriving at the UK. Interlocutors feared that seeking support from immigration authorities would lead to further violence rather than protection. Emenike, said:

> One of the fears we had, especially as we came from the other side of the world, is fear of the unknown. Then two, fear of trust, because obviously given what you've past through, given the experience you've had, torture, trauma, all those things, what you don't want to do is put yourself back into the system where you don't know what is going to happen. So that is the major reason why most of us go straight back into the closet and hide ourselves, until actually we know what is going on.

Emenike's narrative demonstrates that the absence of trust and fear of the asylum system itself causes people to avoid claiming asylum on arrival, especially if they have previously been victims of state violence.

Emenike's case is an illustrative example of the levels of state violence people can face in their search for refuge. Emenike travelled from his CoO across deserts to eventually reach Libya where he hoped of crossing the Mediterranean Sea to Europe. However, in Libya, he was detained by members of the Libyan security forces who tortured and raped him. Emenike said he was targeted because they suspected his sexuality. Spending months in a Libyan prison, he was eventually released, and although he was physically very weak, he was mentally determined to seek safety. Finding passage on a boat to Europe arranged by smugglers, Emenike left Libya. During his journey, the boat capsized, with many of the other passengers drowning. Emenike, rescued by an Italian ship, was taken to Lampedusa, but he said he still felt unsafe there because of his unfamiliarity with the language.

After some time in Lampedusa, he met a group of men through helping to load lorries, who agreed to smuggle him to the UK. Emenike recalled his journey:

> I hid myself inside one of the trucks and they brought me over here, in London. I remember, we landed in central London, so that is how I got myself here. When I arrived in London, I was still very afraid because I thought, in my head, 'Oh, if police are still looking for me, to catch me and send me back'. So, all the torture and, the traumatic experience was kind of in my head, I was completely afraid.

Once in the UK, Emenike was too scared to approach the authorities to claim asylum, both because of his experience with the security forces in Libya and a fear the UK immigration authorities would return him to his CoO. Emenike said his first thought when he arrived in London was to seek support from other people from his CoO. He walked the streets of London until he eventually stopped a man from his CoO. He explained:

> I was asking people, 'Where can I get in the (CoO community) or friends or something?' Anyway, the guy that I saw, he told me that he doesn't live in London, but he lives in (location removed). He knows a church in (location removed) where (name of CoO Community removed) go to, or that Africans go to and if I go there then they will be able to help me.

The man even paid for Emenike's bus ticket to ensure he could travel to the Church in the different city to enable Emenike to seek help. Arriving on Good Friday, Emenike found the church community busily preparing for the religious festival. He said on seeing confirmation that it was indeed an African church he felt safe to ask the congregation members for help, recalling:

> They really felt very sorry for me, but they started helping me in terms of where to stay and what to do next. I was staying with their friend, I didn't trust anybody then, apart from probably these few people I saw at church. I didn't trust the system… I was really afraid of the system, and I was afraid of people because of the experience I have gotten through. But that church they help me to settle in.

Emenike said he it necessary to hide his sexual orientation and he made a deliberate decision to go 'back into the closet' to ensure he could maintain ties with the community. Interestingly, while concerns are often raised about how religious communities are not safe as they can 'force' people back into the closet (Dyck et al., 2019), interlocutors in this research regularly spoke of how being in religious or CoO communities made them feel safe as one of their reasons behind their decision to seek support in these spaces. While informal communities can be homonegative, they do provide spaces of protection in the face of hostile states practices, racism and a growing public hostility towards migrants. Interlocutors' narratives evidence how the primary motivation for flight from CoO was safety and to build security in their lives, not to live openly as LGBTQI+. For interlocutors, living openly was often secondary and generally only happened after living in the UK for a longer period.

Religious communities are also sites of knowledge for people who have newly arrived in the UK. If LGBTQI+ people are living openly in the county they seek asylum, they are less likely to be supported by co-national or co-religionist groups, and this presents a barrier to access local knowledge, for example, becoming aware claiming on SO grounds is a possibility (Khan, 2020). Mary, a practitioner who works with LGBTQI+ people seeking asylum, stated:

> We've known churches who've paid for legal fees, accommodation, but that support is not available to LGBTQI+ refugees, and other types of support that we take for granted like information, what do you do, how do you get support from Migrant Help. It's a huge support network in the migrant community, and that is not available for LGBTQI+ refugees.

A benefit of early contact with informal communities, such as religious groups, is not only related to support, but communities can facilitate and accelerate a person's familiarity with their new social context. Especially useful is knowledge that empowers individuals on the workings of the local asylum process, which are complex and hard to navigate (Zetter et al., 2005; Dustin and Held, 2021). Hazelle, explained how daunted she felt faced with the asylum process:

> The asylum system, for me is complex as a whole. It's very complex. You need to speak with people to understand what it's all about, asylum, if you're not aware. But, for me, I didn't even know what asylum was, so if you don't know, you will not know where to go to and ask for help.

Contact with religious communities not only provides people with the knowledge of how local asylum systems function, but ensures people can present themselves in the right manner to be believed within the RSD process (Greatrick, 2022). Interlocutors said the information they gained through informal spaces, mainly centred on sources where additional help could be found, such as third sector organisation that provided different support services for people seeking asylum.

While, overall, informal support was beneficial to interlocutors, there were incidents where the information provided was inaccurate. However, the consequences of presenting untrue facts within an asylum application can damage a person's credibility. Frequent examples of this, were the types of narratives that should be presented to ensure a successful asylum claim and evidence that was said to be 'needed' to prove sexual orientation. Desire, for example, was told by a member of the Baptist congregation that she should present herself as a victim of domestic violence and female genital mutilation to ensure she was granted refugee protection. Danisi et al. (2021, p. 165) noted how both 'internalised homophobia and/or the proximity of fellow nationals may nudge some SOGI claimants to rely on more familiar narratives of persecution as the basis of their claim' rather than their true circumstances of persecution. This can be due to fear that their sexual orientation will be discovered because they have disclosed it in their asylum claim, such as someone finding their official paperwork or where individuals do not understand the asylum process and believe immigration officials will make public inquiries in their CoO to verify their sexual orientation.

Knowledge and information shared by the states in Europe have been found to have serious deficiencies regarding the information provided by state agencies on how to claim asylum on sexual orientation grounds. Danisi et al. (2021) identified a 'lack of information on SOGI asylum at arrival as one of the most problematic aspects of the system across Europe'. One of the consequences they identified was that insufficient information led to people being exploited within informal communities. For example, one person they cited in their research was living within a church community and carried out much of the cooking and cleaning and at no time had any member of the congregation mentioned the possibility of claiming asylum to them.

Queer Visibility and Informal Support

The legislative measures aimed at making life increasingly difficult for people without legal leave were greatly increased under the former Home Secretary, Theresa May. In her announcement of the Hostile Environment strategy, she said the purpose was to 'create here in Britain a really hostile environment for illegal migration' (Kirkup and Winnett, 2012). A particularly pernicious element of the hostile environment has been the introduction of policies and legislation that have meant local government, private bodies, public servants, police officers, teachers and even ordinary people are complicit in performing boarder enforcement. Griffiths and Yeo (2021, p. 523) described this governmental strategy as 'deputisation' and a means of co-opting 'organisations and people as de facto immigration officers'. The result of these policies is the creation of everyday bordering with ramifications that are both internal and external of the state. Yuval-Davis et al (2019) argues that new immigration policies brought in by the UK government from 2012 onwards, for example the Immigration Act 2014 that introduced the 'right to rent' checks, which means landlords are now required to ensure people have legal leave to be in the UK before renting a property to them. Yuval-Davis et al argue that the raft of new immigration policies brought in by the UK government from 2012 onwards have condemed people to 'grey zones' as migrants are now frequently required to prove their right to be and reside in everyday life. A further consequence of these policies is the increasingly restrictive spaces where people can seek our survival strategies during periods of illegality, created by these state immigration policies.

Support found in religious communities is more flexible and covert, meaning it can more easily circumvent hostile state policies that prevent people from accessing financial and accommodation support (Phillimore et al., 2010; Fletcher, 2016). How asylum support is currently structured, means eligibility can change as people move between different categories of state created illegality relating to their immigration status (Luibhéid, 2008b). People who arrive irregularly and do not claim asylum or those who have been refused asylum often cannot access any form of formal support. As explored above, the ability to access informal support often requires a person to keep their queer subjectivity invisible. The next section of this chapter details examples of what strategies interlocutors used to maintain invisibility and the ramifications on terms of their access to informal support when it was no longer possible to keep queerness hidden.

Emenike remained dependent on the religious community he met on his arrival for many years. He had no means of independently accessing any other form of financial or material support because he had no form of legal leave to be in the UK. He became entirely reliant on the church community for access to informal employment and accommodation. Living within this community gave Emenike the ability to live irregularly in the UK for several years. However, maintaining long-term connections with informal communities often relied on interlocutors to draw on strategies of invisibility regarding their queer subjectivity. Building social relationships in informal settings, interlocutors reported being subjected to intense questioning about their personal lives. Emenike faced questions on his single status and said he felt pressure begin to mount for him to start a relationship. He explained:

> As an African, people always look at you, to have your wife or your girlfriend or something. When people are looking at me, they are not seeing any woman around or I'm not going around holding a woman's hand, and so they question it. So, at the point, I get into the relationship just to impress, just to live up to their expectations.

Afraid his sexuality would be discovered he started a relationship with a woman within the community to ensure his sexuality remained invisible.

While initially, Emenike had imagined the financial and emotional support he received from the church community would mean he could establish a life in the UK without the need to navigate the asylum process. After several years, he began to feel restricted both by the relationships he had built within the community and the constrictions his irregular immigration status imposed upon him, in terms of where he could live and work. Emenike decided his only option was to claim asylum on SO grounds. While he still feared the asylum process, he said living in the UK had given him the confidence to imagine the possibility of living openly as a gay man.

Yet, Emenike's strategy of forming a heterosexual relationship to maintain the support of his religious community had ramifications in his asylum claim. In his refusal letter to his initial asylum claim, the Home Office stated Emenike's claim lacked credibility because he had formed a romantic heterosexual relationship in the UK. Emenike's sexual behaviour was seen as inconsistent with the expectations of decision makers of someone who would claim on SO grounds. Decision maker expectations of sexuality are of a fixed, static and immutable sexuality, and people who claim asylum on SO grounds who present experiences of fluidity can be viewed as inauthentic, especially bisexual asylum claimants (Rehaag, 2009). This is in direct contradiction to scholarship which illustrates the fluid and changeable nature sexuality (Diamond, 2008; Savin-Williams, 2017).

Obligations to embody westernised conceptualisations of queer subjectivity mean individuals must forgo 'their "real nature" to play the (Western) part of the homosexual' (Fassin and Salcedo, 2015, p. 1121). SO claimants are expected to comply with homonationalist stereotypes, where there is a need to assume pure queer identities in line with westernised understandings of sexual and gender diversity (Powell, 2021). Decision making discounts the intersecting factors that shape the necessity to form romantic or sexual relationships as part of a survival strategy, which appear to contradict a person's stated sexuality.

In asylum decision making, there is an absence of understanding of the social reality and experiences that lead people to comply with heterosexual norms, even once in the UK. While the API (2016, p. 13) does state that 'Some will have, in addition to hiding their sexual orientation, evaded detection by engaging in lifestyles that conform to normative cultural heterosexual stereotypes'. It is assumed within decision making this behaviour takes place in CoO contexts and people seeking asylum on SO ground would live openly in the UK. Yet, while a person may be in a country with greater protections and wider societal acceptance of LGBTQI+ people (i.e. the UK), they may be reliant on communities whose own social norms surrounding sexual and gender diversity are not reflective of wider society.

Returning to Emenike's narrative, his decision to claim asylum on the grounds of his sexuality created a conflict for Emenike regarding the relationships he had built with the community that he still wanted to retain. This was because, not only did he depend on the community for his livelihood, but he had formed strong emotional bonds with people, he explained:

> You don't want to upset people that are close to you, you know. You don't want them to find out, that this is your sexuality because you know, the isolation, the emotional isolation and the mental isolation, even physical isolation. You know, so that was why I decided not to be open.

Retaining friendships and emotional support was a key reason behind interlocutors' wishing to keep their queer subjectivity invisible. Nofoto,[2] described the centrality of the emotional support and friendship she had found, and how these relationships sustained her throughout the hostility of the asylum process. Personal relationships and friendships were shown to reduce the day-to-day pressures of having liminal status. In decisions whether to live visibly or not, not only did interlocutors have to consider the consequences of losing material and financial assistance, but also the potential loss of the wealth of emotional support they received in religious and CoO communities. Nofoto, reminiscing on her past relationships, said:

> I was actually part of a dance group. We used to go and perform at weddings and stuff like that. We wear these (location removed) traditional clothes. So, we do the dance, the one where you lift the leg, and we wear those colourful beads. Yes. I was part of this amazing group.

Nofoto's said her decision to live openly was due to her initial claim being refused by the Home Office. In her refusal letter the Home Office had stated that

[2]Nofoto identified as non-binary and utilises she/her pronouns.

her sexuality or the fact she had been trafficked were not believed. However, her choice to live openly had significant consequences for her in terms of her social network. Nofoto said her girlfriend could not cope with her visible queerness, as she was concerned Nofoto's openness regarding her sexuality would cast aspersions on her own and she ended the relationship shortly after Nofoto came out. Nofoto started speaking openly about being queer, such as publicly posting queer content on social media platforms and attending queer events. By living an explicitly queer life. Nofoto said she was cut off from friendships that had previously sustained and supported her, recalling the time when her sexuality became public knowledge She said:

> the rumours were just spreading everywhere. Now I'm not part of them anymore, unfortunately.... But now, gosh. I've actually lost quite a lot of certain things by coming out. I've lost quite a lot of connections, a lot of friends. Even the people from church, I no longer have that connection with them.

The choice Nofoto made to live openly to try to ensure she secured refugee status on the grounds of her sexual orientation led her to lose a significant romantic relationship, several long-term friendships and a rejection from her original religious and CoO community.

Accessing support in religious communities that provided generalised support to people in the asylum system can also be complicated for LGBTQI+ people. Desire started attending an Anglican church, as the community provided destitution support for people seeking asylum. In this community, Desire said she felt comfortable about disclosing that her asylum claim was based on her sexual orientation, as none of the other congregation or attendees were from her CoO. The comfort she felt within the community suddenly changed when other people from her CoO began to attend the church support group. As Held (2023) has argued, spaces can become 'ambivalent' space of support and may be avoided. An example of this within interlocutors' narratives is a sudden appearance of people from their CoO within a support space. These arrivals altered how interlocutors felt able to interact with an organisation or community that they had previously felt safe within.

This was the case for Desire who said the physical space and contact with members of the Angelican community no longer felt safe to her, as she was concerned her sexual orientation would be discovered by members of her CoO, and Desire said she was particularly concerned that church members running the support group would inadvertently out her. She explained:

> I had to step back when I started seeing people that are (West African) coming to that church, that was when I had some bad connections back then.

The 'bad connections' Desire references in the quotation above relate to her ex-husband. Even though he remained in their CoO, she said he had made threats that he would have her killed through CoO contacts who were in the UK. These encounters meant Desire immediately stopped attending the support group, even though she still needed their assistance. This example demonstrates the precarity of informal support contexts for LGBTQI+ people and how, although support can be wide ranging, the stability of the provision is uncertain (NACCOM, 2023).

Interlocutors said they also hid their queer subjectivity while they were in the UK because of the repercussions living openly could have on their relationships with, and the safety of, their family members remaining in their CoO. As discussed in Yetunde's case in Chapter 1, immediate family members can become targets and experience harassment, stigmatisation and violence due to their association with an LGBTQI+ person, due to assumptions that the family is responsible for the creation of a person's queer subjectivity, or the family is thought to be tainted and contact with them would spread the sin/deviation/demon[3] throughout the community.

In terms of maintaining relationships with family members and friends in their CoO. interlocutors raised concerns that family members and friends would disown them if they found out they were LGBTQI+. Sulaiman, a gay man from West Africa, spoke about his concerns about being open about his sexuality during our conversation, saying:

> Even the ones that are here (talking about co-nationalists), I'm close with. I do not tell them my story. Although they are coming very close to asking, 'What is it?' I do not tell them. I say, 'No. Just mind your business'. I'm afraid to tell them. If I tell them, they might know where I came from, and they might know my family, might know my siblings and if they know them, then they will tell them.

Maintaining his connection with his family was very important to him as he said speaking to his family helped to alleviate the isolation he felt while seeking asylum. Sulaiman was certain his family would reject him if his sexuality was discovered, and they were unaware he was claiming asylum. Additionally, as Sulaiman's asylum claim was still pending, he remained frightened of being returned to his CoO and this was a contributing factor which stopped him from wanting to live openly He referred to the 'severe consequences' he would face as a gay man if it was known in his CoO that he was gay if he was returned.

Not all interlocutors reported having to hide their queer subjectivity to access support from religious communities. One example is Jasur, who fled his CoO after he was secretly filmed having sex in his car with another man by a security guard. Jasur became aware of the film's existence when the security guard arrived at his house demanding $10,000; telling Jasur he would release the film on YouTube if he didn't pay. Jasur, unable to pay the blackmailer and knowing the release of the film would place him at great risk in his community, left his CoO.

---

[3]These were all terms used within interlocutors' narratives to describe these views.

When he arrive in the UK, Jasur originally survived as he was living with his long-term partner who had legal leave, and his partner also found Jasur informal work in a restaurant. When the relationship ended, Jasur was left homeless with no means of financially supporting himself. He eventually found assistance in a local synagogue that he had previously encountered through his work as a chef. Jasur said he relied heavily on the material support and informal employment he was offered through the synagogue before he claimed asylum, saying:

> I work like illegal people (meaning informal work paid cash in hand). I work for Jewish people for synagogues. I help him. He's helping me. Always give me vouchers, sometimes money, sometimes clothes, food, everything.

The Rabbi of the synagogue, learning Jasur was homeless, offered him a place to stay within the synagogue. Jasur, while not open with the wider religious community about his sexuality, confided in the Rabbi the reasons behind why he had to leave his CoO. The Rabbi was very supportive and continued to assist Jasur until he decided to claim asylum on SO grounds. This example is an example of acceptance and support.

The Last Bastion of Support: Religious Communities

Another area where religious communities were relied on was when interlocutors found themselves appeal rights exhausted[4] (ARE). It has long been recognised that religious communties and organisations have been a principal gap-fillers of welfare provision due to state retrenchment (Cloke et al., 2009) and are often the only source of support for people who are NRPF (NACCOM, 2023). Dinesh, a practitioner who works with queer people in the asylum process, explained:

> Once your asylum case gets rejected, you literally are relying on people to give you food, clothing, money to get the bus. You don't get any support if your asylum case is rejected.

Those who are in this situation often need to make a further submission to the Home Office for a fresh asylum claim, and to do this, they need to submit evidence which has not been previously reviewed by the Home Office, This type of evidence might be disclosure of sexual orientation or further evidence in support of sexual orientation.

Insufficient support for people in this situation can cause them to seek support in homonegative contexts, such as religious communities. Inaya, a legal practitioner referring to a past client's experiences:

---

[4] The term appeal rights exhausted, is used to refer to people who have no further legal avenues, such as an appeal, to challenge a refusal on their asylum application.

> His asylum claim had failed. He had nowhere to live. On the face of it, it was a very supportive Christian group that would house failed asylum seekers. He was given free accommodation and food. He helped around the house, and he looked after the kids. Yes, he was being financially supported but God knows, he couldn't come out. There was him and several others, almost all of them from Sub-Saharan Africa with a strong evangelical Christian group.

As is seen in the example above, irregular immigration status can tie people to religious communities because they have no alternative means of supporting themselves (Bloch, 2014). Third sector and legal practitioners referred to clients who had had their support withdrawn or were evicted from accommodation which was provided or funded by religious or CoO communities when their queer subjectivity was exposed or discovered. Reliance on informal support networks is precarious and can make people vulnerable to financial exploitation and dependency (Bloch, 2014); this is especially the case for people who are ARE and have no legal pathways to regularise their status (Bloch et al., 2014).

A sudden withdrawal of informal support can have disastrous effects on people, leaving them homeless and destitute. People who have no legal leave have difficulty accessing voluntary or statutory support, as the system is complicated and people do not have the knowledge about the different support available to (NACCOM, 2023). For example, the application for section 4 support is 37 pages long, and while help is available through Migrant Help, it is necessary to have a good understanding of the evidentiary requirements needed to demonstrate eligibility within the limited criteria of section 4. People who become destitute at this point in the asylum process often experience sharp declines in both mental and physical health, which can again impact their ability to engage and negotiate access to support organisations or complete the administrative burden necessary to access this support (NACCOM, 2023).

In these situations, women are especially at risk of SGBV in informal support contexts, for example an interlocutor reported being sexually assaulted by a stranger who had offered her shelter which she accepted because she was street homeless. To avoid street homelessness people can use strategies such as transactional sex for housing, working for low or no pay (Dudhia, 2023).

Additionally, LGBTQI+ people with no legal status are kept in exploitative situations with the threat of either being outed to the wider community regarding their sexuality or reported to the immigration authorities if they try to leave. As one practitioner, Emma, who worked with LGBTQI+ people in the asylum process, explained:

> LGBTQI+ people can also end up in quite exploitative situations where perhaps, either their immigration status is used against them or their sexuality and gender identity is used, and they might be staying with someone because of the risk of being outed, or the risk of being reported, keeps them within that exploitative situation.

People who do not have an active asylum claim are at greater risk of being detained and removed from the UK. People who exploit migrants in this situation use the threat of reporting them to the Home Office and this possibility of being removed back to CoO to keep people working in abusive and exploitative circumstances. People in the asylum process spoke of the trade-offs and continued negotiations people with queer subjectivity had to make to ensure queer subjectivity remained hidden.

Concluding Remarks

Using religious experience as a lens, narratives show the unique complexities for queer people seeking asylum and highlight, far from having the ability to live openly, social experiences often mean LGBTQI+ people must employ strategies of invisibility to ensure queer subjectivity is not revealed to maintain support to survive. While support provided in religious communities can be extensive, it can be conditional and create restrictions on a person's ability to live openly. This, in turn, has implications in their ability to make themselves visibly and authentically queer in the eyes of decision makers and, therefore, can impact the outcome of SO asylum claims.

Religious communities can be a great source of informal support for those with irregular migration a status. They can provide spaces of safety when people have faced sudden departure from their CoO, and religious communities provide a sense of familiarity and comfort in times of trauma and uncertainty. These form of informal support can be central to livelihood and survival strategies. The provision of support provided by, and within, religious communities can mimic the support usually offered by family members, especially if refugees are co-nationals (Nawyn, 2006). Friendship and emotional support found in religious spaces can be particularly significant in providing sanctuary from hostile environments caused by anti-migrant sentiments in reception countries (Allen, 2010).

As discussed in Chapter 2, people claiming asylum are often in the process for many years, with policies surrounding the support available to people claiming asylum designed to enforce poverty and destitution. Therefore, it is understandable as to why someone might make the choice to engage with a queerphobic community, as they can receive multilayered and continuing assistance. For those who do live visibly, negative ramifications are often losing both material and emotional support as LGBTQI+ people are rejected by religious communities and friends established within these spaces. The prospect of losing this support can be daunting in a system which deliberately creates destitution and is inherently hostile towards those in it. Therefore, the choice to live visibly in countries of reception is often a complex and a difficult decision. Additionally, the unpredictability and proximity people have with CoO and religious communities mean it is often safer for them to continually hide queer subjectivity rather than risk the potential harms of living openly when either still in the asylum process or living with irregular immigration status.

Principally, social experiences outlined above demonstrate a tension between living a visibly queer subjectivity and having to present a subjectivity aligned with majoritarian identities, namely, heterosexuality, to ensure safety, social and emotional support, entry to certain spaces and access to knowledge and resources. Importantly, such strategies are not always successful, and as interlocutors' narratives make plain, those with queer subjectivities can face harassment and violence, destitution and double marginalisation if strategies fail or, even if successful in their social context, can have negative consequences within their asylum claims and vice versa. The interplay of visibility and invisibility with regard to social factors and the legal process was a frequent theme, in both interviews with people seeking asylum and legal and third sector practitioners. These understandings are useful not only in a policy context to challenge unjust legal processes but also in contexts of legal provision, support responses and solidarity.

Chapter 4

The Paradox of Faith: Religious Experiences in Sexual Orientation Asylum Claims*

The UK asylum system has been described as 'a heterosexist, homophobic asylum system that violently abandons queer people most in need of protection' (McKnight et al., 2024, p. 5). As seen in Chapter 2, LGBTQI+ people seeking asylum have been targeted by hostile media and political rhetoric. People who claim on SO grounds are accused of making 'bogus' and 'fake' asylum claims. There have been recent attempts by politicians to downgrade the experiences of LGBTQI+ people fleeing persecutory environments, as merely experiencing discrimination. Suella Braverman, a previous Home Secretary, suggested that the harm LGBTQI+ people face in many cases does not reach the threshold of persecution. Stating:

> We have seen in practice is an interpretive shift away from 'persecution', in favour of something more akin to a definition of 'discrimination'.... Where individuals are being persecuted, it is right that we offer sanctuary. But we will not be able to sustain an asylum system if, in effect, simply being gay, or a woman, and fearful of discrimination in your country of origin, is sufficient to qualify for protection. (Zeffman and Francis, 2023)

Accusations that LGBTQI+ people who claim asylum on SO grounds are 'gaming' the system not only impact wider public perceptions, but rhetoric of this nature has wider implications within the asylum process itself. Inferring asylum claims on SO grounds have a higher prevalence of 'fake' claims, not only trickles

* This chapter was developed using material from the thesis: Fletcher, Claire; (2024) Queerly Faithful: The experiences of religion for those seeking asylum in the UK. Doctoral thesis (Ph.D), UCL (University College London).

Queerly Faithful: Queer People's Experience of Religion in Asylum Seeking, 77–96

doi:10.1108/978-1-83797-488-720261006

into public and authorities' consciousness, but makes decision makers sceptical of those claiming asylum on SO grounds (Ferreira, 2022).

Claims relating to sexual orientation are well established in UK law since 1999, with claimants tending to establish persecution under the 'Particular Social Group' (hereafter PSG) grounds of the 1951 Refugee Convention. Before the 2010 UK Supreme Court decision in HJ (Iran) and HT (Cameroon), those claiming on SO grounds were subjected to high refusal rates, 98%–99% (UKLGIG, 2013) due to the discretion reasoning widely applied to SO claimants. The argument used routinely by the home Office was that LGBTQI+ people could return to the CoO and live discreetly. While the Supreme Court ruling saw an end to discretion reasoning, this has been replaced by a pervasive culture of disbelief which manifests in adverse credibility findings against LGBTQI+ people (Millbank, 2013). This is seen in how the Home Office overwhelmingly refuse sexual identity claims on the grounds of 'credibility' (UKLGIG, 2018, p. 9), which is an issue that persists to date (Lopes Heimer, 2020; Dustin and Ferreira, 2021).

Decision maker disbelief is exacerbated if a person states a religious belief and a queer subject position because of assumed impossibility of subjectivities that embody both (Giametta, 2014; Garcia Rodriguez, 2025). This stems from queerness understood predominantly through secular framings, which creates suspicion towards religious LGBTQI+ people (Khan, 2020). Stereotypical views within Western liberal democracies perceive LGBTQI+ people outside of Western geographic contexts to be 'merely surviving in a time of repression' (Giametta, 2014, p. 584). Queer lives are framed as an impossible project outside of the tolerant and progressive West, Credible narratives in RSD interviews are expected to include straightforward journeys from an oppressive religious/culture to the tolerant, secular – read queer-friendly – societies that provide protection and rights for LGBTQI+ people (Lopes Heimer, 2020).

Continued religiosities challenge this narrative. Sustained engagement with 'religion' and religious communities once in the UK is more likely to lead to those claiming on SO grounds to be refused refugee protection on adverse credibility grounds (Dustin and Held, 2021; Garcia Rodriguez and Giametta, 2024; Fiddian-Qasmiyeh, 2016). This is not unique to the UK; Danisi et al. (2021) explored asylum systems in several European contexts (Italy, Germany and the UK) and found that religious upbringings and beliefs were mobilised in RSD processes against LGBTQI+ people.

It is crucial to understand how social factors and experiences provide barriers to the ability of LGBTQI+ people to make themselves intelligible for refugee protection. As seen in the preceding chapter, there are multiple reasons why LGBTQI+ people continue to engage with religious communities, as seen in Chapter 1 religion can play an intrinsic role in individuals' lives. This chapter illustrates how social experiences materialise within a person's asylum claim and how these can lead to an increased chance of their asylum claim being refused. The lens of religious experience was chosen, as religious experience is commonly used to refuse refugee protection in SO asylum reference needed.

In 2016, the Home Office issued the *Asylum Policy Instruction: Sexual orientation in asylum claims (Vol. 6)* (hereafter: API, 2016), to aid decision makers in determining sexual orientation asylum claims. In the API, decision makers are instructed that a 'claimant's religion is not a basis for rejecting their claim' and that lesbian, gay and bisexual (LGB)[1] 'individuals may be adherents of religions that disapprove of homosexuality, preach against it, or indeed forbid it' (Home Office, 2016, p. 35).

Despite this guidance, decision makers still find religious and queer subject positions improbable, and those who retain religious beliefs are penalised for doing so in their asylum claims. Dustin and Held (2021, p. 209) argue that for LGBTQI+ people:

> Keeping their faith was often a factor that prevented them from making a strong claim for asylum and having it heard fairly, as decision-makers were not able to grasp fully the intersections of sexuality and religion.

Research has consistently demonstrated that the API (2016) is not routinely applied in asylum decision making in SO claims. For example research conducted by the UK Lesbian and Gay Immigration Group (UKLGIG)[2] analysed the extent to which the API (2016) guidance was applied in decision making. LGBTQI+ people who retained religious beliefs, particularly if decision were more likely to have their claim refused viewed their religious traditions to be predominantly homonegative. In these incidences decision makers expected claimants to provide detailed reasoning on how they had resolved this conflict for themselves. One judge in their decision stated:

> You are aware that homosexuality is forbidden in traditional Islam as stated in the Qur'an, however you claim to have reconciled this by having your own relationship with God. However, it is considered that the Qur'an is the holy text of Islam and the word of God, this explanation is a contradiction and you have not provided a reasonable explanation as to why you have continued to practice Islam knowing full well that homosexuality is not permitted in the religion. (UKLGIG, 2018, p. 27)

More recently Rainbow Migration's submission to the Women and Equalities Committee's Inquiry into equality and the UK asylum process cited:

> Questions asking claimants how they feel about their religion and how they reconcile their sexual orientation with their religion occur too frequently. This kind of questioning presumes a conflict and also implies an expectation of a complex theological narrative. (2015, p. 5)

---

[1] The UK Government currently only records asylum claims based on lesbian, gay and bisexual people; other sexualities currently go unrecorded.

[2] UKLGIG's name was changed to Rainbow Migration in 2018.

While academic scholarship considering this intersection is limited, scholars who have explored how religious experience manifests within SO asylum claims have found the Home Office regularly issues refusals due to decision makers' incongruence of an individuals' queer subjectivity and religiosity (Garcia Rodriguez, 2025; Fletcher, 2023).

In this research, three main areas emerged as to how social factors (religious experience) intersected directly with a person's ability to prove their need for refugee protection. First, religious beliefs of those claiming asylum on SO grounds were met with a persistent culture of disbelief, especially for those who continued to engage with homonegative religious communities. This was especially evident in the setting of the substantive interview, where if people revealed religious beliefs, decision makers expect claimants to provide a coherent and in-depth explanation as to how they have reconciled their religiosity and their sexual orientation.

Explanations are expected to include both theological details to justify this reconciliation and emotional responses. Expected experiences include shame and guilt of how this conflict has emerged within their emotional journey towards realisations of sexual difference. If a person cannot provide a coherent explanation of how they have reconciled queer and religious subject positions or give a sound reasoning as to why they do not view these subject positions as conflictual, they face an increased likelihood their asylum claim will be refused.

Interviews with practitioners showed how objective evidence is still routinely expected by asylum decision makers in SO asylum claims. The ability to produce objective evidence is attached to assumptions of credibility (Murray, 2016). Decision makers assume determining credibility is 'premised upon the assumption that truth can be deduced through the analysis of factual evidence...primarily oral narratives and written documents' (Murray, 2014, p. 22). A person's narrative is expected to be consistent with external elements, namely, objective evidence that decision makers have access to. This can include country information reports and objective evidence, such as witness statements, photographs and medical reports (Ferreira, 2023). Decision makers not only expect people to be living openly in countries of asylum, but that they can objectivity evidence this, such as proof of attendance at LGBTQI+ organisations, Pride or evidence of sexual or romantic partnerships (Gaucher and DeGagne, 2014; Berg and Millbank, 2009; Giametta, 2014).

The ability to produce objective evidence is directly related to social factors and experiences, for example a person's ability to be 'out' regarding their queer subjectivity within the country openly as LGBTQI+. As discussed in both Chapters 2 and 3, social experiences such as being housed with CoO communities within the asylum support system have implications for a person's ability or willingness to live openly as LGBTQI+. The remainder of this chapter discusses these themes in more detail, to illustrate how social experiences can prevent individuals from meeting decision makers' expectations in RSD processes.

Religiosity, Disbelief and Narrative Expectations

All practitioners who were interviewed, referenced a prevalent culture of disbelief within the Home Office towards SO claimants. As one legal practitioner said, 'with sexuality, there's a culture of disbelief. I mean it's absurd'. The substantive (main) interview, according to practitioners, is where this culture of disbelief is most evident.

In an initial asylum claim, the substantive interview is the part of the asylum process where a person presents their case to the Home Office to establish the grounds of their persecution and why they fear returning to their CoO. This interview is with a Home Office caseworker and claimants can submit additional objective evidence in support of their claim.

Legal practitioners noted disbelief tended to increase if a person claiming on SO grounds stated a religious belief and is evidence of the prevailing assumption among decision makers that religious LGBTQI+ people are not genuinely queer. Rachel, a legal practitioner, stated:

> If somebody has a strong religious identity usually the Home Office tend to perceive them as they are lying, they're not really LGBT because they say, how do you reconcile your religion with the fact that you are queer.

Decisions on SO claims are often grounded in decision makers' subjective position and knowledge base which often ignores, or cannot comprehend, the lived realities of claimants (Spijkerboer and Jansen, 2011; Millbank, 2002). As Cohen (2001) has argued subjectivity is at odd with consistency, which is necessary in legal decision making to ensure every individual receives equality of treatment.

Despite this, overall, decisions by the Home Office were viewed by legal and third sector practitioners as often subjective, with evidence to suggest negative decisions were reached on decision makers' own preconceived understandings of how religious and queer subjectivity *should* intersect, rather than the person's narrative or evidence presented before them.

As religion is seen as an oppressive force towards queer subject positions, SO claimants who embrace queer secularity and present narratives in their asylum claims that reify tropes of illiberal, backwards and homophobic CoO are more likely to be believed (Dustin and Held, 2021; Giametta and Havkin, 2021). Giametta argues, that it is only when LGBTQI+ people present themselves as an 'absolute victim' do they become 'intelligible and therefore audible to the UK society in general and British jurisprudence in particular' of needing protection (Giametta, 2014, p. 59).

Broadly, responses from both interlocutors and practitioners illustrate there is a systemic issue within asylum decision making that views religious experience as always, an oppressive force in the lives of LGBTQI+ people. Farah, who runs an organisation supporting LGBTQI+ people in the asylum process, explained:

> There's an assumption that every religious experience that a queer person has had will be negative, because they should've been rejected by this community, but that's not the case, it's not that simple, or black and white. There are so many different overlapping

> things, and not every religious experience is going to be terrible because of your sexuality.

This ignores the many queer affirming communities, religious teachings and beliefs and the positive benefits LGBTQI+ people receive through religious encounters, especially in times of trauma and distress (Kilpatrick, et al., 2005). As noted in Chapter 1, most interlocutors were from geographical locations where religion holds a primary importance for most of the population; therefore, even if LGBTQI+ people lived within homonegative contexts, expecting a person to simply abandon lifelong religious beliefs is simplistic.

Typical lines of questioning LGBTQI+ people encounter in asylum interviews follow the line of questioning in Njema's interview transcript: 'You say you are a Catholic, can you tell me about your religion and sexuality and if they cause you any conflict' (Njema, Transcript 1). Legal practitioners reported that LGBTQI+ people who professed a religious belief are often subjected to more intense questioning. Questions concerning a person's religiosity were especially prevalent in cases where individuals were still actively involved in religious communities and attended religious institutional settings, such as a temple, mosque or church in the UK.

People who are able to provide detailed and eloquent responses to this form of questioning are more likely to receive positive decisions in their claim, as their retelling is seen as the 'right' narrative to prove sexual orientation. Conversely, extensive scholarship has explored how claimants whose narrative does not meet the expectations of decision makers are more likely to receive an adverse credibility findings (Jansen, 2013; Powell, 2020; Middelkoop, 2013).

An issue raised by practitioners, and linked to expected narratives, was the incorrect use of terminology or that the claimant had used unfamiliar terminology to describe their sexual and gender diversity. While, the API (2016, p. 22) states:

> Concepts of 'sexual identification' or 'orientation' is not represented in all languages, and that certain words in such languages can imply that the behaviour to which they refer is inappropriate or 'sinful'. As a result, claimants may use unfamiliar words and phrases. Some people may not identify with the labels 'LGB'.

As seen in Chapter 1, previous religious encounters in CoO, terms used to refer to LGBTQI+ people often had negative connotations and people were labelled as 'abominations' or 'devils'. (see Chapter 1). Additionally, language used in the Global North to refer to the variety of queer subjectivities, and again, can negative connotations in peoples' CoO. Furthermore, words that are assumed to have universal meaning by decision makers can have divergent meaning or are used to describe different identities and behaviours (Clare, 2015). As Rachel, a legal practitioner, explained:

> One problem, people that come here for the first time they use these words to identify themselves and there is no neutral word, not a word that doesn't have any bad meaning you know. Sometimes

> there is not such word as 'gay' you know it is a derogatory word and so it's difficult and sometimes difficult for people to identify themselves in this way….I think that this is an issue because I remember people are not prepared to even identify themselves in this way simply because, first it would be the first time if they'd been hiding their sexuality, secondly because there is no such word that doesn't have a meaning that isn't offensive.

Those with queer subjectivities may actively reject Westernised terminology entirely becasue terms have negative connotations in their CoO contexts and causing problems for people who use or have subjectivities labelled with Western terminology (Otu, 2022).

Rachel's quote highlights how expected terminology can create barriers for people seeking asylum. Previous scholarship has warned of the dangers of labelling queer subjectivity and using terminology that is divorced from the realities of the socio-cultural, geographic and historical contexts (Gaudio, 2009). Queerness understood in this way ignores the diversity of non-normative subjectivities and is vastly inadequate to capture the global diversity of sexualities (Manalansan, 2006). Rigid identity formations made legible within RSD frameworks, such as the UK asylum process, delimits who is eligible to be granted protection.

Familiarity with localised terms used to describe queer subjectivities is linked to a person's ability to access local knowledge. For people seeking asylum this is often gained through LGBTQI+ communities, organisations and specialist services. As discussed in Chapters 2 and 3, for LGBTQI+ people accessing support within informal communities and the formal asylum support system are barriers to engaging with LGBTQI+ communities and organisations. Not being able to access these spaces can restrict a person's ability to become familiar with local terms used to describe sexual and gender diversity.

There is a common belief that if a person is 'genuinely' lesbian, gay or bisexual (LGB), they will experience 'a sophisticated internal conflict with their religious beliefs' (UKLGIG, 2018, p. 27), which is only resolved through 'a deep intellectual process' (Dyck et al., 2019, p. 13). For LGBTQI+ people who retain and reveal their religious beliefs, especially if their religious tradition is viewed as homonegative by decision makers, conflicting feelings, such as guilt and shame, surrounding their sexual orientation and how it transgresses religious norms is expected. In relation to conflicted feelings, practitioners stated this line of questioning on religious and queer subject positions is expected to garner an emotional response from the claimant.

Decision makers anticipate that LGBTQI+ people can provide a detailed explanation of how they have reconciled this supposed conflict between their queerness and religiosity within RSD processes (Garcia Rodriguez, 2024). Those who can do this to the satisfaction of decision makers have an increased likelihood of being found credible in RSD interviews. Rachel, a legal practitioner, explained this:

> I had a client recently, he said (in his asylum interview) he is very religious, and he is a gay man, and he said God made me this way,

> so there is no conflict there. Why, that's the way I am because God made me like this. He was Christian and happy in his religion and didn't perceive any conflict. And he said, yes there is something in the Bible that says otherwise, but I think that's not what it is about.

Answers are expected to first recognise there is a conflict if a person's religious faith is aligned with conservative views about sexual and gender diversity. Second, explanations are expected to draw on theological reasoning. Claimants are expected to explain why they have no conflicting feelings about their sexuality or provide theological evidence of how they have resolved any such conflict. If individuals show no signs of conflict, decision makers often question the genuineness of their stated sexuality.

In this research, practitioners' referred to LGBTQI+ people who did not exhibit any signs of conflict between their sexuality and their religious beliefs or were unable to provide a detailed explanation about this lack of conflict were more likely to have their asylum claim refused.

These assumptions by decision makers are underpinned by queer secularist understandings. Queer secularism has positioned religion as a subjugating and repressive force against those with diverse sexualities and genders and has discounted the possibility of agentic constitutions of subjecthood, where both religiosity and queerness are central (Puar, 2007). This exclusionary process of determining who is an 'authentic' queer is particularly difficult for those 'whose racialized identities are associated with "problematic" sexualities or attitudes towards sexual diversity' (Murray, 2011, p. 130). This is seen in the RSD process where individuals claiming on SO grounds retain homonegative beliefs or continue to be involved with homonegative religious communities.

For example, when Desire received her initial decision refusing her claim, the decision reasoning stated it was implausible she would continue to attend a homonegative religious space as a lesbian woman. Desire said she was questioned extensively about her engagement with a Christian religious community in her substantive asylum interview:

> They tried to use the religious aspect that, being a Christian, that I know that it's against the law of my Bible that I shouldn't practice lesbianism. So, why do I forge ahead? They didn't accept it based on that. Because this is something that, I'm aware of in the Christian way…they didn't like the idea of my religion not making me change.

There has been a tendency within Western-centric sexuality scholarship to centre the importance of sexually and gender diverse identities as ones of primary individual importance. The desire for public openness should not be an assumed need for everyone and it is important that the absence of such expressions should not only be read as evidence of remaining oppression (Decena, 2008). In reality, queerness is only one part of a person's subjectivity, which is also in contestation with competing and conflicting identities and subject positionalities. As in this research, people are mothers, sons, Christians, Muslims, friends, persons seeking asylum, congregation members, with different subject positions taking precedent, either permanently or temporarily depending on the different temporal, geographical and situational factors of the time.

Practitioners highlighted the problem of how the primacy of religion in LGBTQI+ claimants' lives often led to misunderstandings about the perceived conflict between their religion and sexuality. As Rachel, a legal practitioner, explained:

> In terms of 'how do you reconcile your religion with the fact that you are queer' what!! What does that even mean. Some people find it very difficult to say – they are like how I reconcile what!! And you can see that the answer is like I don't have an issue, and then they (Home Office interviewer) say 'oh you don't have an issue, but you were not able to explain why you have religion, and you are a religious person, and you are gay'.

Practitioners raised how claimants' just did not understand questions on whether they had experiences conflicts about their sexuality and religious beliefs as it was often something they had not considered before. Saafir, who saw no conflict, said this line of questioning from the Home Office made him feel angry. He viewed the decision makers as passing a form of judgement on him for being both LGBTQI+ and religious.

> They asked me, 'Are you a Christian or Muslim?' I said that I am a Muslim. And they said that you are calling yourself a gay. How do you react to that question? I said 'Are you God? You are not a God. You can't judge me, and I can never judge you. Because God doesn't. Just leave all my sexuality to God, not you'.

Islamic beliefs were discussed more frequently by legal practitioners, and practitioners believed LGBTQI+ Muslims experienced higher levels of disbelief compared to other religious traditions. This was the case even when Muslim claimants were eloquent and well-versed in Islamic theology and had the ability to narrate detailed reasoning of their reconciliation of religious belief and queer subjectivity. While there is no statistical data available to corroborate these claims of bias, previous scholarship has highlighted elevated suspicions surrounding the possibility of a queer Muslim subject position and indicates there is a widespread bias towards queer Muslims (e.g. see El-Tayeb, 2012; Fiddian-Qasmiyeh, 2016; Held, 2016). Research by Danisi et al. (2021) argues that LGBTQI+ Muslims within the asylum processes in the Global North are expected to reject either their queerness to retain their religion or their religion to maintain their queerness.

The homogenisation of 'Muslims' as a homophobic presence in Western contexts is often positioned as a 'threat' towards the tolerance enjoyed by 'queers' within Western liberal democracies. 'Muslims' are constructed as a 'cultural opposition between liberal sexuality and racialized religiosity' (Akachar, 2015, p. 174), with Muslim populations positioned as opposing liberal freedoms, especially in relation to gender and sexuality. These stereotypical framings create and support myths of the impossibility of a queer Muslim subject despite wide-ranging evidence to the contrary (for example see Habib, 2019; Yip and Khalid, 2010; Shah, 2018) and the importance of religion for queer Muslims (Garcia Rodriguez, 2024; Gaudio, 2009; Peumans, 2018).

Heightened levels of suspicion against queer Muslims in RSD processes have been located in how Islamic religiosity and, therefore, Muslims have been constructed and associated with traditionalism, barbarism and oppressive stances towards gender and sexually diverse minorities. These stereotypical assumptions increase scepticism towards queer Muslims by decision makers (Yip and Khalid, 2010; Puar, 2007). By homogenising 'Muslims' as one whole religious community completely ignores the multiple re/presentations of religious identification within the category of 'Muslim' and the multiple ways people define and externally represent themselves to others' (Fiddian-Qasmiyeh and Qasmiyeh, 2010 p. 302). El-Tayeb (2012, p. 80) specifies the problem succinctly, arguing:

> Queer Muslims, if such an identity can be envisioned at all, occupy a place close to that assigned to Muslims, i.e. they are perceived as being too oppressed and alienated from their own needs to speak up as long as they still identify with Islam. It is only when they can make the step into western modernity – a step that necessarily requires the break with, the coming out of the Muslim community – that they can claim an individualized identity as feminist or queer, usually by expressing gratitude for being saved by their 'host society'.

This bias towards LGBTQI+ Muslims has led asylum claimants who occupy these subject positions to pretend, for the sake of their asylum claim, to have rejected their religious beliefs as they believe declaring religiosity would lead to a rejection of their claim (Garcia Rodriguez, 2025).

Finally, in relation to expected narratives and decision making, and the assumption of an incompatibility of queer and religious subject positions, practitioners believed decision makers can choose to wilfully misunderstand the enduring importance of religious experience in the lives of SO claimants. Instead, the aim of this line of questioning is intented to create a range of adverse credibility findings to reject claims for protection. As Mia, a legal practitioner said:

> You will find some perfectly reasonable judges who you know for a fact don't actually believe this nonsense about religion, and who have added that in, as it is one of the reasons to add to an adverse credibility finding. Every judge knows that the more reasons you offer the less appealable your decision will be. If you find 20 rubbish reasons to disbelieve someone it is highly likely that determination will hold up unless you've made some kind of other different boo-boo.

This is suggestive of broader institutionalised trends to identify reasons to disbelieve people seeking asylum on SO grounds. Maintaining notions that religious identity and queer subjectivity are inherently conflictual is beneficial to decision makers as it can be used to contribute to refusal reasoning and deny refugee protection. This finding is replicated in other research, with a participant in Danisi et al. (2021, p. 191) research suggesting the incompatibility if religiosity and queerness was used by the Home Office interviewers to 'just… to shake them[claimants] up'.

Concerningly, in a minority of interviews, the religious subjectivity of the decision maker, both in the Home Office interview settings and in the First Tier Tribunal (Immigration and Asylum Chamber) was suggested by practitioners to influence the outcome of a person's claim. Mia, a legal practitioner, said:

> I represented a guy who actually explained how he found it really difficult to deal with all these things and in quite an articulate way. But the decision maker was basically taking a different theological view of Christianity.

Because of a difference in theological understanding, the decision maker refused the person's asylum claim. Another legal practitioner, said there were certain judges who were more likely to refuse a person's asylum claims if a claimant's understanding of their religion did not reconcile with the judge's own understanding of the religion in question.

Shortage of Legal Advice

Linked, but separate to the issue of disbelief, is the shortage of legal advice in the UK. In November 2024, it was found that 57 per cent of people claiming asylum in England and Wales were unable to secure legal representation (Wilding, 2021, 2024). While it is impossible to know how many LGBTQI+ people are represented during their SO claims, a report by African Rainbow Family in August 2024 highlighted how only 57 per cent LGBTQI+ people they supported had access to a solicitor African Rainbow Family, 2024. Legal practitioners in this research, all referenced how important it is for SO claimant to access quality legal advice as SO claims are considered complex. The difficulties claimants have proving sexual orientation means it is crucial LGBTQI+ people have access to 'sound legal guidance' to ensure claims are presented in line with decision makers expectations (Alessi et al., 2025, p. 789). Yet, this is challenging in light of the current shortage of legal representatives.

Considering specifically the intersection of religiosity and sexuality, practitioners raised how legal advice was important as advisors are able to prepare people to expect questioning on how they have reconciled their sexuality and religious beliefs. As seen above, this form of questioning can surprise claimants, which can impact their ability to give a sufficient response. As Rachel, a legal practitioner explained:

> I mean you can expect questions about a conflict and so it is better for the client's representative to pre-empt and explain these

> in the statement. And so, ask questions about it because if left unexplained, chances are it will crop up in the interview, and then I think the client, if somebody doesn't perceive this as a conflict at all they wouldn't be prepared. It would be difficult to give an answer simply because there's no issue there. So, if you make them think before about the possible answer then they will have a chance to elaborate a little and it will be easier to answer a question on this. So, I'm not talking about coaching your client, that is not it, it is just making you think about something that could be an issue so they can be aware of it.

The current shortage of legal advice means access is often based on social connections, such as those formed in queer organisations. For example, Njema, was introduced to her solicitor who specialised in SO asylum cases through a queer organisation she was a member of and, at the time, she was living relatively openly as a lesbian in the UK.

However, in her narrative, she referred to friends who had to rely on legal advice from solicitors who were part of their CoO or religious communities. Njema spoke of one friend who felt unable to disclose their sexual orientation as the grounds of their asylum claim. This experience is reflected in research carried out by third sector organisations who support people in the asylum system, with findings revealing that people fear disclosing their sexual orientation if their legal advisor has a connection with their wider CoO and religious communities (Dudhia, 2023).

Another issue related to the provision of legal assistance from within CoO is the quality of the legal advice, as legal advisors may not have the expertise in asylum, especially claims based on sexual orientation or gender identity. Other issues that are raised regarding the quality of advice were, the provision of inadequate information on the asylum system and process, and solicitors providing no, or limited time, to help people to prepare for an asylum interview or tribunal hearing (NACCOM, 2023).

In the absence of legal advice, individuals often look for advice within support spaces. This also raises concerns, as McGuirk (2018) has argued, that NGOs and support groups risk reproducing decision-makers' stereotypical assumptions of LGBTQI+ people, rather than trying to eradicate them. Her findings also noted the important role NGOs and support groups can play in SOGI claimants' preparation for judicial hearings, especially for those who only contact LGBTQI+ groups after an initial refusal.

Communities and organisations can act as translators of the local contexts and knowledge gained in LGBTQI+ organisations can be used by individuals to ensure they are identified as the right 'fit' to be recognised within the PSG category in RSD interviews (Greatrick, 2022). In the UK context, workers within NGO's supporting LGBTQI+ people seeking asylum have been found to help claimants 'verbalise' why queerness and religion can be reconciled. While help found in NGOs can provide a lifeline to people who are unable to secure legal advice, the quality of advice found in NGOs can vary (Danisi et al., 2021).

In the UK, there are a range of very good organisations, such as Right to Remain, who provide general knowledge about the asylum process and access to this is invaluable to help people to prepare for their asylum claims. However, there are a limited number of organisations who specialise in supporting LGBTQI + people claiming asylum on SO grounds (Wilding, 2021; Alessi et al., 2025). This leads to people seeking help with more complex issues within informal religious communities, and religious practitioners raised how they were increasingly trying to assist people to navigate the asylum system who had been unable to find a solicitor. There was evidence in practitioner interviews that, however well-intentioned, practitioners were running the risk of straying into providing legal advice, especially in the areas of constructing witnesses' statements and answering questions about evidence needed to 'prove' SO orientation.

Several practitioners mentioned they were already working with people in the asylum process but wanted to ensure their support was helpful and were exploring gaining further training to ensure this type of service could be expanded effectively. This is important as volunteers responding to people seeking safety through informal means often lack the training and preparation for the unmet needs they encounter. Douglas (2023) highlighted that groups and communities in this space found training on supporting asylum seekers on humanitarian grounds difficult to find and access. Furthermore, Local Faith Communities are often volunteer-run and have limited funds for training volunteers and staff. This, combined with high volunteer turnover, can make it difficult to maintain institutional knowledge.

Evidentiary Expectations

The API (2016, p. 19) states, a 'claimant's oral testimony is usually the most important evidence, and often the only substantive evidence that relates specifically to their individual protection needs'. It was suggested by practitioners working with SO claimants that the reason claiming asylum on SO grounds is harder than other grounds is because a person's narrative can be the only source of evidentiary proof (Berg and Millbank, 2009). There was a clear consensus among legal practitioners that it is beneficial for a person claiming on SO grounds to either be in a same-sex relationship or have objective evidence of a previous or current relationships, such as photos, phone messages or evidence of activity on dating apps to support their claim.

This expectation creates a barrier for LGBTQI+ people who are unable, often related to social factors, to acquire supporting objective evidence. This is especially concerning given the evidence that SO claimants are expected to provided is a often set at a higher evidentiary burden than is legally required (UKLGIG, 2010, 2018). This is an issue likely to increase with the higher standard of evidentiary proof established under section 32 of the Nationality and Borders Act 2022 (Powell and Rifath, 2023; Hasan, 2025). Practitioners regularly mentioned the issues surrounding 'objective' evidence in SO asylum claims and cited the following types of expected evidence. Inaya, a legal practitioner, listed common evidentiary expectations which included sexual activity and public expressions of sexuality, such as attendance at Pride marches, by the Home Office.

While the API (2016, p. 23) guidelines state that the 'provision of any extrinsic supporting evidence is not a prerequisite for a genuine claim', legal practitioners said the absence of such was more likely to lead to refusals. This is reinforced by findings by other scholars, who have argued evidentiary requirements are an essential part of successfully 'proving' SO in an asylum claim, and is frequently expected (Berg and Millbank, 2009; Wessels, 2011; Jordan and Morrissey, 2013). Concerningly, Powell (2023) has argued, in sexual orientation asylum claims, objective evidence is given more weight and deemed more credible by decision makers than an individual's own self-identification. Barriers to obtaining objective evidence and how social factors can impede this are now discussed.

Same-sex Relationships

The importance of being able to provide evidence of current or past relationships or proof of engaging in same-sex sex is heavily reliant on social experiences. Social factors can affect a person's ability and/or willingness to be sexually active or become romantically involved while seeking asylum. As discussed in Chapter 3, hiding queer subjectivity was a common strategy for interlocutors to access support in informal religious communities, however, this strategy has ramification in a person's SO asylum claim, as for instance, as it can prevent LGBTQI+ people pursuing sexual or romantic relationships.

Choosing or being forced into heterosexual relationships was a common experience from people in their CoO (see Chapter 1). Practitioners all referenced heterosexual relationships, regardless of motivation, as damaging the credibility of a person claiming on SO grounds (Giametta, 2017). Previous scholarship has suggested this is more problematic for lesbian women who are more likely to have had a heterosexual marriage and/or children due to societal pressures and expectations in their CoO (Lewis, 2013; Tschalaer, 2021). However, in this research, all interlocutors, regardless of gender, experienced pressures to accept heterosexual marriages.

Interlocutors spoke of how decision makers seemed to expect evidence of same-sex relationships that were in line with stereotypical Westernised understandings. For example, Jamilah had avoided a serious relationship due to the precarity she faced in her CoO. Jamilah said her family were abusive towards her for not meeting heteronormative expectations and her employment and living situations were insecure. Her situation in her CoO meant Jamialh was very cautious in terms of entering into same-sex relationships, and this lead to an intense line of questioning in her substantive interview. She explained:

> I said something along the lines of how secrecy was very important, and I tried to explain to my partners that it's light, keep it light. So, she was, like, 'What do you mean by keep it light?' I said-, because in my head, there was no future for it and we need to keep it a secret from people because if people got to know, I'm going to be in trouble and then, that was somewhere in the first question. Then, later on, in another question, she was, like, 'How

> would you feel living in the UK would it be different for you? How would that make you feel?' I said something about safety, security and then I said something along the lines of, 'And having a proper relationship'. She was, like, 'Can you elaborate about that?' I said, 'Proper because in my head, these were not proper. Proper as in to experience everything that I didn't experience before and having the expression that there is a future. Why not, maybe, I'm going to find a woman that completes me, and we get married, hopefully have the two dogs that I always dreamt of'.

Jamilah's idea of a 'proper' relationship was seemingly at odds with the interviewer's expectation of how a romantic relationship should be characterised. Jamilah said, that after describing her previous relationship in this way, she thought the interviewer's further questions insinuated that she believed that Jamilah had lied about the nature of the relationships. Jamilah said she had labelled her past relationships in that way as she did not view her previous affairs as 'proper', as, because of her social experiences in her CoO, she could not envision a future. Legal practitioners cited how decision makers' subjective understandings of 'proper' or 'meaningful' relationships can be used to undermine a person's credibility in terms of the assumed authenticity of their queerness.

Additionally, as discussed in Chapter 2, in asylum accommodation LGBTQI+ people are often housed with CoO or religious communities that they have had persecutory experiences with. This creates a barrier to seeking out romantic or sexual relationships or platonic connections with other LGBTQI+ people. During conversations with legal practitioners they spoke of working with clients whose accommodation created limitation on their pursuing romantic connections. Ali, a legal practitioner, talking about a previous case, said:

> He was really scared of people in his asylum accommodation. He was uncomfortable, just didn't accept himself for himself, you know? He said he was on some dating apps, but he didn't want to put his face on there, so obviously if you don't put your face on the dating app no one is going to want to date you, because they want to know what you look like. So yes, that was another reason I think he went to review (meaning the initial asylum claim was denied).

While the result of their asylum claim is still uncertain and interlocutors were not sure they would be able to remain in the UK, they often choose to keep queer subjectivity hidden due to the risk they could be returned. As Sulaiman said:

> When I have my refugee status, then I have nothing to worry about. Because now I'm so worried, by my status here. But I need my protection first, I want my security first, before I can go into any relationship.

In this worst-case scenario, pursuing a relationship in the UK without a secure legal leave to remain, puts LGBTQI+ people at risk if they were eventually removed to their CoO.

However, Repeated refusals from the Home Office can force people to enact their queer subjectivity visibly, as it is assumed that visibility is more likely to result in a successful outcome in their asylum claim. An assumption that was supported by all practitioners, who all stated it appeared easier for people to have SO claims granted who were living visibly and were connected to LGBTQI+ organisations and communities. These findings are evidence of a scarcity of empathy within decision making for external social experiences that might complicate the ability to provide 'objective' proof of romantic or sexual relationships.

Social Experience and Barrier to Procure 'Objective' Evidence

Non-engagement with LGBTQI+ organisations is a reason often given in Home Office decision letters for refusing to believe a person is genuinely queer. However, the production of 'objective' evidence relating to attendance within LGBTQI+ communities and organisations can often be problematic for SO asylum claimants to obtain. The necessity for objective evidence was noted within initial claims, and at appeal. In appeals, practitioners said there was often an expectation from the judge that if a person is claiming on the grounds of SO, there would either be a representative from an LGBTQI+ organisation present or a present/previous partner in support of the claimant. Practitioners said the absence of either was often noted by adjudicators, both during tribunal hearing and within written determinations.

Expected evidence is often framed by Western expectations that a person has 'come out' and would want to engage with LGBTQI+ organisations and communities. This expectation is often at odds with the cultural and social context of a person's CoO. Mary, a practitioner who worked at an LGBTQI+ organisation supporting people in the asylum process, said:

> Western stereotype or the Western way of having to come out, it's completely different because there's a lack of cultural understanding or consideration, some cultures you don't even talk about any sexuality until you're 18 or above, or until the day you get married. So, they expect you to say that's how I knew and explain that in depth, when you can't even talk about sexuality. It's a real lack of cultural consideration.

The inability to engage with LGBTQI+ organisations is caused by social experiences, such as support from religious communities and living within asylum accommodation. As Desire said:

> 'How am I going to be able to prove that I'm a lesbian?' I have not been in any relationship; I have not been for any activities.

Non-engagement with LGBTQI+ organisation raises doubts towards an individual's credibility and interactions with LGBTQI+ organisations were shown to increase the likelihood of a successful claim. Mary, a practitioner who worked with LGBTQI+ people in the asylum process, said:

> You know that you had to produce evidence, right, so obviously depending on your circumstances, if you're out, or you're not out, you have to be playing in the middle where you want to be out enough to be able to get that evidence, or to prove your life as a gay person, but at the same time, if you're relying on someone for a roof over your head, or if you rely on your community or family for something, then you are also hiding in that space. I know that in many communities' people rely on support from either their religious spaces, or from their family or friends, and they might actually not want their friend to know that they're claiming asylum because of their sexuality.

However, if a person claims asylum on SO ground and references continued engagement in religious communities, there is often an expectation that there will be a presence of a religious authority figures in court, either providing an oral witness statement or attending court to provide emotional support to a person during their tribunal hearing.

As discussed in Chapter 3, interlocutors' narratives clearly laid out the ramification of visible queer subjectivity, including the loss of informal support, friendships, romantic relationship, with visibility opening individuals' up to the risk of further violence. This tension and concerns about the ability to collate 'objective' evidence was a key source of stress for SO claimants. The pressure of providing objective evidence can force LGBTQI+ people to live openly, even when they do not want to or there is a risk to their safety to do so. Practitioners detailed hard choices people had to make between living openly regarding their queer subjectivity and securing 'objective' evidence. As Mia, a legal practitioner, said:

> You might have friends, and your only friends are homophobic or trans phobic.... And you have to make some hard choices in the knowledge of the consequences.

Which was also supported by Inaya:

> They all rely entirely on family and friends and if you're asking somebody already in a very vulnerable position to reject their family and friends by coming out, or face rejection from them, it's a very big ask. It shouldn't happen.

This was seen in the cases of both Emenike and Nofoto in Chapter 3 who lost the support of the informal religious communities when they made the decision to live openly as LGBTQI+. Considerations of safety due to social factors, are consistently not taken into consideration by decision makers.

Finally, engagement with LGBTQI+ organisations themselves revealed there were barriers to access for LGBTQI+ people. People who feel able to approach LGBTQI+ organisations, find that these organisations are not able to, or do not understand how to adequately support people in the asylum process. Practitioners referred to claimants facing barriers in obtaining objective evidence, even if they were involved with LGBTQI+ organisations. This was because organisations did not understand the requirement of those subjected to the asylum process to require proof of attendance at LGBTQI+ groups or organisations. This is frequently asked for by legal representatives to be in the form of a letter or witness statement that independently confirms attendance. Requests for this form of evidence are regularly refused, mainly due to staff capacity limitation within the organisations or an unwillingness to become involved in a person's asylum claim. Not being able to produce objective evidence to support claims of engagement with LGBTQI+ groups is used by decision makers to cast doubt on the reliability of the person's account of attendance at LGBTQI+ events and activities.

Conversely, some interlocutors experienced similar expectations by LGBTQI+ groups about the impossibility of the coexistence of queer subjectivity and religious beliefs. One practitioner, spoke of the experiences of previous LGBTQI+ Muslims he had support. He said that racism and religiosity presented barrier to belonging in certain spaces. Dinesh used his own experiences to describe this barrier, saying:

> I wouldn't be allowed in because I looked too straight. I would get stopped and they would say, 'This is a gay bar', and then I would have to explain myself, it was quite exhausting. And then when you get past the door somebody would approach you and they would start a conversation around, 'Where are you from?' and I would have to explain myself and then the conversation always leads to, 'but you know you can't be gay and Muslim?' If you can imagine being in a sweaty nightclub with lots of gay men and having a discussion about Islam and sexuality, it really put me off the gay scene, to be honest....that's why I work with (organisation identity removed) and volunteer for them because I really felt like there needs to be a space for people who identify as Muslim and queer.

His own experiences as a gay Muslim man demonstrates how queer subjectivities that are in contrast with homonationalist understandings of queerness are challenged in queer nightlife spaces, which are predominantly reflective of gay, male, white and middle class people (Held, 2016, 2023). Shah (2020), in his research with queer Muslims, explored the dynamics of racialisation in queer community spaces, with interlocutors reporting facing disbelief regarding their queerness. One interlocutor stated: 'We're brown and look like this – we couldn't possibly be gay, so we must be up to something else, right?' (Shah, 2020, p. 36).

Dinesh, in our conversations, also referenced the prevalence of alcohol in the UK queer scene, which was not one that many of the LGBTQI+ Muslim people he supported wanted to be involved with. This finding is replicated in other studies; in Bennett's (2014) research, she referenced how a lesbian woman was extensively questioned as to why she did not attend LGBT nightclubs, which, as a Muslim woman with small children, was not something she wished to do. However, her lack of knowledge regarding the 'gay scene' was detrimental to her asylum claim on the grounds of her sexual orientation (Bennett, 2014). These examples illustrate how both social experiences and religion can limit a person's ability to source expected objective evidence from LGBTQI+ organisations and communities, either because of hostile racialisation processes that prevent people's ability to access certain spaces or a limit of LGBTQI+ affirming spaces where people are comfortable expressing both subject positions (Danisi, et al., 2021).

Concluding Remarks

This chapter has illustrated how social experience have direct implications in SO asylum claims. Religious experience was used as a lens to demonstrate how those who do not fit within decision makers expectations of what the experiences of an SO claimant should be, find it more difficult to be seen as genuinely queer. Analysis in this chapter shows how queer subjectivity can intersect with religious experience and create barriers for people both to be recognised as in need of protection and how inequalities emerge and persist.

The ability to 'prove' a sexual orientation, is often reliant on the production of expected narratives and objective evidence. As Dustin (2018) has argued, stereotypical expectations deprive individuals the opportunity to have their claims of persecution individually assessed. Moving towards RDS processes that allow for individual assessment and self-identification of queer subjectivity would prevent people from having to mould their experiences to the stereotypical expectations of Westernised conceptualisations of sexual and gender diversity. Dustin and Ferreira (2021) argue this could be achieved from RSD processes that focus on 'proving' sexual orientation one that explores the intersecting factors that can come together to form persecutory environments.

Religious experience was used as a lens to demonstrate how those who do not fit within decision makers expectations of what the experiences of an SO claimant should be, find it more difficult to be seen as genuinely queer. Stereotypical imaginings of queerness limit and ignore the complexity present within lived experiences (García Rodríguez, 2023). The examples above make it clear how the importance of religious beliefs for people claiming asylum on SO grounds are not fully comprehended or understood by decision makers. Religious illiteracy amongst asylum decision makers, means, more often than not, LGBTQI+ people who express religious belief have their credibility called into question.

Regardless of an individual's motivation, continued encounters with religious communities can cast a shadow of suspicion, as this is viewed as unaligned with the stereotypical oppression to liberation narratives that construct LGBTQI+ people as only truly 'free' once they have shaken off religious and/or cultural traditions from their CoO (Chossière, 2022). This increased scepticism towards people who engage with religious communities is especially concerning, as religious venues are increasingly key sites of support in the UK, as people seeking asylum often experience high levels of destitution and poverty. Furthermore, as will be discussed in Chapter 6, engagement with religious communities is not directly correlated to a person's religious subject position, as people seeking asylum engage with religious communities for a wide variety of reasons.

The findings in this chapter demonstrates the need for greater training for decision makers to understand the diversity of experience for people claiming asylum on sexual orientation grounds. What is more concerning, is evidence from both interlocutor and practitioners points to a systemic culture for looking for reasons to refuse claims rather than to provide a thorough assessment of the protection needs of the individual.

Chapter 5

Redoing Religion: Religious Experience as a Resource for Healing Among LGBTQI+ People Seeking Asylum*

Chapter 1 highlighted how interactions with 'religion' led many interlocutors to interpret their queer subjectivities negatively and harmful experiences and trauma were intertwined with religious encounters. Subjectivities that deviated from heteronormative expressions of sexuality and gender in individuals' pre-migration contexts were often framed within religious terminology as deviant, sinful and abhorrent. Religiously inspired negative framings of LGBTQI+ people led interlocutors to experience both homonegative occurrences and internal conflicts regarding their queer subject positions.[1] While several interlocutors spoke of starting to re-configure the negative framings used to understand their religious and queer subject positions in their CoOs, for many, this process only began once in the UK. This chapter shows how religion can provide a framework to redress and ease the influence of homonegativity and internalised homophobia stemming from previous religious encounters.

---

* This chapter was developed using material from the thesis: Fletcher, Claire; (2024) Queerly Faithful: The experiences of religion for those seeking asylum in the UK. Doctoral thesis (Ph.D), UCL (University College London).

[1] This chapter only focuses on the narratives of those who experienced negative feelings towards their queer subjectivity. As discussed in Chapter 1, personal negative feelings and/or internal conflicts regarding queer subjectivity were not experienced by every interlocutor. It is important to highlight the importance of acknowledging a diversity of authentic queer experience. Therefore, it should not be expected or needed with SO asylum claims for those who come from geographical contexts where there are higher levels of homophobia and homonegativity to display internal conflicts or a level of distress around their sexuality or gender diversity.

Queerly Faithful: Queer People's Experience of Religion in Asylum Seeking, 97–122

doi:10.1108/978-1-83797-488-720261007

Individuals' past history of religious stigmatisation left an enduring, negative impact on their views of themselves as LGBTQI+ people. While Religious experiences in countries of asylum were found to assist LGBTQI+ people to move past harmful understandings of their queer subjectivity that were grounded in religious stigmatisation. Existing scholarship has established the positive contributions that religious experiences can have on refugee populations in terms of individual resilience, mental wellbeing and the healing from traumatic events (Fensham, 2021; Alessi et al., 2021; McGuirk and Niedzwiecki, 2017). However, currently, very limited literature considers the intersections of LGBTQI+ people seeking asylum, mental wellbeing and religion, especially responses that involve intercultural spiritual care for LGBTQI+ people (Fensham, 2021). Even less research considers religiously inspired care towards LGBTQ+ people specifically from the viewpoint of people seeking asylum (García Rodríguez, 2023).

The positive examples of religious experience within the narratives provide an empirical counter to simplistic tropes that position religion, in relation to sexually and gender diverse people, as purely restrictive and oppressive influence (Nynäs and Yip, 2016). Much has been made of the religious harms metered out against LGBTQI+ people, enacted by religious groups, communities and individuals, and this should not be ignored. However, I would argue these dominant assumptions have hampered consideration of religious resources as sites of alternative provision of welfare, comfort and protection (Knibbe and Spronk, 2022). While conservative religious interpretations are often used to justify the persecution of LGBTQI+ persons, religion, faith and spirituality can simultaneously be used to motivate people to help those in need and be a source of strength in times of uncertainty (McGuirk and Niedzwiecki, 2017).

Fensham (2021, p. 9) has identified how internal dissonance of queer subjectivity is particularly high for people who hold religious beliefs, but argues:

> For many people this inner dissonance or experiential-spiritual rupture may never completely ease. Progress can be made by normalising and embracing embodied experience including sexual attraction and sexual expression. This is not just a personal journey but, in important ways, also a spiritual journey. Finding resources in the person's own religious tradition and finding an affirming community that supports those resources is therefore important.

Yet the significance of religion is often ignored by secular NGOs and third sector actors in responses provided to LGBTQI+ people seeking asylum (Fletcher, 2016). The oppositional positionalities of the religious and secular have resulted in limited support provisions which centres and attends to both the queer and religious subject positions in displacement contexts (Danisi et al., 2021). Complicating considerations of how religious experience can be situated within broader responses to LGBTQI+ people seeking safety in the Global North are westernised assumptions that assume support provided to LGBTQI+ people should be secularly framed.

The dominance of secularism within support spaces is due to a scepticism surrounding the motivations of religiously inspired responses and religious actors in humanitarian contexts (Farnell, 2009; Lant, 2017). While religion is viewed as a restrictive element towards progressive and liberal developments regarding gender and sexuality, secularity is seen as 'exceptionally amiable to queer subjecthood in comparison to religious modes of being' (Khan, 2020, p. 136). Khan argues a secular self is seen as 'the only possible way to be successfully *liberal* and *liberated*' (*ibid*, italics in the original). It is assumed that the further a LGBTQI+ person moves away from their traditional religious upbringing and beliefs, the freer they will be (García Rodríguez, 2023).

Encouraging a consideration of religiously inspired care, Fensham (2021, p. 1113) argues that for those who have experienced harm at the hands of religious actors, while secular care is thought to be more appropriate, if trust can be established with a spiritual caregiver, there is a chance for 'extraordinary potential'. Care provided by a caregiver who is able to attend to a person's spiritual needs is more likely to lead to the LGBTQI+ person reaching internal acceptance of themselves. Dyck et al. (2019) argue that religiously inspired aspects of the discrimination and psychological difficulties LGBTQI+ people endure is a reason why support from religious communities can be particularly valuable, although it should not be ignored that they can also be sites of continued harm (Schlager and Kundtz, 2007).

The first part of this chapter focuses on religious experiences, that interlocutors had on reaching the UK. These were are often a catalyst for individual's to reconceptualise their queer subjectivity. The shift of emphasis to an individualised level of enquiry on how religion is meaningful (or not) facilitates a more nuanced understanding of the part religion can play in the lives of LGBTQI+ people in an asylum-seeking context. Narratives in this chapter show how individuals reinterpreted their previous understandings of religious doctrine and shifted towards an individualised relationship with Allah/God. Interlocutors also distanced themselves from previous institutionalised forms of religion, although individual spiritual practice usually resulted in a re-engagement with communities of faith. The centring of a personalised relationship with both their deity and religious doctrine allowed for a reinterpretation of dogma that removed the negative framings of queer subjectivity previously understood within their CoO contexts (McGuirk and Niedzwiecki, 2017; Alessi et al., 2021).

While individuated practices did play a key role in how people started to reconceptualise and reconstitute their subjecthood, this frequently happened in conjunction with meeting queer-affirming religious individuals and communities. Therefore, the second section of this chapter moves to exploring interlocutors' experiences within both non- and queer-affirming religious communities in the UK. Interlocutors sought out religious communities for a variety of reasons (see Chapter 3) and religious encounters helped people to achieve a removal or reduction in conflictual feelings between their religiosity and queer subjectivity. The quotation below from Neil, a priest and a volunteer with an LGBTQI+ organisation that supports people in the asylum process, captures this unique positionality:

> Sometimes you find that there are people in the wider LGBT community who are very anti-religious, and even some of those with

> me as volunteers don't approach that side of it at all, and for them, it's meaningless. But, I think, if you take people where they're at, and they've suffered discrimination in some other country, but they've grown up with a basic frame of life with them praying several times a day, honouring Ramadan, those things have meant something to them. And if they could still be Muslims and know something about the Qu'ran and have ability to practice their faith, at the same time not disavowing their own identity as LGBT people, that's really, really important....So I think it's really important that we help LGBT refugees and asylum seekers to claim the two parts of their identity, their religious side and who they are as individuals, as there's no contradiction between them.

Interlocutor narratives presented in this chapter reveal how, for people with strong religious beliefs, involvement in a queer-affirming religious community or a relationship with a queer-affirming religious individual provides a way of overcoming dissonance between their religiosity and queer subjectivity, leading to increased wellbeing and self-acceptance. Responses that were religiously literate and, therefore, attune to the particulars of harm and trauma stemming from religiously inspired rejection had the ability to respond in ways that other types of responses could not. Both forms of religious experiences and encounters resulted in interlocutors having a new way to imagine the relationship between their queer subjectivity and religious beliefs, and will be explored in the proceeding sections.

Individualised Re-conceptualisations

The reshaping of religious beliefs towards a personal interpretation of religious teachings included distinguishing between a belief in a deity – God/Allah – and institutionalised forms of religious doctrine and practice. Research has found LGBTQI+ people who hold religious beliefs are more likely to embrace a form of 'religious individualism' in how they interpret, construct and live their religiosity (Wilcox, 2009). Strength, in displacement contexts, is sourced from within religious practice, especially practices that develop a 'deeply personal and individual relationship with God' (Alessi et al., 2021, p. 179). Interlocutors who moved towards an individualised religious belief that superseded previous institutionalised forms of religious understandings, did so in diverse ways, and there were substantial differences in how people encountered and experienced religion or continued their religious practice. This section illustrates the variegated ways people observed, understood and lived their religious beliefs outside of institutional religious framings.

The main way interlocutors started to develop their own individuated understanding of religion, was to first distance themselves from institutional religious spaces or communities connected to religious teachings from their CoO. In a minority of cases, this had started to happen in people's CoO, but more often, it was through leaving their CoO that people were finally able to achieve distance. The creation of distance provided people with the space, both physical and metaphorical, for a self-exploration of their religiosity. Migrations to other geographic contexts allowed interlocutors the time and temporal space to research, reflect and reconstitute religious beliefs and understandings of previous religious teachings. Previous research has highlighted how dissonance for a person between institutionalised religious teachings and their own queer subjectivity can cause them to react in this way, creating both psychological and physical distance from religious institutional spaces to protect themselves (Yip, 1997).

For example, Fillemon, a gay man who had been residing in the UK for five years at the time of our conversations, had grown up in a Seventh Day Adventist community in Southwest Africa. As the religious community was very small, he had no friends or family outside of this community. In Fillemon's CoO, LGBTQI+ people were considered to 'have demons'. At home, throughout his childhood, Fillemon was a regular attendee at church, but he said:

> I started exploring other churches because the whole time I went to that church, it never felt like home I would say. So, when I got into my teenage years that's when I started exploring other churches, maybe I would feel at home.

For Fillemon, his disconnection and dissonance towards his religious community started in his CoO and worsened as he began to acknowledge his own queer subjectivity. His awareness that he was different led to his slow rejection of familial religious spaces as they were homonegative. To try to relieve this conflict, Fillemon began to independently engage with religious scripture and teachings, which was also driven by his desire to find somewhere he felt 'at home'. Fillemon's independent engagement with Christian scripture led to the beginning of his questioning of the 'absolute truth' of the religious teachings of his childhood. Yip and Khalid (2010, p. 37) have argued that religious texts are often 'the source from where the venom of homonegativity originates'; therefore, it is unsurprising how individuals will often return to religious texts in search of new ways of understanding their queer subjectivity. Religious passages are often used to justify the condemnation of LGBTQI+ people and prove the naturalness of heterosexuality (Yip, 2005). Therefore, a common exercise for LGBTQI+ people, who want affirmation that their deity does not disapprove of them, is to seek proof of this within scripture (Yip, 2016).

Fillemon explains his research mainly took the form of re-readings of the Bible, searching for answers and guidance about same-sex desire. Fillemon said he especially struggled with how 'sin' and how hierarchies of sins had been conceptualised by religious leaders in his CoO, saying:

> The Bible says sin is sin. That never even made sense to me when I was young, because it just never made sense to me until I started, like, researching my own journey and trying to find God in my own way.

Fillemon's personal interpretation of sin in relation to biblical scripture was that, while he acknowledged the existence of sins and sinful behaviours, he disagreed with the explanation given by his religious leaders that there was an evident hierarchy of sinful behaviour. Religous leaders in his CoO preached that same-sex desire was seen as the 'ultimate sin'. However, Fillemon understood sinful behaviour as actions that had no differing degree of severity. Yet, when sin and sinful actions were preached on in the churches, he attended in his CoO that 'homosexuality' was spoken about as being a sin worse than any other. Fillemon's later re-readings of the Bible led him to an understanding that there was a lack of doctrinal evidence for 'homosexuality' being 'the ultimate sin'.

His new understanding caused him to question the way LGBTQI+ people were positioned as 'abominations' by religious leaders in his CoO. For him, his new understanding was confirmation of a conflict between God's word and institutionalised religious preaching. This difference created a doubt in Fillemon's mind as to whether institutionalised religious teachings were actually in accordance with God's word. This doubt created the beginning of his rejection of institutionalised interpretations of the Bible that had been taught throughout his childhood.

Consequently, teachings from his CoO stopped resonating with him. He reasoned that to understand his faith, he had to take an individualised approach, saying, 'If the Bible says itself that God is love, then I've got to develop my own relationship with God'. Instead of attending religious services in his CoO, Fillemon sought out religious leaders he felt an affinity with online and began to watch and engage with a variety of religious sermons in this way. More broadly, the internet has encouraged and allowed people 'to tinker with their religious affiliations and beliefs in ways that have gone mostly undetected' (McClure, 2017, p. 482). The internet was used by interlocutors to gain access to different interpretations and teachings within their religious tradition, on sexual and gender diversity.

In the UK, Fillemon still maintained his Christian convictions, and a belief in God, and he continued to explore different interpretations of his Christian faith online. By accessing different teachings, this helped him to work through and create his own personalised religious belief system. The freedom to use the internet as a tool of exploration of the sheer variety and diversity in Christianity meant Fillemon could find religious teachings and worship that matched his own subjective religious beliefs. The pastors he found connections with were based in West Africa and he was drawn to teachings that focused on God's love, rather than preaching about religious restrictions on behaviours or subjectivities. While the pastors he referenced in our conversations are not queer affirming, they do not condemn LGBTQI+ people, and instead put their focus on God's loving individuals regardless of who they are.

Fillemon complemented his online worship by individual readings of the Bible, and centring on parts of scripture that spoke of God's love. This helped him to move towards self-acceptance and a more positive understanding of himself as a gay man. Explaining this, he said:

> Reading the Bible myself and searching the Gospel myself, I started to realise that, for example, in John 4:8, it says 'God is love'. So, that alone to me was like, 'Okay well, if God is love, how can anybody else tell me that because I'm this (meaning a gay man), God does not love me?'

Yip (2016) argues that 'empowering statements of faith and ontology, underpinned by the unshakable certainty that one's sexuality (and gender) – no matter how despised and persecuted – is not just a choice or random genetic predisposition, but divinely willed and planned' (Yip, 2016, p. 40) helps individuals towards self-acceptance. Interlocutors who came to believe in the certainty of divine love, a love that would remain, despite how they were disapproved of and rejected by family and communities, helped them to accept their sexuality. This unshakable certainty was often grounded in the belief in divine will and an all-knowing divinity. As Fillemon said:

> The book of Jeremiah where God talks about how he knew you before he formed you. To me, that alone lets me know that if God knew us before he formed us, right now if we go to, let's say, 2025 and God even knows what we were going to be doing in 2025, then to me it's like, 'Why not just live your life in a way?' Because God already knows who you are. Because God already accepts who you are, then, logically, live your truth.

Fillemon's belief that his existence was divinely planned alleviated his fear of divine disapproval or intolerance inspired by religious teachings in his CoO. This form of understanding was replicated in other interlocutors' narratives of a religious deity that was omnipresent and all-knowing, but there were several slight differences within this type of reconstitution of religious beliefs.

Individual reinterpretations of scripture provided interlocutors with a new theological knowledge base, in which they came to understand that God had not forsaken them. Understanding themselves as still a consideration within God's divine plan gave interlocutors' both a feeling of strength and hope. For Fillemon, as God had created him this way, his queer subjectivity couldn't be against God, as God was his maker and he was part of God's plan. Therefore, his existence was beyond his or anyone else's rebuke.

A common belief among interlocutors was that God is the ultimate judge and is the only authority on the religious piety of lives lived. This is replicated in other scholarship, such as Bonthuys and Erlank (2012, p. 272) and in their research interlocutors spoke of a belief that 'judgement belonged to Allah' alone. Those who had reframed their religious beliefs towards a more sympathetic consideration towards their queer subjectivity drew comfort from understandings that if God/Allah was truly displeased with them, then they would not have been permitted by God to live queerly. This allowed them to believe that, regardless of their queer subjectivity, if God judged them to have lived good lives, then they would still be welcomed by God in death.

In a similar vein, interlocutors spoke of the inherent goodness of God and this was used as a justification by interlocutors that as they were created in God's image, and God is good. For example, Saafir said:

> All this is natural. It is only God that will know the best thing for us. He is the God that created me. That's what I believe. It is God that created me in this, and I will never fear any other man.

> Because I do believe in God, he is the one that created me. If it is not good, he won't have created me.

As a creation of God, Saafir views his queer subjectivity to be outside of the purviews of societal *and* his own control. Believing God viewed them as valuable and part of his creation or divine plan, in spite of how their queer subjectivity was positioned in their CoO religious communities they themselves must also be good (McGuirk and Niedzwiecki, 2017).

Theological research and reengagement with scripture was again an avenue interlocutors used to move past negative feelings, about queer subjectivity, Emenike, said:

> I was kind of feeling very guilty, let me put it that way, and that was based on what I was taught, preached by other people, ok. By some homophobic pastors or reverend fathers or, you know, whoever. I was kind of feeling very guilty and blaming myself. However, as I became older and started doing my research and, you know looking into things, I found out that my sexuality hasn't got anything to do with religion. As far as I am concerned, there's a very big gulf between your sexuality and your religion. You can be anything and practice whatever religion you want to practice.

Separating queer and religious subject positions helped people to detach themselves from previous homonegative teachings, and this helped them to move past negative self-beliefs. Separation in this way enabled individual re-engagement and reconciliation with their religiosity.

Reconciliation of religious beliefs and queer subjectivity was not always an easy thing for interlocutors to do independently. While interlocutors did come to a personal understandings and ways of living in terms of their religious beliefs and queer subjectivity, reconstitution of their religiosity was still often heavily influenced by institutionalised religious norms, These influences left lasting negative feelings regarding their queer subjectivity. As Ammerman (2016) argues, even if a person has ceased contact with all institutional forms of religion, their rejection of institutionalised religion in its totality cannot be assumed. Previous religious influences cannot and should not be ignored in individualised and personal religious interpretations, beliefs and practices. Ammerman argued that it is impossible to draw distinct boundaries around lived religious practices and how previous or current influences from institutionalised religion can shape current religiosity. This is especially evident in the ways interlocutors sought out institutionalised religious spaces that held affirming theological positions.

For example, Njema, spoke of her contradictory feelings in relation to her religious beliefs and her sexuality, saying:

> Njema: Even back home, even with R, she would say, 'It's God. God is going to judge us, let us leave everything in his hands'. So, yes. It always comes back, honestly. It's not easy to believe in God

> and to be gay. It's not easy. Especially when you know that you came from somewhere that was against it completely. You always have that. It's something that you know in yourself, like, 'The Bible is against this. God is against this'.
>
> CF: Do you think God is?
>
> Njema: Honestly, I don't think he is. I think he loves us all no matter what. I don't think he is, no. I know that when you talk about it, people try to convince you that's why maybe he destroys Sodom and Gomorrah, because it was infected with gay people and paedophiles. But for me, if he doesn't accept that, he's going to punish us.

In Njema's quotation, it is clear that the institutionalised religious belief system she grew up within continued to influence her view that same-sex attractions and relationships were against God's wishes. This caused enduring conflictual feelings for Njema. And that at the time of our conversation she was still struggling with previous religious teaching, even while she was certain she was loved by God. Njema's example illustrates how past religious experiences can create a tension for interlocutors within their religious beliefs, even though they have come to understand a difference between institutional teachings and how God sees them.

A common concern presented in the narratives was the belief that, because they were LGBTQI+, the past and current hardships they were facing – being forced to leave CoO and family rejection – were seen as a form of divine punishment. This belief caused people to stop attending religious spaces and additionally, individuals believed that they were being punished and this led them to assume their deity no longer protected them or wanted them to be part of the religious community. One religious practitioner, Kit, explained:

> It can be really hard for people. They want to turn to God in prayer because they're hurting, they're lonely, they're worried about their case or whatever, but they've got this little niggling feeling that God doesn't like them because of what their pastor has said about them being gay.

Evident in Kit's quotation is how difficult it can be for people in times of crisis or hardship – such as being in the asylum process – to feel an inability to turn to their deity and religious beliefs for comfort. A significant element of interlocutors arriving at an affirming understanding of their religious faith meant they were, once again, able to draw on their religious beliefs as a source of strength.

Interlocutors who moved to personalised interpretations of religious doctrine rarely resulted in an avoidance of religious spaces altogether. However, a willingness and a wish to attend religious spaces to worship should not be interpreted that the religious space is queer-affirming and a person has the ability to be open as LGBTQI+ within the community (McGuirk and Niedzwiecki, 2017).

Fillemon, for example, did not regularly attend church or interact with any religious communities, but at the time of our conversation he had not rejected the idea of returning to religious spaces or religious communities in the future. However, while Fillemon expressed a desire to return to a physical space for worship, he was still reticent about revealing his sexuality in a religious setting, because of a previous experience at a friend's church. Reflecting on this interaction he said that he recognised that his whole self – meaning his sexuality – would not be welcome within the Church community. Stating, 'Like all the things that I've been through since I was a kid. You can kind of sense it and can't really open up there'. Therefore, while he wanted to return to worship he recognised these space could be ambivalent in terms of acceptance of LGBTQI+ people.

The above excerpts have explored how both individualised reinterpretations of religious beliefs, and distance from CoO religious communities, facilitated people to reject past institutional religious framings that queer subjectivity is deviant, sinful and a contradiction for a morally religious person. The creation of personalised beliefs provoked a reconstitution of how people understood and lived their queer subjectivity and, most importantly, allowed them to begin to heal from past trauma. This is of significance, as evident in narratives, is the long-lasting impact homonegative institutional religious teachings can have on LGBTQI+ people. The healing of religious doctrinal fractures freed individuals from constant feelings that they were acting discordantly with God/Allah's wishes. This freeing was not only articulated as a sense of relief for earthly life but also relieved fears about a divine retribution because of their life of 'sin' on their death. Generally, the ability to reconfigure religious doctrinal interpretations removed significant levels of anxiety and distress for interlocutors.

Religious Individuals and Communities

Histories of homonegative pasts remained intertwined with interlocutors' temporal presents, which were illustrated in the re-telling of their narratives. McGuire (2008, p. 12) argues that while lived religious beliefs and practices can be intensely individual, people can also share 'vivid experiences of intersubjective reality' which can shape how religious belief systems are formed. Fensham (2021, p. 1113) further contends, that religious resources, especially if combined with accepting communities that support divine affirmation, can create environments where individuals who have previously experienced religiously inspired harm can 'grow and flourish'. In light of this, this next section explores how experiences within religious communities helped interlocutors to come to terms with religiously inspired harm.

Hazelle, who grew up in a Catholic community, struggled to accept her sexuality as a bisexual woman. In her CoO, Hazelle attended church regularly with the rest of her family, and she explained that religious adherence was a familial expectation. Non-attendance of church was not tolerated in her family and if she missed church she would be punished, such as meals being withheld. During our conversations, Hazelle confided about how she started to hate attending church in her CoO, explaining

> I hated going to church.... back home they would force you to go to church, you have to hear all of the crap that they always say, Sodom and Gomorrah, all the same bollocks. So, it just made me to, just hate church. I was, like, 'God, if this is not normal just change me, let me just be'. My prayer was like, 'Just let me be a normal person'. Because I feel, you think that there's something wrong with you, or maybe you are mentally not stable in your brain, when I grew up that's how I felt.

Evident in Hazelle's excerpt is how attendance at church contributed to her negative feelings about herself, which were directly related to the religious teachings she heard when she attended church. Religious leaders drew on religious texts and scriptures to justify the normative violence meted out to those who acted outside of permitted sexuality and gender norms (Goss, 2002; Habib, 2012).

In Hazelle's case, she internalised religious teachings, which framed LGBTQI+ people as abominations and evil and who were acting outside of permitted social and gender norms, which in her CoO were grounded in the naturalness of heterosexuality. This form of religious discourse led Hazelle to feel alienated from and unwelcomed within her church community and that she was not 'a normal person'.

At the time of our meeting, Hazelle had claimed asylum in the UK as she had been caught by her husband with her girlfriend Fendee, who she had met while studying in the UK. One weekend, Hazelle's husband who had been visiting family in a different county, returned home early to find Hazelle and Fendee asleep together. Hazelle's husband told her family back in her CoO who immediately disowned her, Hazelle explained:

> They see that being gay is evil. You are bringing curse upon the family and because they are from a very Christian background. For them, it's an abomination, basically, so they just looked at me as an outcast, an abomination.

The pain of her family's rejection caused her years of emotional distress, which was compounded by Hazelle's previous religious experiences that framed queer subjectivity as sinful. Hazelle said she struggled for years to find peace and self-acceptance as a bisexual woman and avoided attending religious spaces in the UK.

Several years after her husband's discovery of her affair with Fendee, Hazelle was introduced to a queer-affirming church by a friend. Hazelle began to attend worship on a regular basis within this community, and slowly her perspectives about her religious beliefs started to shift, especially in relation to her sexuality. Evident in Hazelle's narrative was how the Reverend of this community was a particularly important figure in Hazelle's reconceptualisation of her religious beliefs, as she explained:

> I would always go before the service started or even stay when we finished the service. I would approach Reverend and I was, like,

> 'Okay, I am struggling with this, this is how I was brought up, and this is what I've been taught. That being gay is not normal, how can you help me to accept this?' Because they say God is love, I don't see God loving because people used to turn to this verse, and say, 'Oh, no you are an outcast', and everything. But she said (the Reverend), 'No, God just loves you the way you are, there's nothing wrong with you, you are born that way. If God came and died for all sinners, why would you think that there's something wrong with you? We are born that way; you didn't make yourself that way'. So, she helped me too slowly accept myself, my sexuality, my sexual relationships, and yes, reading sermons. She would always send sermons, like, 'Read this passage, it will help you understand and help you with more clarity'. So that's how I, kind of, reconcile my sexuality with religion, because I know that God loves me just the way I am, I am born like that. If he wanted me to be a different person, I would be a different person.

This excerpt illustrates how her relationship with a queer-affirming church started a process that enabled a renewal and reconfiguration of her religious subjectivity and beliefs. Having a person who was religiously literate allowed Hazelle to bring up specific Bible teachings and sermons which had been used to frame queer subjectivity as a sin. These teachings had been used in her CoO religious community to cast out people who transgressed heterosexual social norms. Hazelle's ability to question her previous religious beliefs with a person she viewed as having a religious authority meant she believed the validity to the alternative religious interpretations of biblical teachings put to her. In other narratives it was found the perceived truth of alternative beliefs and different interpretations of religious doctrines were deemed more credible when interlocutors perceived the person who preached them to be a religious authority figure.

The importance of an authoritative religious person in supporting individuals to move away from negative understandings of queer subjectivities was regularly referenced by interlocutors. Njema, said that she initially questioned herself constantly

> You start asking yourself a lot of questions. 'Am I doing a good thing? What am I doing?' ...You know, you question yourself all the time.

In the UK, Njema regularly attended a Catholic Church whose religious community was heavily involved in advocating for the rights of, and supporting refugees and migrants. Njema attended this church as a source of both spiritual and material support, and in our conversation she recounted a particularly difficult day when she grappled with her religious beliefs and sexual orientation. Feeling overwhelmed, she sought the priest's guidance to understand God's perspective on her. As she explained:

> I spoke with a priest there for a long time. And I say to them, 'What do you guys think of homosexuality and religion'. I said,

> 'But in the Bible, it says this. We all read the Bible; you ask us to live according to the Bible, but in the Bible it's against'. But he said, 'No, God is okay with that'. I think it was good to hear a priest telling you that. So, since that day, I just did, no matter what. I know God is there and I know he exists. I know he loves and looks after me and he's been there. He loves everyone, no matter how. If you are just nice to people.

Njema's excerpt again underscores the significant impact of how people with religious authority can provide reassurance and relief to LGBTQI+ people who have been subjected to religiously inspired harm. Religious authority figures can provide assurances to people that God/Allah still loves them and has not abandoned them.

Religious authority figures can play significant roles in either providing different theological interpretations of religious doctrines or introducing people to affirming religious communities. Re-interpretive work was seen to hold particular weight if carried out alongside a religious authority figure. Religious practitioners who led, or were involved in affirming religious groups, faith practice/prayer or social justice projects said they were often involved with queer-affirming interpretative work with scriptures and doctrine with people seeking asylum.

Re-interpretive work is often undertaken to find affirmation of acceptance of sexual and gender diversity (Fensham, 2021). There were two main types of interpretive work present within interlocutors' narrative. The first is the practice of a re-examination of religious texts for examples of same-sex intimacy and for religiously sanctioned guidance for expressing it (Yip, 2016). The second involves a reversal of 'religious discourse that challenges the truth claims of the heteronormative dominant discourse' (*ibid*, p. 38). Yip notes the common examples included in the Bible, are Genesis 19, Leviticus 18:22 and 20:13, Sodom and Gomorrah, and the Qur'anic suras 6:85–87, 38:11–14, 54:33–40. These passages have been employed by conservative religious traditions as evidence of the naturalness of heterosexuality and the unacceptability of any forms of sexual and gender diversity which transgresses heterosexual norms. Re-interpretive work is seen as broadly beneficial as it removes the religious stigma associated with LGBTQI+ people (*ibid*).

Practitioners commented on how this type of religious activity seemed particularly healing for LGBTQI+ people who had faced religiously inspired normative or actual violence because of their queer subjectivity. A violence that was justified through religious texts and scripture. Kit, a pastor of a queer-affirming church group, said:

> We actually devote a certain amount of time, whether it's in personal discussions, study groups, sermon series, whatever, in tackling the anti-LGBT theologies and scriptures and beliefs, and actually just head on confronting them and talking and explaining why we think that God is totally cool and onboard with people being LGBT.

Kit's description illustrates how responses dedicated to the reinterpretation of religions texts are one of the unique types of support found within religious communities. This type of religious encounter can provide an environment where people who have felt at odds or shunned from their religious community have a space where, not only are the negative impacts of religiously inspired harm understood but also provides a space for people to heal.

Robert, a priest leading a Catholic community, referred to this type of encounter as a 'healing ministry'. Robert led a queer-affirming mass, which he explained was developed to provide a place where LGBTQI+ people who had been excommunicated from other religious communities could come and find welcome. The idea was to ensure the community affirmed the whole person, with all elements of a person's subjectivity welcomed. Robert said that within these services he had met and supported many people seeking asylum in the UK who had faced rejection in other religious spaces.

Religious practitioners did raise concerns about a power imbalance that needed to be considered when thinking of religious responses to people seeking asylum. Practitioners felt conversations they had with people held greater weight and influence because they were viewed as a religious authority figure. Kit explained this in one of our conversations:

> I have to be very careful because, in essence, they take very seriously what I tell them and if I tell them that God definitely doesn't hold whatever it was against them and that God is definitely on their side, that seems to hold real weight. Which is something of a responsibility.

Kit's excerpt provides a caution about the impact religious authority figures continue to have in the UK. It is important to also note that there was evidence in interlocutor narratives of continued experiences of normative violence perpetuated within homonegative religious communities. One of the limitations in this research is that it did not engage with any religious communities who were not queer-affirming and, therefore, reflections on negative experiences within religious communities are only from the standpoint of interlocutors within the asylum process. An area for further enquiry would be to explore responses provided to LGBTQI+ people within non-affirming religious communities, especially given the ever-increasing responses to people seeking asylum by religious communities due to the significant shortages in the formal asylum support system and within the third sector.

Generally, religious communities played a central role in shifting interlocutors theological understanding to one that was more affirming of their queer subjectivites. Interlocutors who were or had been involved in affirming religious communities in the UK, viewed these experiences as significant in how they had resolved or moved away from negative feelings about themselves. Hazelle attributed her involvement with a queer-affirming religious in altering her perspectives on how she understood her relationship with God, explaining:

> When I came here (referring to the religious community), and meeting other LGBT people who believed in God, and there's a church

> for the LGBT community as well! Why would you think that God does not love you? Because he said in his word that he is love, and he loves you despite-, even before you were even born, there's a scripture that says, 'I love you even before you were born'. So, he knew you even before you were born, so the way you come out, whether you are trans, whether you are gay, whether you are lesbian, he knew that you were already going to be like that. So, why would people say no, the way you are is not what you should be, the way you think is not what you should be, or it's an illness, no. So, coming to understand that helped me a lot to, like, reconcile some of the thoughts that I had as a child when I was growing up. So, no need to condemn yourself, because God does not condemn people that way.

Hazelle's beliefs and theological understandings were changed and reaffirmed through her interactions with other members of this community, who practiced an affirming theology, and were also LGBTQI+ and religious. Worshipping with other LGBTQI+ people who held strong religious beliefs gave her the conviction and belief that God still loved her, despite her identity as a bisexual woman.

Emenike said he developed his religious understandings when he joined a new religious community when he was seeking asylum in the UK. He said:

> The benefits are quite rich. One is, really even the opportunity to study more, about, you know, divinity, about God, you know? Casually giving me the opportunity to seek deeply, as well, you know, about our journey here on Earth as human beings. And it really made the opportunity, as well, to look and see that no matter how you are, what you are, that God himself sees all of us as the same.

Emenike's excerpt reflects the greater degree of freedom people had to explore different tenets of religious belief, which interlocutors said was an impossibility in CoO contexts. This freedom and religious flexibility allowed interlocutors to interrogate their own beliefs and have an environment in which they could challenge and question homonegative religious teachings and interpretations of scripture. Yip (2016) argues that when individuals' theological understandings transcend religious authority structures and their official pronouncement, people can begin to develop their own subjective understanding of their religiosity in which they see God on their side and as their Creator.

Another repeated theme which emerged in regarding religious communities was their ability to, once again, take part in communion and other religious rituals and shared worship. For example, Bunkechukwu had stopped receiving communion before he left his CoO because, as a gay man, he felt he was a sinner and unworthy of participating, saying:

> When I realised, look I'm a gay man and that's a sin. In fact, it's the worst sin they've ever said you can commit as a Catholic, because it's a sin of Sodom and Gomorrah. To be honest, I started withdrawing,

Religious practitioners who worked with LGBTQI+ people seeking asylum who had been victims of religiously inspired harm often referenced how banishment from certain religious rituals and worship was used as a form of punishment. Frederick's excerpt demonstrates the awareness religious practitioners can have regarding the experiences That LGBTQI+ people seeking asylum might have faced:

> We offered communion every Sunday, because the first thing that churches which were moving against you tended to do was to ban you from communion. So, if you had been discovered kissing your boyfriend and the Minister found out, the first thing they would do is say, 'You are no longer worthy of communion'. So, we thought it was important that the principal worship service on a Sunday should always include communion, even if it's a very simple communion, because that is the first thing that is used as a punishment in churches that are punishing you.

Many of the religious practitioners who worked with queer people seeking asylum had themselves been targets of religiously inspired harm including being excommunicated from religious communities. The motivations of religious practitioners to provide support to those with queer subjectivities in the asylum process was often framed by their own past homonegative experiences within religious communities.

Being publicly prevented from taking part in religious rituals was cited as a public form of punishment. Religious practitioners who had experienced, or had knowledge of these forms of harm, because of their own sexuality provided practitioners with wide-ranging understanding and empathy for people seeking asylum who had experienced similar forms of persecution.[2] For example, Frederick, a Methodist minister from a queer-affirming Christian community, said:

> I think, in a sense, it goes back to the old Jesuit saying, 'Give me a child until the age of 7 and I will give you the man', in the sense that, if you hear enough hatred about sexual diversity within the highly influential sphere of religious teaching, it's going to take a long time to get over that self-hatred. … I would say that one of the contributions that a faith space can make is to help people make that journey of self-understanding, away from hatred and persecution and towards self-respect, self-esteem, and a healthy relationship with the faith that they choose to follow.

Therefore, they were aware of how significant it would be for a person who had experienced this treatment to be welcomed to once again take part in religious

---

[2] Within the narratives of religious practitioners who also identified as LGBTQI+ all reported experiencing homonegativity and religiously inspired harm in at least one religious community in the UK within a diverse range of religious traditions.

rituals. Interlocutors spoke of how being invited to take part in worship, rites, sacraments and prayer had a significant impact on reducing their negative self-perceptions and feelings of isolation, created by feeling their queer subjectivity was viewed negatively and as something sinful.

Bunkechukwu, when he was dispersed to another part of the UK, found an LGBTQI+ group who supported people in the asylum process. The group was headed by a Methodist minister and on learning of Bunkechukwu's Catholic beliefs, referred him to a pastoral support group for LGBTQI+ Catholics. Through this group, Bunkechukwu was introduced to a queer accepting Catholic priest and Bunkechukwu said on learning the priest was queer-accepting he felt able to reveal his queer subjectivity. Bunkechukwu explained:

> A priest, one of the chaplains at (organisation's name removed), I told him a summary of my story and all that. I had a confession, and after the confession I just felt relief, and the priest told me, 'Look, you are in this country, you're going to be accepted for your sexuality, don't mind about what people say. Just be focused and then come back to your faith. And then be happy with yourself', I was so happy, I said, 'Oh my God, really, so I can come back to my faith?' You know, because I used to think, 'Oh, as a gay man, I'm the worst sinner, there's no hope, just living as a sinner'. He said (the priest), 'No, no, no, no. Everybody is a sinner, okay, just come, and any time you want confession, just come with me, and I will have your confession'.

Evident in the excerpt above is Bunkechukwu's joy at feeling he could return to a religious community.

The priest's reframing of LGBTQI+ people as something that should not be treated any differently from any other sinful behaviour reassured Bunkechukwu that everyone in their own way transgressed. The priest's framing provided Bunkechukwu with the permission he felt he needed to re-engage with his religious community. His conversations with the priest, not only brough Bunkechukwu a sense of joy but a sense of self acceptance, he said:

> In the past, I used to have this self-guilt, 'Oh, why am I gay, I wish I was never born gay' and all that. But now, if you ask me if there is any world to come after this world, I would want to come as a gay man, to be honest, because now I understand. You know, it's just out of ignorance that a lot of people act the way they do and all that. If really, they are informed and understand nature, I don't think they would be saying these things, you know. If they're call homosexuality a sin. There are a worse sin than homosexuality. I mean, for instance, murderer. What could be worse than killing your fellow human being? Yes, so (name of priest removed) really, really, helped me, and now I'm getting stronger and stronger, and I'm very happy.

In Bunkechukwu's own description of his queer subjectivity, he now has a positive view of himself as a gay man. At the time of our conversation, he was a member of a queer accepting Catholic group and was fully engaged with his religious community. Bunkechukwu was attending Catholic conferences where he spoke openly about his sexuality and felt able to challenge negative doctrinal interpretations on sexual and gender diversity.

The narratives above highlight the importance for LGBTQI+ people to, once again, take part in religious rituals, such as communion. Re-engagement within religious communities was regularly mentioned by interlocutors as a source of joy. Practitioners who are religiously literate provide a shorthand of common experience for people seeking support and can understand how intersections of queer subjectivities, religiosity, family and community relationships can be deeply interconnected within individuals' experiences or religiously inspired harm without the need for in-depth discussion.

While queer-affirming religious encounters are still relatively limited in the UK, there are a growing number of responses where people can find support and communities, where it can feel safe to reveal both their religious and queer subject positions, such as the Inclusive Mosque. Dinesh, explained his own battle to find help when he was struggling with his own religious and queer subjectivities, saying:

> At that point, before I joined (organisation name removed), I had reached out to organisations, LGBT organisations, Samaritans, anybody that could help me because I was struggling. However, there wasn't anyone who could understand my situation. When I contacted LGBT Switchboard they said, 'Look, all we can say is that you must be struggling', and although they listened to me, they couldn't grasp the concept that I was culturally still not able to detach myself from my community and my family.

Dinesh's example shows how there is often an incomprehension surrounding the importance of religion for LGBTQI+ religious people within queer support spaces. For people whose religious and queer subject positions are of equal importance, it is hard when their queer or religious subjectivities are viewed negatively within communities they engage with. For example, religious practitioners referenced working with other practitioners who did not hold religious beliefs and who were dismissive of, or could not understand why, LGBTQI+ people would want to retain contact with homonegative religious communities, especially if they had experienced religiously inspired harm.

It was not only communities and religious leaders, but also individual people of faith who responded to interlocutors seeking asylum. In narratives, a common theme was the help and support people received from individuals they had connected with through religious communities. It should be noted that the experiences presented here are from the perspective of the interlocutors and, therefore, it is impossible to know the religious beliefs or attitudes of these individuals, or if religion played any part in their motives to respond. However, for the interlocutors, the religiosity of these individuals was of significant importance to them.

Desire, spoke of a couple, Sandra and Jason, who provided a hosting space for her when she experienced a period of homelessness when her asylum claim had been refused. Desire said, that because her hosts were also Christian she was originally wary of how they would respond to her if they knew she was a lesbian. However, Desire found her host were only ever accepting and welcoming towards her. Desire attributes meeting Sandra and Jason as responsible for changing her previous perceptions of her Christian beliefs as entirely homonegative and unaccepting of LGBTQI+ people. In our conversation, she told me she believed that being hosted by Sandra and Jason was a divine intervention from God to help her return to her faith.

On learning of Desire's Christian faith, the couple invited Desire to attend services with them at their church. Desire explained:

> God wanted me to still have the connection with Him, despite who I am. That's why He made me come to them, and start living with them, because I've already totally given up hope on anything religious, because I'm scared of not having my freedom in the church…. So, Sandra, the way they accommodated me and accepted me, they made clear to me there is nothing in that way, that God loves me for who I am. She always showed me a Bible passage. Sometimes I'm feeling guilty for who I am, that I'm bad, because that's the way my husband makes me look like, that's the way my father, everybody, the society, that I'm bad, that I'm, an abomination, that is the language they used. She (Sandra) makes me feel, God would never inflict us with anything that is called bad. I started going to church with her. And I was even able to join online churches as well.

Desire's experience with Sandra and Jason, helped her to re-evaluate her view that her queer subjectivity was as a barrier to being able to follow and practice her Christian beliefs. The time she spent with Sandra talking and reviewing scripture helped Desire shift her perspective on how she had previously believed she was perceived by God, as an abomination. In the safety of Sandra and Jason's home, Desire said she could talk to Sandra and disclose how she felt, that she would never be accepted by other Christians and God because she was a lesbian. Desire said, Sandra would always reassure her that this was wrong and provided Desire with evidence from the Bible as to why she believed this to be the case she explained:

> With the conversations I have with Sandra, she makes me feel that I should not downsize myself, no matter what people say, I should still be able to follow what I want to follow. Even if I want to serve God, I should serve God for who I am.

Desire's increased self-acceptance created a greater confidence in herself as a lesbian and, in her words, she did not feel the need to 'downsize' herself anymore. Desire said She was able to let go of feelings of guilt and self-condemnation that she had held within herself for a long time because of her sexuality.

Yetunde, was introduced to another lesbian Muslim woman who had offered to be a mentor through an organisation that supported queer Muslims. She explained the importance of this experience during our conversations:

> I have a mentor that usually calls me every time, and she is Muslim, so having someone that is a Muslim do that to me almost every week, every two weeks. It made me feel like 'okay yes, I'm not the only one going through stuff as well'. Because she also told me that, when she came out to her family it was the same thing. Like they actually left her, they didn't contact her. So, I know 'okay, I'm not the only one in the same situation'. Because the fact that she is a Muslim, yes, it is a good feeling.... I actually discuss everything with her, my asylum case and everything. Whenever I'm down and thinking about my parents, I'll just send a text message if she could call me. And then she calls me and tries to get me to feel better.

The interpersonal dynamic between Yetunde and her mentor provided an empathetic source of support for Yetunde. Primarily, the common ground of their queer subjectivities and mutual religion, and how this intersected with other factors, such as family and friends, meant Yetunde felt understood.

Yetunde spoke of how she had struggled with the rejection and loss of contact with her family when they discovered she was a lesbian. Yetunde's mentor grasped and understood the reasoning behind her family's rejection. Yetunde said she did not have to give detailed explanations, such as the source of homonegative attitudes and beliefs within her family, as her mentor had a similar social frame of reference and common experience. This was particularly important as her mentor did not judge her family's rejection, and Yetunde said she felt uncomfortable and was negatively impacted by other people who were from either a different religious or cultural background speaking negatively about her family. Yetunde's mentor provided her with an understanding and empathetic space to resolve and heal from her family's rejection and Yetunde attributed these conversations as pivotal in coming to terms with the loss of contact with her family. There is often a hostility to religion and religious subjectivities from within secular queer communities, and as a result, the needs of those with religious subjectivity are not properly understood or met within secular responses (Held, 2015, 2023).

In conclusion, re-entry into religious communities for interlocutors was not something that was that tangibly manifested (as in physically returning to religious spaces and communities). Narratives showed that what was equally important to people was how re-entry was internally realised. Interlocutors articulated how the vindication that their queer subjectivity was not in conflict with their religious belief system felt like a release of an inner burden. Not having to deny or suppress their queer subjectivity and to be included within a religious community, or to have a relationship with God, was one of the repeated outcomes for interlocutors who engaged with queer-affirming communities. The presence and interaction with a religious leader were central to some interlocutors' reconfiguration of their religious beliefs, and, as a direct consequence, their queer subject positions.

Experiences above demonstrated how religious responses provide specialist understandings of the religious frameworks that people who experience displacement often draw upon to help make sense of their situation (Kirmani and Khan, 2008). This is a unique advantage of religious literate responses, and it is rarely replicated or considered within secular provisions. As people seeking asylum often come from places where religion and religious experience play a significant role in society, it is important that service provision and responses consider incorporating and acknowledging the importance of religious belief and praxis for displaced populations (Fiddian-Qasmiyeh et al., 2021).

Religious Diversification and Conversion

The final significant experiences that were present in interlocutors' narratives, in relation to how people reconfigure religious beliefs, were in terms of religious conversion or religious diversification. Religious conversion, in the context of this chapter, should be taken to mean the complete abandonment of previously held religious beliefs and the adoption of a new religion. Religious diversification is a concept to explain how interlocutors retained some elements of their previous religious traditions and beliefs, but adopted elements from, or worshiped within a religious community different from their own.

While most of the interlocutors I spoke with wanted to seek out religious spaces that were aligned to their own religious beliefs, a minority of interlocutors sought out alternative religious spaces for worship. Sulaiman, wanted to avoid religious spaces belonging to the same religious traditions of his CoO, due to his past experiences with his Muslim community. He feared a repeat of past harms and would experience mistreatment in any Islamic religious space, Yet, Sulaiman still had a desire to attend a religious space as he said worshipping in a religious space made for him to feel closer to God. Due to his discomfort of mosques, but his wish to be in a space that he considered sacrosanct, he decided to attend a Christian church. The Christian church he chose was one that he was introduced to through a friend, who was also a Muslim, but had made the decision to start worshipping in a Christian community. Sulaiman explained his reasoning behind his decision:

> The friends are not in the (country-of-origin removed) community. Some of them go to church but they came from a Muslim background. So, they started going to church, (name removed) church. The (name removed) church, it's very nice, so sometimes I do join them on Zoom, but I've never been to a mosque (in the UK). The Muslims all around the world, they don't like

> gay people, no matter where they are. Even if they're here in the UK or in America where LGBT is legal, to them it's always illegal, Muslims. They don't have that tolerance. Definitely if you're gay, you will not be comfortable. They will say, they are not praying with a gay person but the Christians, they are more or less helping LGBT communal prayer, and it was the absence of this communal worship in his life which led him to seek out an alternative religious space, saying:

Another motivation for Sulaiman to seek out another religious community was the fact that he missed communal prayer. It was the absence of this communal worship in his life which led him to seek out an alternative community, saying: Sulaiman brings to the fore the often-ignored importance of religion for LGBTQI+ people. While it was clear from our conversations that Sulaiman did not personally feel safe seeking out an Islamic community, both of Sulaiman's quotations are homogenising and repeat essentialising assumptions about Muslim people as intolerant towards people with queer subjectivities. This is even though Sulaiman's own positionality as a gay Muslim man challenges the assumption that Islam is a homogenously queerphobic religious belief system and this does not represent the wide range of diversity within Muslim communities around the world (García Rodriguez, 2024).

The primary importance of being in a religious space to worship was present in other narratives. Emenike, who identified as broadly Christian, explained he was content to worship within various denominations, be it Pentecostal, Anglican or Catholic. What remained important to him was to be able to worship God, which for him needed to take place in a religious space as he viewed this as essential to be closer to God. His reasoning shows that while religious spaces still held an importance to him to be able to commune with God, Emenike had rejected the boundaries of different religious traditions and denominations as important. He conceptualised his religious faith as a direct relationship with God.

Sulaiman, even though he regularly attended the Christian church said he had not consider converting from his Islamic faith, and his Islamic beliefs remained of continued importance to him. His engagement with Islam moved to the realm of the private, and he said he only engaged with Islamic teachings online and through solitary prayer.

Abdul, who came from a Muslim community, had a similar experience to Sulaiman. Abdul also attended a Christian church for worship and fellowship, but his engagement with this community led to his wish to convert to the Christianity. He explained his decision to convert was grounded in a belief that he would never be accepted in any Muslim religious community as a gay man, explaining:

> Christian faith, they are more or less welcoming compared to a Muslim community. Even they are making things so complex compared to the Christian people. They make things so complex for people, you know, like always telling negative things about the LGBT, like back home, you know.

While both make homogenising assumptions about the intolerance of *all* Muslims towards those with queer subjectivities and refer to Muslim's in the UK as a whole community, they do reference homonegative experiences within Islamic communities in the UK. However, these homonegative experiences were not unique to Muslim communities and many interlocutors in this research referenced homonegativity they encountered in a variety of religiously inspired settings and religious traditions, which is supported in other scholarship (Moon, 2014; Yip, 2007).

However, Islam is more commonly framed as traditionalist, conservative and especially restrictive in terms of the rights of women and gender and sexually diverse individuals (Puar, 2013; Abu-Lughod, 2015; Bracke, 2012). These essentialising trope ignores the multiple subject positions and representations of religiosity and queerness found within Muslim lives and communities (Shah, 2018, 2020; García Rodriquez, 2023; Peumans, 2018; Yip and Khalid, 2010). While in the UK there are currently more theological resources to support queer Christians, compared to those within Islamic theology Yip (2007), there has been a growth of Islamic responses providing queer-affirming support to those seeking asylum. Such as the Inclusive Mosque and Hidayah LGBTQI+.

All faith traditions are constituted by a diverse range of people from different socio-cultural, geographical and historical backgrounds, with the potential to hold queerphobic views and opinions, and is the same for those who hold no religious beliefs. While conservative religious communities have higher incidences of homophobia, these experiences are not restricted to Muslim and Christian communities (Templeton, 2010–2019). The growth in queer-affirming religious spaces does not mean we should ignore the problems that LGBTQI+ people face in religious communities, such as harmful conversion practices (Ashe and Mackle, 2024). Nonetheless there is a need to recognise the diversity within religious communities and traditions, as in even just one community, and there can be a multitude of perspectives and interpretations of religious doctrine (Schlager and Kundtz, 2007).

Finally, Nofoto, in her narrative, discussed in detail her conversion from Christianity to Islam, which, she said, had been a desire of hers since her teenage years. She had been prevented from converting in her CoO due to her family's religious beliefs, which she described both as a 'Christian and traditional religious background'. Nofoto explained that converting to a different religion was just, not done, in her CoO and to pursue this would have led to her being disowned by her family. Interestingly, when explaining where her desire to convert to Islam came from, Nofoto said it had started when she fell in love with a Muslim girl during her teenage years. While the relationship remained platonic, Nofoto said the time she spent with this girl were some of the happiest moments in her CoO. Therefore, the Islamic faith held deeply personal and positive associations for Nofoto.

When Nofoto claimed asylum in the UK, she shared her room with a roommate who identified as Muslim. Nofoto explained how this was exciting for her as she viewed their shared space as an opportunity to be able to learn as much as she could about Islam. In our conversation, she recalled this experience:

> This girl, she was from Sudan, a serious Muslim girl, she prayed. So, that's where my journey started with her and, for her, she showed me

> how to pray, how you dress up as a Muslim and I saw from her how they pray, five times a day, but for me I was like, 'I can't do this', but I was determined, 'You know what, I need to learn because this is the religion that I want to follow and this is the way I want to be', but she never knew the other part of my sexuality.

During an Eid, Nofoto said, how she had wanted to accompany her roommate to the mosque, but her roommate refused to take Nofoto as she had not formally converted to Islam.

While Nofoto wished to convert to Islam, she said she felt a barrier vis-à-vis her queer subjectivity. Not only did Nofoto experience same sex attraction, but she identified as non-binary and it was her queer subjectivity that she regularly cited in our conversations as to why she did not view herself as 'a complete' or 'proper' Muslim. Nofoto said it was the social expectations that prevented her from formally converting, and explained:

> As a Muslim, there are barriers. Especially when you have a sexuality. So, at this minute, I have never been into mosque because I know that if I go to mosque, I have to be married. It's a must that you have to be married. The moment you are a Muslim woman so they will connect you (to be married). So, I decided not to even create that relationship with the Imam here, because I had the feeling that if I do that, it means that they're going to get to know who I am....The lady that was helping me at (name of accommodation removed), she moved out and she was like, 'When lockdown is over, I'm going to take you to the mosque so that you can be able to do the whole procedure properly' But, for me, I knew that it's not going to happen because of my situation and we still keep communication and she keeps asking, 'We have to go to the mosque because then you know you have to be married' I'm just in a position whereby I'm not going to do it but I'm just going to keep my religion where I am and be in a space where I'm accepted and I'm safe.... the mere fact that as a Muslim woman, we are all obligated to put on a certain dress code and if we don't wear that, then it becomes a problem.

Nofoto assumed that because of her queer subjectivity she was unable to be part of any Muslim community as she did not want to conform to the heteronormative expectations, she thought were an essential part of her becoming a 'proper' Muslim. Nofoto's assumptions draw on conservative interpretations of Islam, and there are a wide range of smaller local religious communities which are affirming towards queer and Muslim subject positions. An example of these communities in the UK would be Imaan and Inclusive Mosque.

As discussed above it is clear there is a wide range of ways people engage with religious communities who seek asylum. While some interlocutors converted to the faith of the religious community, they became involved with, others found were only seeking a religious space without an aspiration or desire to convert. In fact, retaining their own individual religious beliefs was important to some, and it was separate factors, such as fear of hostility, which drove people to seek out alternative religious spaces for communal worship, fellowship and the physicality of a space which they viewed as bringing them closer to God.

Concluding Remarks

In this chapter, I have demonstrated that interlocutor's experiences of religion in the UK can assist in a reconfiguration and building of a different understanding of their religious beliefs, which are removed from homonegative framings. As evidenced above religious communities can play an important role in assisting people in coming to terms with religiously framed harm. I argue this is one of the central areas that is underrepresented currently when considering responses to LGBTQI+ people seeking asylum in the UK.

The importance and the place of religion for LGBTQI+ people seeking asylum is presently overlooked in the responses provided by the third sector. Even large NGOs, whose mandate is faith-based, still provide responses that are more in line with secular organisations due to deep-rooted suspicion of faith organisations in the humanitarian sphere (Fiddian-Qasmiyeh and Pacitto, 2019; Fiddian-Qasmiyeh, 2015; Ager and Ager, 2016). Narratives presented in this chapter showed how the development of an interpersonal relationship with God is used by the interlocutors in this research as a way of providing them with comfort and a way to process religiously inspired harm.

Narratives in this chapter highlight the value in religiously inspired responses for those who have been subjected to normative and physical violence, and rejected by communities whose justifications for both are drawn from religious doctrine, propagated by religious leaders and institutions. Religious communities can help those who have experienced this type of violence by providing a way to re-imagine themselves that depart from conceptualisations of 'abominations', 'demons' and 'sinners'. In terms of the religious spaces themselves, while some chose to reject religious spaces attributed to their religious tradition, they did not abandon their religious practices but choose alternative ways and spaces in which to worship.

The benefits of these religious encounters that led to a reformation of belief were plainly visible in the healing interlocutors experienced and discussed in relation to the violence suffered in their CoOs (Dyck et al, 2019). Interlocutors' engagements with queer-affirming religious communities allowed a space for the consideration of varied ways of contemplating how religion is practiced, performed, experienced and negotiated, outside of, or in association with, institutionalised doctrinal teachings.

While in their CoOs, religious communities had often became associated with negative feelings that led some interlocutors to avoid them altogether. Yet, in the UK, interlocutors reconnected with religious spaces and beliefs, demonstrating the ways that religious beliefs and practice changed over time and space.

Narratives illustrated how, even if a person has experienced rejection from members of religious communities, they can, and do, reconceptualise their religious belief systems to navigate away from past homonegative religious persecution and discrimination.

Chapter 6

Thick Solidarities: Local Faith Community Support for LGBTQI+ People Seeking Safety*

'Religion' has long motivated, inspired and framed responses to the discriminations faced by people forced to flee and seek refuge in countries other than their own (Marfleet, 2007, 2011). Religion, from its historical roots to current times, is intertwined in challenging social injustices faced by migrant populations (Ager and Ager, 2016) and providing sanctuary for those who have been displaced around the globe (Blake, 2021; Boudou et al., 2021). As discussed in the previous AQ1 chapter, in the Global North, religiously inspired groups, communities and individual responses to people seeking asylum are often met with suspicion, due to the dominance of secular ideology within humanitarian spaces (Ager and Ager, 2016, Ferris, 2005).

In terms of providing support responses, generally, 'rightly or wrongly', there is often a lingering perception that faith-based organizations are 'somehow inherently less professional or business-like than equivalent secular organisation' (Lant, 2017, p. 55). Concerns also stem from anxieties that support might be used as part of proselytising missions or provided on conversion conditionalities (Thaut, 2009). These assumptions have created an unease, and there is concern that, for people seeking asylum, especially those who are destitute, their involvement in religious communities cannot be freely chosen because of the significant shortage of support (Wheeler, 2021).

In relation to LGBTQI+ people having to seek sanctuary in other countries, religion and religious experiences are often overlooked when considering responses to displaced LGBTQI+ people (Alessi et al., 2021). The affirmative role religious

* This chapter was developed using material from the thesis: Fletcher, Claire; (2024) Queerly Faithful: The experiences of religion for those seeking asylum in the UK. Doctoral thesis (Ph.D), UCL (University College London).

Queerly Faithful: Queer People's Experience of Religion in Asylum Seeking, 123–146

doi:10.1108/978-1-83797-488-720261008

experience can play in support received is often 'obscured by overarching assumptions that religious values and LGBTQ+ identities and practices are diametrically opposed' (Greatrick, 2022, p. 1919). While secular spaces are assumed as more appropriate to provide support for LGBTQI+ people, as Yip (2015) argues, secularity as a condition of ensuring spaces of freedom is not proven, provides no guarantee of queer inclusivity or acceptance (Taylor and Peter, 2011). Secular spaces can also oppress and restrict LGBTQI+ people (Yip, 2015). For example, devout LGBTQI+ people can encounter hostility in secular queer spaces, particularly those from racialised minority backgrounds (Held, 2023). There is currently insufficient consideration or knowledge on the experiences of LGBTQI+ people seeking asylum and assistance that is religiously inspired.

In the UK, there remains a separation between more formalised third sector provision and the informal support found in local faith communities (Fletcher, 2016). The aim of this chapter is to consider the positive and beneficial experiences found in religious communities for LGBTQI+ people and to explore the various types of solidarities they provide. Evident within my interlocutors' narratives is the complexity surrounding the navigation of religious spaces, with both positive and negative aspects found in responses of support and solidarity. Encounters within religious spaces were sometimes unwelcoming and hostile, yet others found community, welcome, love and friendship, and for some LGBTQI+ people religious communities were vital sites of sanctuary.

As seen in Chapter 2, there is limited support available to LGBTQI+ people seeking asylum. Therefore, religious responses, and the nuances of such, are an important consideration given the current shortage of capacity in support specifically assisting LGBTQI+ people. Limited support spaces attend to both queer and religious subject positions and LGBTQI+ organisations offering general support to the wider UK population often do not have specialist knowledge of supporting people in the asylum process. For people racialised as non-white, they can face exclusionary practices in queer spaces (Brotman and Lee, 2011; Powell, 2023). Danisi et al. (2021, p. 70) found people claiming on SO grounds often have to choose between LGBTQI+ or migrant support groups 'rather than groups that can address the totality of their experience'. As a result, LGBTQI+ people seeking asylum are faced with difficulties due to the lack of spaces which they are deemed to belong.

However, more understanding is needed, as there is evidence that religious responses to people seeking asylum have not developed without controversy. In 2019, it was revealed that 21 Home Office immigration surgeries had been embedded into community centres and places of worship to assist the Home Office to locate people with irregular immigration status. Religious and community organisations received thousands of pounds from the Home Office in return for assisting immigration enforcement teams (Taylor and Busby, 2019).

The Sikh Council, one of the organisations that took part, argued that their involvement was in a 'direct response to the need on the streets where people were sleeping rough' (*ibid*). The charity argued that there was no conflict in their accessing this form of government funding as its goal was to alleviate poverty and homelessness. However, migrant rights and legal charities argued that faith communities who were targeted to take part in the scheme suggested there was a degree of racial profiling. Fizza Qureshi, the Co-Chief Executive officer of the Migrants' Rights Network, criticised this scheme, stating that 'These kinds of practices destroy trust within and between communities'. Arguing the scheme would leave already marginalised people with no place to turn in times of crisis because of the lack of trust schemes of this nature instilled (*ibid*).

This chapter specifically focuses on provision provided in local, grassroots, religiously inspired community responses towards people seeking asylum, which is currently an underexplored area of academic inquiry in the UK context. I use the term Local Faith Communities (LFCs) to describe these communities, rather than faith-based organisations (FBOs). This is because FBOs are used to define a wide variety of organisations, ranging from large, multi-million operations such as the *Catholic Agency for Overseas Development* (*CAFOD*) and Christian Aid to tiny community organisations running out of a mosque or church (Benedetti, 2006; Berger, 2003; Ferris, 2011). FBOs often have headquarters situated in western liberal democracies and commonly resemble their secular counterparts, and while FBOs often start from religious foundations, they have often undertaken a 'form of trajectory from explicit religious beginnings through processes of professionalization and secularization' (Ager and Ager, 2015, p. 5).

LFCs will be used to refer to the religious communities discussed in this chapter, due to their size, geographic localisation and the informality of responses provided. LFCs are defined as communities 'whose members reside in relatively close proximity, such that they can regularly meet together for religious purposes, often in a dedicated physical venue' (Fiddian-Qasmiyeh and Ager, 2013, p. 11). This definition is intentionally flexible but has two key elements which are important in terms of the experiences considered in this chapter, which are 'proximity' and 'meet together for religious purposes'. However, it should be noted, it is impossible to know the levels of religiosity of the individuals within LFCs. As with scholarship on FBOs, a certain degree of religiosity cannot be assumed (Benedetti, 2006; Berger, 2003).

To explore the encounters between interlocutors and LFCs, I borrow from Fiddian-Qasmiyeh et al.'s (2021, p. 1) reference to 'thick social solidarities' from their discussion on LFCs local responses to forced displacement in towns and camps across Lebanon, Jordan and Turkey. Fiddian-Qasmiyeh et al. identify that 'thick social solidarities' are an important element underscoring how LFCs respond to those in displacement contexts. Thick social solidarities 'provide opportunities for rapid, effective local responses' and 'long-term solutions, rooted in long-term relationships, in situations of protracted displacement and hosting' (*ibid*, p. 1). LFC responses are identified as larger in scale, in terms of provision and timescale and with responses transcending purely material considerations, which Fiddian-Qasmiyeh et al. (*ibid*) argue is essential in upholding the dignity of those affected by displacement.

People seeking asylum in the UK often face long delays for their decision, often facing situations of limbo and liminality for years. The concept of 'thick social solidarities' is valuable in analysing how religiously inspired responses are mobilised as an essential part of responding to those in limbo, created by the structures that govern the UK asylum system. This chapter considers how religious responses could perhaps provide a more flexible form of solidarity, which is not as easily impacted by hostile state policy making.

In conjunction with the concept of 'thick social solidarities', I also draw on Fiddian-Qasmiyeh's (2021) notion of 'poetics of undisclosed care', which she conceptualises as discrete actions of care given towards those in need and encompass private acts of solidarity that often go unrecorded and unannounced. Religious encounters of this nature are under researched, due in the main to their informality, as many LFC responses are run by volunteers and operate 'below the radar' (Phillimore et al., 2010). LFC responses often start spontaneously through chance or increased encounters with people in the asylum process. Support provision is rarely publicly advertised and happens within the confines of religious congregations and communities (Fletcher, 2016). Therefore, the intention of this chapter is to shine a light on the various forms of the undisclosed care taking place within religious communities in the UK.

Religious communities play a pivotal role in responding to destitution among people subjected to the asylum system in the UK (Crawley et al., 2011; Rowlands, 2018; Mayblin and James, 2018). As discussed in Chapter 2, destitution is a deliberate policy making tool within the UK asylum system, and as Mayblin et al. (2020, p. 108) argue:

> While policy programmes focused on the reception of asylum seekers are meant, within the framework of human rights law, to protect, some other unspoken logic makes the systematic impoverishment of asylum seekers – living in poor housing, banned from working, dependent on meagre welfare support payments – acceptable.

A growing body of scholarship has considered the intersection of religious encounters and asylum seeking in the UK context (Snyder, 2011a, 2012; Douglas, 2023; Loul et al., 2016; Fiddian-Qasmiyeh and Qasmiyeh, 2010; Rowlands, 2018). However, less considered is the intersection of LGBTQI+ people within the refugee support context. While a burgeoning body of scholarship has challenged the assumptions of the impossibility of religious and queer subject positions (Giametta, 2014; Brennan, 2020; Garcia Rodriguez, 2024; Peumans, 2018; Greatrick, 2022), there is still limited research that provides a sustained focus on support provision to LGBTQI+ people seeking asylum in religious spaces (Dustin and Held, 2021).

In Giametta's (2017) research with LGBTQI+ people in the UK, he describes both the positive and negative ways 'religion' can be experienced by LGBTQI+ people. Interlocutors spoke of religion as a source of hope and solace, despite their religious experiences being intertwined with physical and normative violence individuals had lived through.

In terms of support contexts in the UK, Greatrick (2022, p. 8) has used the concept of 'transformative accommodations' to encourage a consideration of multicultural difference and argue for a recognition of the tensions and negotiations arising within this difference. Importantly, Greatrick identifies that when LGBTQI+ people seek sanctuary and support in churches and mosques, while interlocutors did negotiate their queer subjectivity within these religious contexts, these negotiations did not result in a reduction or persistent conflict with their own religiosity. Therefore, he argues, there needs to be a reconsideration of religious and queer subject positions as constantly in contention and they are better considered 'mutable rather than inherently conflictual' (*ibid*).

For LGBTQI+ people, reliance on informal communities, such as religious communities, can have an added layer of complexity. Often, for LGBTQI+ people, spaces of support can be ambivalent spaces (Held, 2023), and places which are safe and welcoming for other people seeking asylum can be hostile and unsafe for LGBTQI+ people. Powell (2023) argues that for sexually and gender diverse people accessing informal support is not straightforward and can require complex negotiations in terms of accessing different spaces. For example in Dyck et al (2019)'s research, one interlocutor stated:

> Being African and homosexual, nobody else helps me. Nobody else helps me in the community. Everybody is trying to abstain from me as much as possible… Me being an African, and also a homosexual, a gay, I find it difficult. I can't go to people. I am always alone, in a tight corner. (p. 28)

Therefore, obtaining informal support can come with conditions; for example support located in religious communities can mean a person has to hide their queer subjectivity (Dyck et al, 2019). Generally, in the UK, there is a shortage of adequate support for LGBTQI+ people in the asylum system, in terms of formal state, third sector and informal support (Danisi et al., 2021). This shortage forces LGBTQI+ people to seek support in homonegative communities, which can expose them further incidents of discrimination, violence and exploitation (Rainbow, 2025).

Queer Visibility in Religious Spaces of Solidarity

Rafael, at the time of our first conversation had been in the UK for one and a half years, was seeking asylum because of his political activism for the rights of sexually and gender diverse people, which had led to his exile from his CoO. Rafael came from a large Catholic family, and in his CoO the Catholic church had taken a homonegative stance towards LGBTQI+ people. Despite this, he had become involved with a local Catholic community in the UK, after he was introduced to the priest through a refugee rights organisation he was being supported by.

Before his involvement with this community Rafael had stayed away from religious communities, believing them to be no different from the ones he had experienced in Central America, saying, 'the Catholic church, they don't kill people who are gay, you know, but they don't accept'. However, Rafael's encounter with an affirming Catholic community made him realise that the Catholic Church as an institution could be separated from individual Catholic communities, and Catholicism could be experienced in a variety of different ways within independent communities of worship.

Rafael invited me to attend his religious community's LGBTQI+ affirming Mass, before we arrived at the service he told me:

> The homily, when the Father talks about an interpretation about the Bible this is beautiful, because it is his word, because the Father talks in this language, inclusive, respectful, very humble, because he doesn't want to offend anybody. This is beautiful because you're like, 'Oh, it's new. This is comfortable'.

While the familiarity of the homily and religious rituals made Rafael feel connected to a community in an unfamiliar place, it was the affirming nature of the sermon and religious teachings which affected him in the most positive way. The inclusivity of the priest's sermon ensured Rafael felt comfortable within the religious community and reduced the isolation he was confronted with as a person seeking asylum.

Interlocutors also referenced the attempts by religious communities to be inclusive, not only to LGBTQI+ people but also to those who are seeking asylum. Emenike described the approach of an LFC he was a member of, explaining:

> Our church here, we are very inclusive. Very, very, very inclusive. If you come to church here, sometimes we pray in every language. You know what I mean? You're encouraged to pray in your language. To sing in various languages, Kurdish, in some Nigerian languages as well. Even though it's Church of England.

As can be seen in Emenike's example, it was not only important for religious spaces to be affirming to sexual and gender diversity, but welcoming of cultural diversity as well.

While interlocutors more often sought support from within their own religious traditions, others were offered support from members and organisations of a different religious faith. Desire was provided support by a progressive synagogue, who had started a monthly drop-in service for LGBTQI+ people in the asylum system. Desire was referred to the drop-in by another LGBTQI+ organisation who supported people in the asylum process. On originally learning it was a religious space, she said:

> I couldn't believe, honestly. I couldn't believe it, I was shocked. But this is something that if you don't have an experience…I had never been part of the group and you tell me, 'Oh you can go there and tell them you're a lesbian'. I would have said, 'You are putting me in the mouth of a lion. You want me to be beaten, or you want something bad to happen to me'.

Desire had previously faced religiously inspired harm in her CoO and this made her extremely wary of attending religious spaces, and she only willingly attended the drop-in after a support worker she trusted confirmed it was a queer affirming space. Desire said because of her past experiences within religious communities she needed the reassurance of someone she trusted that she would not be at risk of harm within the community because of her sexuality.

Having to vouch for the safety of queer-affirming religious organisations was also referenced to by practitioners who worked with LGBTQI+ people in the asylum process. Kieran, a Support Services Manager, who worked at an LGBTQI+ organisation supporting people in the asylum system, spoke of his own experience of this, saying:

> An organisation got in touch with me called the Inclusive Imams. I spoke with service users about going, they were absolutely petrified, no way, and I said, 'No, it's inclusive, women and men and people with disability and LGBTQI+ people can attend'. No way would they go, even the ones that have a faith, and it means something to them. I had to go, basically, a recovering Catholic, had to go, and if I survived, I could come back and tell them it was fine, which I did, of course, come back and tell them it was lovely. Then some of our service users joined them for Ramadan. But they had an absolute fear about that, even though it was called an inclusive mosque, and they reached out to us, they had a fear.

This example shows how religiously inspired harm can prevent people from wanting to seek support in religious spaces and it was important that interlocutors were able to establish the safety of the space before attending.

Safety assurances for LGBTQI+ people were not only provided through partner organisations. Njema, for example, was dispersed to a small rural town away from her established support networks. A local Anglican community was offering support for people who are being accommodated in the large accommodation site. Njema said she started to attended church services there and that she made the decision to be open with the vicar about the grounds of her asylum claim due to a small Pride flag sticker displayed in one of the church's windows. Njema's example suggest for organisations who are considering providing queer-affirming support in religious spaces, explicit visibility that the space is safe for LGBTQI+ people can make people feel secure in both attending the spaces and revealing they are LGBTQI+.

However, in contrast Desire said she would have been too scared to attend the queer drop-in at the synagogue, if there had been any external evidence on the outside of the synagogue that the drop-in was being held for LGBTQI+ people, saying:

> The only thing that encourages me to come in is there is no evidence of what we're going to do there. There is no evidence of who we are. But then for example, we put a flag up there. And then the next building is a (name of country of origin) building. I would be scared.

This was because Desire was living in a location which was close to her CoO community and she was fearful that she would be seen entering a visibly LGBTQI+ space. These two examples show the complex decision making LGBTQI+ people must make when assessing the safety of accessing support spaces.

Practitioners reported that spaces identified as trustworthy and queer-affirming quickly became popular though word of mouth. This could cause problems as LFC responses could easily became overwhelmed with the numbers of people seeking asylum who needed support. This was particularly a problem in LFCs who relied on ad hoc volunteer staff, who were untrained in providing support for people with complex needs. Religious practitioners who had developed responses to people seeking asylum on SO grounds referenced the speed of which their provision had to evolve, both in terms of resources and capacity. Increased capacity could not always be achieved, meaning people had to be turned away, which is evidence of both insufficient state support and a shortage of responses that attend to both queer and religious subject positions.

Provision of welcoming and inclusive spaces was often cited as a key factor in a reducing feelings of isolation for LGBTQI+ people seeking asylum. People forced to leave their CoO find experiences of isolation and loneliness are exacerbated by language and cultural barriers (Kahn et al., 2017). The familiarity of religious rituals, prayers and services provided interlocutors with a way of bridging language barriers and building new social networks through the connection of shared religious practice (Allen, 2010). Interlocutors' narratives demonstrated that religious responses and acceptance into a religious community – whether the person was open about their queer subjectivity or not – was a significant source of emotional and social support.

Isolation is a common occurrence for people subjected to the asylum process and is often compounded for LGBTQI+ people who have already experienced rejection from CoO or religious communities (Fensham, 2021). Jasur, for example, said:

> I am almost 40 years. I want family, I want somebody living with me together. Almost six years I've lived alone and it's very hard, this life if you're alone, very hard.

Interlocutors who were members of religious communities' spoke of how relationships with other community members reduced feelings of isolation. Commonly interlocutors' made reference to LFCs as a space where they had found a new community or a new family. This was the case for Desire, who explained:

> The synagogue makes us feel like you are in a family, a loved space, where you can be who you want to be and forget about your status for a moment. Forget about that depressed night. Forget about not having money, forget about not really being able to eat good food for a while. It's like a love place.... It's just where love is shared openly, and you can come, and you don't have to hide anything. You can just be who you want to be at that moment. That's the way I feel. I always look forward to it no matter what.

While initially concerned about the drop-in being within a religious space, Desire's reflections on her experiences with group did not consider its religious geography, as a space that was specifically Jewish and religious. Her central reflections focused instead on the fun she had with the group and how safe she felt to be herself, and in the quotation she articulates a clear sense of belonging.

Danesh, spoke of the importance of local community groups, including religious ones for people in the asylum process. He said:

> Having that social community is so important because a lot of the people were so isolated, because you're not allowed to work. If you don't have access to facilities, you can't read English, you can't access a course or do anything, you're left to just wander the streets and if you're alone, and you don't have anybody at all to speak to. This is why it is really important that there's community groups out there that are doing the amazing work that they do with refugees and asylum seekers.

The importance of a sense of belonging and acceptance was reflected within other narratives when conversations turned to their experiences with LFCs. Interlocutors spoke of feelings of care and comfort provided, especially in relation to outings and invitations to special events, which are not in the financial reach of most people in the asylum process. Interlocutors referred to the ability to engage in social activities, such as an outing to the beach or going bowling, allowing them to forget, even momentarily, the difficulties of facing the asylum process.

Religious Solidarity and Support

Interlocutors were aware that many religious groups provided support to people seeking asylum, with churches, mosques and synagogues mentioned specifically in the research. Support provision varied widely within each LFC and included financial, emotional, spiritual healing and material assistance, and a mix of these different forms of support at any one time. Communities often helped people in the asylum system to source equipment such as laptops, bikes and items needed in housing, such as fridges. For people who were destitute LFCs had provided regular financial payments and accommodation. Religious communities would also advocate for people in relation to their asylum claim and help advocate for people to access asylum support. Individual within LFCs attended tribunal hearings (either in terms of emotional support or to give evidence) and groups would contribute or pay for private legal advice and representation.

For example, Sulaiman told me that he had asked several different charities, to help him source a laptop to allow him to attend college, but none of the organisations could assist him. On confiding his problem to someone in his church community, in a matter of days, he was provided a laptop allow him to continue his college education. In religious settings, communities can often provide individualised responses to people in need. In more formalised spaces, there can be more formalised processes in place to ensure people who access services receive equal treatment, often driven by funding and capacity constraints on resources.

Religious communities can also be spaces which can counter the negative impacts of hostile state policy making on people seeking safety (Snyder, 2011b). As LFCs are often informal sources of support, they are more able to resist hostile immigration policies. LFCs are also not bound by the restrictions found in NGOs and the formal charitable sector, who are often obliged to comply with funding restrictions on where funds can be allocated.

People seeking asylum often move between legal and illegal statuses (Luibhéid, 2008b) and lack of access to any forms of support increases the likelihood people will experience secondary harms (Parekh, 2020). During periods where a person has no asylum application under consideration with the Home Office, many avenues of support within the third sector can also be closed due to funding requirements, which only permit funds to be spent on certain 'legal' categories of people, such as 'asylum seekers' (Zetter, 1991). The ability to prove membership to formal legal categories is frequently insisted upon to enable access to support, both in the asylum system and the third sector. This leads to people seeking asylum being subjected to different forms of epistemic and symbolic violence created by systems of labelling and categorisations (Zetter, 2007). Informal responses provided within LFCs are often not bound by these requirements and can be the only survival strategies available to those caught between il/legality (Fletcher, 2016).

This can also be seen within LGBTQI+ organisations, where the LGBTQI+ acronym is used as a category to delimit service provision. Those who are seeking asylum who have diverse sexualities and genders are often forced to fit within narrow gender and sexuality classifications, despite the terms not representing their queer subjectivity (Powell, 2021). This form of categorisation acts in a similar way to the category of 'asylum seeker' when seeking access to services from charities or the third sector. Labelling criteria found in third sector responses are responsible for perpetuating and reproducing credible queer subjectivities, and are also complicit in replicating exclusions and marginalisation created by the asylum process (McGuirk, 2018).

Formal third sector responses are governed by safeguarding and risk assessment processes which can again limit who is eligible for the service. Emergency hosting provisions for people who lose access to statutory asylum support often require a confirmed move-on plan for a person seeking emergency hosting. This can be difficult to provide, especially for people who are ARE and are in the process of gathering further evidence to make a further submission to the Home Office for a fresh asylum claim. Gathering fresh evidence can take many months, and during this time only a minority of people are able to access asylum support.

There is limited service provision for people who have an asylum claim refused and lose access to formal asylum support. LFCs for people in these situations can become lifelines. For example, Jasur was supported and accommodated by a synagogue, after he became homeless due to a breakup of his relationship when his boyfriend returned to his CoO. Jasur's irregular immigration status meant he could not formally secure alternative accommodation. Had the synagogue not provided him with a place to stay, he would have become street homeless.

Incidences of crisis provision were replicated in religious practitioner interviews who recounted their experiences of responding to people in the asylum process. Kit, a pastor in a religious-affirming community, said:

> There's not one of us that hasn't had somebody living with us for at least a while who's seeking asylum, but there's far more people who are without an income and a safe home than there are who have them in our community. I had a guy who stayed at my house for a year because when his landlady, at the place where he was staying, found out he was gay and that was why he'd come to the UK, she didn't throw him out. She made him sleep on a chair in the kitchen. Gave his room to someone else. He told somebody who he'd gone to for prayer support at church and they came over to me, and he said look 'Has anyone got a spare room?' And I'm like 'Well right now yes, I've got some space'.

People seeking asylum are more vulnerable to 'shocks' as irregular status provides barriers to the possibilities of constructing social worlds and support networks (Bloch et al., 2009). People seeking asylum are less likely to have the ability to alleviate crisis points due to a lack of access to material and financial capital, as livelihood strategies people in the asylum process can pursue are bound by the structural constraints imposed upon them by immigration policies, such as the asylum support framework (Crawley et al., 2011).

For example, Emenike's life hit crisis point, because of the unexpected death of his partner, David, from a heart attack. Before his death, Emenike had been totally reliant on David for his housing and financial support, as he had been refused asylum and was attempting to make a further submission to the Home Office for a fresh claim. Due to his irregular immigration status, on David's death, he became homeless with no ability to financially support himself. For many years, Emenike's partner had been a long-standing member of a local church congregation.

At his partner's memorial service, the Reverend discovered Emenike's situation and that he now found himself with nowhere to live. On learning of this, the Reverend offered Emenike a room within the church compound, and Emenike, at the time of our conversation, was still living since there. He said:

> When my friend died, oh my god I was lost. I feel especially the day he died. I just thought that's it. The church kept me going. It was the worst thing. So, without them I don't know where I'd be, I'd probably be dead.

Emenike was given a private room within the grounds of the church itself and he had 24-hour access to the church building, and he told me he how he lived within the Church grounds:

> You come to my room; you wouldn't even know that this room is being occupied by an asylum seeker. It feels like a normal, relaxing

> room. It feels like heaven, and the vicar himself, Reverend, he gave me the privilege, the space I need to do what I'm meant to do. I'm doing my best, so it's been beautiful. The church now, they will never abandon me or leave me on my own. They were treating me as one of theirs, they have embraced me as one of theirs. I'm part of the ministry team.

The church not only provided Emenike with a secure space to live, but he was supported by the congregation in terms of his emotional wellbeing after David's death, saying the members of the congregation provided him with comfort and supported him while he grieved the loss of his partner. Emenike, was clear, that in his interaction with other members of the congregation, he was not made to feel that he was just a beneficiary the church supported, but was an equal member of the community.

After Emenike had been with the church for some time, he said he became more involved with the running of the community. The support he had received inspired him to want to help other LGBTQI+ people in the asylum system. He explained, 'I've been given the encouragement to read and become a leader'. Emenike took the initiative, alongside another LGBTQI+ faith leader, to establish a support group for people seeking asylum, hosted in the church building. The remit of the group was to provide support for other LGBTQI+ people in the asylum process, and Emenike said members who attended the group came from a diverse range of religious traditions and were at various stages in the asylum process.

Activities of the group included a discussion space for members, which Emenike said participants mainly used to speak about, reflect on and seek support regarding their queer subject positions. As members mainly originated from homonegative geographical contexts, where they had not been accepted, they were finally in a space that gave them access to a network of other individuals who understood their experience. In the group, participants knew they could freely and safely discuss their feelings and experiences, which, even in the UK, was often difficult. It has been found that processing trauma through groups, particularly those comprising of other LGBTQI+ people seeking safety, is not only effective in building trust within the group but creates a potential space where friendships can develop (Fensham, 2021).

Emenike's example demonstrates how the provision of thick solidarities can build capacity within systems of support, as those within the asylum process who are well supported have the capacity to support others. Emenike, in his narrative, displayed a firm conviction that his religious community would not abandon him regardless of the length of time it took for him to receive the final outcome of his asylum claim. This conviction shows the trust and strength of the relationships that can be built between LFCs and people seeking asylum. People with experience of the asylum process have the knowledge to build more effective responses to people seeking asylum. However, they need to have adequate emotion, material and financial support in which to build this capacity.

The examples listed above highlight how responses found in LFCs provide versatility to assist people who hit crisis points when seeking asylum. Furthermore, examples of LFCs responses spoken about by interlocutors illustrated how they were not required to fit certain criteria to be supported. LFC responses were extended by contact with LGBTQI+ people in the asylum process. As with Emenike's example this can increase support available to LGBTQI+ people seeking asylum. These examples are illustrations of the 'thick social solidarities' found in religious responses (Fiddian-Qasmiyeh et al, 2021).

Religious Solidarity and Belonging

LFCs often resisted policies created by the hostile environment. Religious experiences can be used to foster inclusion, and religious communities are actively involved in challenging dominant state ideologies that frame people seeking asylum negatively, such as blaming them for society's problems (Wilson and Mavelli, 2016). Involvement with LFCs allowed people to step away from marginalising and oppressive labels, such as 'asylum seekers' or 'refugee' as in LFCs, background and citizenship status are often irrelevant and unremarked upon (Snyder, 2012; Sveen et al., 2022). LFCs provided spaces where interlocutors were able to engage in activities meaningful to them and which improved their wellbeing, such as the ability to engage in informal employment and volunteering.

Most people in the asylum process are prevented from working, and it has been regularly reported that this prohibition on employment and long periods of waiting for asylum decisions have significant negative impacts on individuals' mental wellbeing (LGBT Health and Wellbeing, 2025). Involvement in religious communities can provide people within the asylum process a way of integrating in local communties, where hostile government policies increasingly seek to separate people in the asylum process from the wider UK population. Additionally, low levels of asylum support also prevent people from taking part in social activities within social spaces. LFCs are shown to offer protective and resistant spaces from the UK's state-sponsored hostile environment.

Volunteering and working in LFCs provided people with a space where they felt treated as equals, as one member of the community to another, in contrast to the dehumanising process and policies they were subjected to as people seeking asylum. Within religious communities, interlocutors often referenced feeling viewed as a person and not an 'asylum seeker' or 'refugee' as their individual personhood was seen and valued.

Volunteering opportunities took people away from the everyday monotony of the asylum process. Umaru described that while volunteering at his local church helping to run the food bank, he did not have to identify himself as someone in the asylum process or reveal his queer subjectivity. Having other members of the community treating him the same as any other volunteer, with nobody prying into his immigration status, meant Umaru felt part of a community and that he had space where he was free from the confines of the asylum process.

Emenike was widely embraced by the community and given roles and responsibilities within the set-up of the church, its daily schedule and religious rituals. After living at the church for some time, the reverend nominated him for church membership, and he was given the position of Sacrist. This gave Emenike responsibility for the care and organisation of all sacred objects within the church and he was involved in the preparation of liturgical celebrations. It was clear during our conversations that he felt very privileged to have been awarded this role saying, 'I feel very honoured actually to be a sacristan of a great church like this. You know, I feel very confident'.

Jasur worked as a cook within an LFC; being part of this community provided him with a route to informal employment and a means of supporting himself, even though he was permitted him from seeking formal employment. As a chef, he prepared meals at the synagogue, which were then distributed to a nearby hospital to feed elderly patients. During the Covid pandemic, Jasur said people stopped volunteering to deliver the meals and he then took over the responsibility for delivering the meals as well.

Avenues of informal employment provided people with much needed sources of financial and material capital, as in Jasur's example. Research conducted by Fiddian-Qasmiyeh and Qasmiyeh (2010) shows that employment is not necessarily pursued only for financial support. An interlocutor in their research who was prevented from engaging with formal employment, due to his irregular immigration status, continued to work for free, as it was the act of being employed and not the financial compensation that was linked to feelings of self-worth. It was the employment itself that provided him with assurances that he was seen as an active participant in society, and this created a sense of belonging (Sveen et al., 2022).

While Jasur, Emenike and Umaru framed their experiences positively, there is a need to be alert to the power imbalances present in such encounters, where people are heavily reliant on forms of support found in LFCs. For example, Jasur, through his informal work at the synagogue, was placed in a position of vulnerability, as not only was he working through the Covid pandemic when other staff did not work in order to protect their health, if he had been caught working illegally by immigration enforcement teams, this would have had serious ramifications on his asylum claim. In other interlocutors' narratives, there was evidence of other exploitative employment arrangements, such as care work within private homes and domestic work in exchange for food and accommodation.

Additionally, sources of informal financial support are becoming increasingly restricted and criminalised for people with no legal leave to be in the UK (Yeo, 2022; Yuval-Davis et al., 2018). Current asylum support policies deliberately create destitution amongst people seeking asylum (see Chapter 2). This form of structural oppression exposes people to exploitation and risks of harm.

One final themes, raised in interlocutors' narratives, was how religious communities enable those in the asylum process to create new friendships and build connections outside of the asylum system, this not only helped people to feel part of communities but can assist them in finding employment on grant of refugee leave and provide access to local knowledge. Boudou et al. (2021, p. 100), while not explicitly exploring the experiences of LGBTQI+ people seeking safety, did identify religious communities as spaces where people found a 'sense of optimism and provided possibilities of forging social bonds'.

For example, Umaru had come to the UK to be with his partner, Daniel, who Umaru had met when he was on holiday in his CoO. When Umaru's sexuality was discovered, his situation in his CoO became untenable and Daniel had promised to look after him if he came to the UK. However, on his arrival in the UK, Umaru said Daniel became possessive and controlling, explaining:

> For me, when I was with Daniel, he seized my freedom, he did not allow me to go out, he did not allow me to make friends, it's like he just infringed on my rights. I don't know what he really wanted from me. I just thank God for rescuing me from that man, I don't know his intention, his plan for my life, I just thank God. He always left me at home 'don't go anywhere, I will give you whatever you want, just stay here'. I thought that, because we were in a romantic relationship, he loved me, so it's just like he was trying to protect me, that was my perception. When he's telling me, 'Don't go out', I thought that oh this guy, he's showing love to me. He doesn't want me to get cold. I was just having that perception, not knowing that he had a hidden agenda for me….when he came along with another friend and he wanted to have a threesome, I said, 'oh Daniel, this is not our plan'.

Because Umaru refused Daniel's request to have sex with this other man, the relationship ended. However, since coming to the UK, Umaru had mainly been in Daniel's house and had only been allowed to leave the house with Daniel. On the sudden end to the relationship, Daniel drove Umaru to another part of the UK and abandoned him there. Leaving him street homeless and alone. It was only through the help of a passerby from his CoO that Umaru found out that he could claim asylum, the passerby even showed him where he could find the AIU. Umaru explained how lonely he felt after claiming asylum:

> I was at home, lonely, I had no-one to talk to, so it's like going to church will give me the opportunity to talk to people and also give me the opportunity to make friends and feel I belong… I was seriously depressed. Let me say, from Monday to Sunday I had no friends, I don't know anyone, so it's like, me going to that church, I see it as a big opportunity for me. That is the place where I started having some white friends and they invited me to some programmes, to some Bible studies. So, it's like I feel okay now, I'm trying to integrate myself with the community. Because as I'm going to church now, most of the members of the church, they live within the community, so by then I started knowing more about the community, when I went there, I integrated myself with the people in the church. Some of them gave me their number, some of them gave me their address where they live. So, it's like I started exploring around (location removed). I started knowing places, I started visiting friends from the church, so it's like I explore. I know so many places through the friends I got from the church.

In the above excerpt, Umaru describes how he built friendships in the local area through a local LFC. Often, those in the asylum process are separated from local communities especially if they are accommodated in large-site accommodation which is often located in rural areas. (Danisi et al., 2021). However, while Umaru began to build friendships with people within the religious community, he kept the fact he was a gay man claiming asylum on the grounds of SO hidden. Yet, having to hide this part of himself started to bother Umaru and this highlighted for him how important it was for him to find friendships where he could be open about his sexuality. Umaru started to look for queer-affirming communities which he did eventually find. This example shows how individuals can utilise their faith to build connections and friendships. While there are inherent power dynamics due to their insecure immigration status, interlocutors vocalised that the friendships formed in religious communities overall, had a positive influence in their lives.

Queer Uncertainty in Religious Support Contexts

Despite a wide range of positive examples of interactions with LFCs, not all interlocutors felt they could be open within the LFCs they encountered. For example, Bunkechukwu, through an educational charity, was put in touch with a Catholic community when the charity discovered he was religious. Bunkechukwu decided to keep his sexuality hidden because of his past experiences with religious communities in his CoO made him wary of the reaction he would receive if he was openly gay, saying:

> I didn't even tell them about my sexuality. The reason is because I heard that there's still some priests who still don't support the gay Catholic members, and I don't know which of the priests, except the ones I know, that are gay-friendly, and I know the (organisation's name removed) know them, because they've had, maybe, interaction with them. So that's why I don't even open up to the Catholic community, because I still feel they are just similar to that of (Country of origin removed).

After the organisation made the introduction, the priest visited Bunkechukwu at his asylum hotel to offer pastoral support. When he was dispersed to another part of the UK, the priest even made sure Bunkechukwu was connected with another Catholic community. When he arrived, members of the new church helped him source bedding, clothing, food and a bike. However, while Bunkechukwu said he felt emotionally supported, as members of the congregation would regularly contact him to ensure he was ok, he did not disclose his queer subjectivity to them as he did not feel safe to do so.

Bunkechukwu said his reasoning for hiding his subjectivity was that he was aware that the Catholic church in the UK still had members who had negative views of LGBTQI+ people. Bunkechukwu said how it was impossible to know who was a safe person to disclose his queer subjectivity to. As he was reliant on the community's support, he did not want to take the chance of disclosing his sexuality for fear the support would stop. Interlocutors who were receiving support from co-nationalist religious communities, were more likely to keep their queer subjectivity hidden. This was driven by a fear they would face a repetition of harm they had experienced in their CoO and/or they would no longer receive assistance from the community.

Only two interlocutors expressed a desire to avoid religious spaces altogether. For example, Farid stayed for several months in an asylum hotel when he first claimed asylum. He started to notice a lot of the other residents in the hotel attending a church opposite. Farid assumed that they were people who had converted to Christianity and were claiming asylum as apostates. One night, there was a fire at the hotel and all the residents were evacuated and were unable to return to the hotel that night. This same church opened its doors and provided a place for the hotel residents to sleep. It was because of this incident that Farid discovered that the church provided clothing, hot food and other activities for the people staying in the asylum hotel regardless of their religion. He said:

> The church was really supportive, but I never went there because I was afraid, I mean, I really try not to really judge people, but I've been in that situation before, and I didn't want those things to happen to me again.... Even now, I try to avoid strict religious people because I don't feel safe. It could have posed more danger than doing good for those people to know about me, because people ask about each other's stories.

Farid expressed a continuing suspicion of 'strict religious people' due to his previous experiences in his CoO, and his perception that religious spaces would not be safe for him as a gay man. In his quotation, for Farid, it was not just the space itself, but he assumed that both the people providing the support in the Church and those receiving it would be religious and, therefore, he assumed likely to be unwelcoming towards LGBTQI+ people. His assumption about the religiosity of those seeking support is also seen in his original presumption that the people attending the church were apostates and, therefore, Christian. Support provisions provided in religious spaces do not always provide an accurate indication of the religious tradition or even the religiosity of individuals involved in providing the support responses. For example, interviews with religious practitioners referenced non-religious individuals contributing to responses headed by a religious community, as they were motivated to help for nonreligious reasons.

Farid's quotation does raise another concern, which was also present within other interlocutors' narratives. It was not only the space that prevented LGBTQI+ people from seeking out support. Interlocutors referred to the subsequent questioning of why you are seeking asylum from other people seeking help that can be problematic. This is not unique to religious spaces but is a dynamic raised by those with queer subjectivities regarding any spaces that people from their CoO, or other people in the asylum process may attend and access.

Religious practitioners also referenced this issue of assumed religiosity and a generalised fear of religious people by LGBTQI+ people seeking asylum. Frederick, a Methodist minister, and a gay man, provided a weekly support group for LGBTQI+ which he originally held in a church building. However, Frederick referred to the difficulty that entering a religious space can prove for some LGBTQI+ people. In our conversation, he spoke about providing support in religious spaces:

> If you hold it within the worship space, within a church building rather than a community hall then it adds something to the need to be quite brave to cross the threshold for some people, especially if those people have been hurt by a church in the past and have quietly said to themselves, 'Christianity is not for me, I'm not going to darken another church's door as long as I live'. And that is certainly the case for some people.

This can show how providing responses within religious buildings is potentially marginalising, as hosting responses in a religious space will prevents some people with queer subjectivities from attending. Due to this, Frederick moved his group to a queer secular space. While the group's foundations remained religiously inspired, the fact that the sessions were no longer held in a religious building encouraged more people, both from a non-religious and a different religious background to attend. Frederick's example of moving his support response into a space to ensure it was perceived as secular does not remove the religious motivation behind the encounters. This example demonstrates how it is often too simplistic to imagine how 'religion' and 'secular' can be separated (Knott, 2005).

Even outwardly queer-affirming religious spaces are avoided by people who need support because of past experiences and trauma with religious communities. A minority of interlocutors stated how they would rather avoid any engagement with religious organisations and to avoid the possibility of coming to harm. Farah, a practitioner who worked with people seeking asylum on SO grounds, recounted her experience with people accessing her organisation:

> I've had experience of people accessing faith spaces that they know are safe, so for example, Imaan, the House of Rainbow, and there are other organisations that we're aware of, and people go there, and they know it's safe. But I also encounter a lot of people who aren't willing to, or don't want to try that, just because of what they've experienced in the past, they don't even necessarily want to try and find out if that place would be welcoming, because their experience has always been that it isn't. Or a fear, or a suspicion that there's something else going on as well, that it might not necessarily be as safe as they think it might be, and there'll be other people there who might not be sincere, or safe to be around. So, there are definitely really good experiences, but then there are

> many people that just avoid religious spaces altogether, even if they are practicing their religion.

These examples demonstrate how those who have experienced normative or physical violence from religious communities or organisations have often lost trust in anything inspired by, or linked to religion. Therefore, building trust is an important factor in providing an effective response within a religious space or one founded within an LFC (Fensham, 2021). It is not only the religious environment which can cause a mistrust of support spaces but concerns regarding the other attendees who are sharing the same spaces.

These vignettes of interlocutors' experiences of hiding their queer subjectivity reveal important factors to be taken into consideration when reflecting on or providing responses within religious spaces. First, how precarious this support can be for LGBTQI+ people; however, it is also important to stress that perceived queerphobia that was feared by interlocutors in certain religious spaces was not evidence that the spaces were definitely unsafe. Interlocutors did read strict religiosity in certain people due to their outward appearance, or their location within a visibly religious space, but there was no independent verification as to the degree of a person's religiosity or their views on those with queer subjectivities. Finally, when considering providing a response in a faith space, it is important to consider how visible signs of queer affirmation can make a difference as to whether a person feels they can be open within religious spaces.

While none of the interlocutors in this research referred to pressure to convert or engage with religious practices against their wishes. Dinesh, referred to people in the asylum process being pressured to undergo a religious conversion in exchange for support:

> There are sometimes places, for example churches that offer free meals, but I've been to some of these places, and you get a Bible with it, and I always think, as a Muslim, I wouldn't want to, how do I say this, push my faith on to someone. If somebody wants to be Muslim they come along, you shouldn't need to, how do I say this without sounding offensive? I don't like people pushing religion on someone, anyone, and giving them a meal and saying to them, come to our church recital or our mosque venue, listen to our mosque talk. If you're going to help somebody, you just help them. You shouldn't be asking for something in return. I found out where a lot of these place were just, through just talking to some of the asylum seekers and refugees, People would say to me, I'm going to a church, I feel terrible because I'm not being honest with them because I don't really enjoy the sermons and that I'm a Muslim, but they're offering me food.

This is an example of why people can be suspicious of religiously inspired support, especially in terms of destitution alleviation (Wheeler, 2021). One of the limitations of this research was that it took place within the Covid pandemic; therefore, there was only limited opportunities to attend a physical religious spaces where support responses were being provided, and this would be an interesting area for further research.

Religion as a Source of Strength

Interlocutors articulated how their religious beliefs gave them a sense of strength and hope from which to draw on during the process of seeking asylum. The system is hostile, and those who experienced it articulated feeling exhausted, dehumanised and isolated. Religious beliefs were cited by interlocutors as one thing that was reliable in a time of uncertainty and that provided them with a source of comfort. As Emenike said,

> So, my religious faith, you know, I have really, really gained a lot from it, spiritually, emotionally, even physically as well, you know. So, as I said. Sometimes when I sit back and reminisce about my journey, where I started and where I am now, I just become very emotional and, at the same time, very grateful to God and to people around.

Religious beliefs also brought hope to interlocutors and a way of making sense of their displacement, reassuring themselves that their current insecure situation would be resolved. Common refrains in interlocutors' narratives are like Saafir's quotation below:

> I am just being hopeful to have my application will be granted. Because I try my best and I leave the rest to the almighty God.

Within interlocutors' narratives, they often referred to the fate of their asylum case to be in the hands of God/Allah. They believed that if God/Allah deemed them to be deserving then their asylum claim would be granted. As there are no set timeframes for asylum decisions to be made in the UK interlocutors spoke of feeling like they had no sense of control over their lives and what was happening in their asylum claim. As Rafael said,

> My faith has helped me in all this time. When you make a difficult decision because it is clear that you cannot return to your country of origin for a long time, That you cannot see your family and friends and you start from scratch. But you hope that asylum will be granted, faith is an elemental ingredient in patience. All this time I have not lost faith that I have not lost hope that I must start living again.

Believing in a divine plan, and that their fate was part of God's divine will provided comfort even while in the asylum the process which they had little control over. In Hazelle's reflection, she articulates that she felt the constant presence of God throughout her life's experiences and, again, this was a common theme in relation to the harsh realities of the asylum process, that interlocutors drew comfort from the belief that God/Allah was there with them through times of hardship:

> I always had that belief, like, he will always be by my side, and there's always a scripture that I always, like, he will never leave, if God is for you, nobody can be against you. I think that's one of my favourite scriptures, like, even if I go through the deepest, hardest, toughest time, he will still come through for me, and he has not proven me wrong until now.

In her statement, saying 'nobody could be against her' is Hazelle's way of resisting the negative experiences inherent in claiming asylum. Loneliness and rejection from family and community meant interlocutors often felt alone. In countries of asylum, if they had not built any social connections from which they could seek comfort and solace when facing hardship and adversity, interlocutors often spoke about connecting with God. The way Njema speaks about this is a good example:

> I always believed that in this life it's good to have something which gives you hope. No matter what it is, because there are some people that don't believe in God, and I have no problem with them. I always say, 'You choose what you believe', but for me you have to believe in something. You have to hold onto something that gives you that strength, that hope. The church, for me, is God. It's not only a church, but it's God. When I was in (location removed), that was one of my worst moments in the UK. I needed that place where you can keep on giving me that hope that everything is going to be okay. When I was in church it was, for me, hope. There's someone, I'm not alone. Most of the time I'm so deep into prayer, this is when I'm suffering.

Njema found her belief in God provided her with a sense of hope after she was dispersed to an unfamiliar location in the UK that separated her from her social support networks and friends. In the new location, Njema found solace and hope in a local Church, and while unfamiliar to her as a space, it still provided her with comfort as the Church made her feel closer to God.

In addition to finding support in terms of their current circumstances, interlocutors also drew on their religious beliefs to help them to process and come to terms with trauma in their past. Nofoto refers to how she drew on her religious belief to come to terms with painful past events, saying:

> I had to go through a closure of so many things. Closure of losing my parents, closure of losing my sister, closure of losing her as well. I mean, for her dying, it brought back all the memories

> and closure of losing my partner in (location remove). So, there was quite a lot of series of incidents that I had gone through and closure of having to raise a child without the father that was killed, so, it was just a lot. So, I guess, when I fully got the chance to get into the Muslim religion, for me, it's just not about the religion, it's about giving me that hope, that life. It's like I've been given a second chance to live again and any time when I do the Ramadan and I see all the good things that happens in my life, like, I get a second chance, so, for me, it's just beyond.

Nofoto drew on her religion as a way of processing and providing closure to many difficult experiences. In Nofoto's except, she not only drew on her religion to come to terms with past events, but through her religious beliefs, she felt hopeful for the future. Using religious practice, she could review events in her life and focus on the positive things that happened to her, while moving past and leaving behind the negative experiences.

Religious spaces were also referred to by interlocutors as where they could go to process their thoughts and feelings. Terminology used by interlocutors to articulate this included terms such as 'safe' or a 'sanctuary'. For example, Desire sought out religious spaces in the UK when she was facing a particularly challenging event in her life:

> I just want to feel that, okay I'm in your (God) presence… I feel I need that thing at that moment, which is I want to be in His presence and I count that being in His space, sometimes, it's not a matter of going to that church, it's a matter of having a confined place that you can say is a sanctuary.

Desire referenced having found sanctuary within a variety of religious spaces. In her narrative, she reflected on a particularly dark period in the asylum process when she had become ARE and was homeless and eating food out of bins. At the time of this recollection, Desire was gathering evidence to make a further submission to the Home Office for a fresh asylum claim. As part of this process, her solicitor had asked her to attend an assessment for a new psychological report, and as part of the assessment, Desire had been asked to relive many instances of past trauma. Desire said the experience with the psychologist sent her into a downward spiral where she felt she could not face being with anyone. At the time, Desire was living in a hosting placement, which had been offered to her through a third sector organisation that worked to relieve homelessness in people seeking asylum. However, after the appointment, Desire said she could not face having to pretend to be ok in a house with strangers. Instead, Desire sought sanctuary in the church she had originally attended when she first arrived in the UK. Recalling this time, she said:

> My system was everywhere, my brain was just everywhere, I was unsettled. I don't even know what to do in between. You know, I was

going through all the fresh things and all that has transpired back in (location removed). Suicidal thoughts came up. Lots of things came up. The priest that did baptism for me in (location removed) when I was in the hostel there. So, I just went down there. I can just be in that presence. Just be alone because I know that priest, they were accommodating based on how long you want to be. They just give you whatever. There's toilet, there's bathroom. So, I just wanted to just be in that, kind of, vicinity at that moment. Somewhere that you can go and lie down, sleep for a while. All the peace, like, the celebration, the ceremony of church, of being in God's presence will be going on around you.

By seeking sanctuary in the church, Desire felt she was allowed to just be and was able to experience her feelings without pretending to be ok. As seen in her quotation, the regular ebb and flow of church life provided her with comfort, and the church community allowed her to remain in the space for as long as she needed. People in the asylum process are often forced to occupy spaces with strangers. In the majority of asylum accommodation people are forced to share bedrooms and living spaces. This lack of privacy can be particularly difficult for people when they experience periods of hardship.

Religious beliefs also provided interlocutors with ways of dealing with unexpected negative events while seeking asylum. Rafael, while in the asylum process, discovered he was HIV+ which increased his feelings of isolation and depression. At the time, he had only one friend in the UK, and he said it was his faith that helped to keep him strong on learning of his diagnosis.

Rafael: I feel, I felt very close about my faith.

CF: Why do you think that was?

Rafael: Very close. Because it's like the, I need to hold on to something.

Rafael's said his religious beliefs strengthened him and his relationship with God ensured that he never felt alone in what he was facing. These examples show that in some instances a divine relationship can provide a replacement for friendship and community, especially when a person is isolated from social connections. In times of hardship, interlocutors spoke of how their relationship to God/Allah meant that they did not feel they were facing these circumstances alone. In addition, interlocutors revealed how religious spaces provided safety and sanctuary, and places where they felt able to be themselves.

Concluding Remarks

For LGBTQI+ people in the asylum process, religious communities are an undervalued and under-researched resource. Understanding the complexity of these responses and why interlocutors choose to engage in religious spaces or not can provide valuable insights in terms of designing holistic responses for LGBTQI+ people seeking asylum in the UK. The narratives in this chapter show how LFCs provided solutions to problems of liminality, isolation, loneliness and destitution caused by the asylum process and hostile policies towards people who seek safety.

Interlocutor's experiences challenge stereotypical assumptions that religious spaces are overwhelmingly hostile to LGBTQI+ people. In fact, experiences provide a deeply complex picture of religious experience and how religious belief can provide a source of resilience and solace during the process of seeking asylum. Interlocutor experiences presented in this chapter show how religious spaces can surmount the need to categorise people, with needs met discreetly, without fanfare or lengthy processes of form filling and a justification of need, often required within third sector spaces. Due to the informality and unnoticed responses of small LFC's support, there can be spaces where people can find sources of informal work or undertake daily activities which give meaning and purpose to their lives. A reoccurring theme within interlocutor narratives was notions of feeling equal within LFC spaces, where labels such as 'asylum seeker' were not relevant or needed to be disclosed to access support.

The flexibility of LFCs expressions of solidarity allows for the provision of responses outside of the confines of state policies which aim to restrict access to public funds to those who have unsettled immigration states. LFCs, due to the informality of responses, can provide accommodation, financial support and employment opportunities to individuals which fly under the radar of state policies and sanctions. While having spaces that attend to both subject positions is important, interlocutors' experiences have shown how completely affirming spaces are not always needed, as interlocutor can construct their outward identities to navigate spaces to meet their needs, for example seeking material support in homonegative religious spaces.

Final Remarks

The overriding aim of this book was to present the complex ways religion intersects in the lives of LGBTQI+ people seeking asylum. Narratives presented in the preceding chapters firmly challenge the positioning of religion and queerness as diametrically opposed. Interlocutors' experiences portray the diversity of religious experiences for people, both in CoO contexts and in the UK, and show how religious experiences are intertwined with the self-understanding of queerness, material and emotional support and harm. Interlocutors drew on religious experiences strategically as part of survival strategies and sought safety and support in religious communities.

However, the evidence shows how these experiences create tensions within individuals' SO asylum claims, as reliance on religious communities is instrumentalised against LGBTQI+ people in the RSD processes, these encounters show how social factors create barriers for LGBTQI+ people in terms of accessing a fair RSD process. Yet, one of the principal findings of this research is how religiously inspired responses can provide spaces for LGBTQI+ people who have been subjected to religiously inspired harm to heal from and move past negative self-understandings.

Intersection of Queerness, Asylum Seeking and Religion

One of the core reasons for continued engagement with religious communities is the hostile nature of the asylum process and the design of the asylum support system. Chapter 2 highlighted how states in the Global North are continually motivated to create increasingly hostile policies to prevent people from seeking asylum in their states. As discussed in Chapter 2, the UK's asylum system has been purposely designed to cause destitution and poverty for people seeking asylum. Yet, for LGBTQI+ people, there are distinct barriers which create greater marginalisation and risks of harm created by harmful policy making, such as enforced room-sharing in asylum accommodation. At the time of writing these concluding remarks, the current government is attempting to introduce further changes to the asylum support system.

Queerly Faithful: Queer People's Experience of Religion in Asylum Seeking, 147–152

doi:10.1108/978-1-83797-488-720261009

From June 2026, the provision of asylum support moved from a duty to a power, meaning the Home Office no longer has a legal duty to provide asylum support if legal conditions are met. The Home Office has stated this is to ensure support is provided through a conditional approach. However, the intention behind this form of policy measure is to increasingly restrict people who are in the asylum system accessing any form of state funds.

The Government also intends to bring in provisions which are outlined in the Immigration Act 2016 (IA 2016 c. 19); This act in its entirety aims to drastically reduce support provided to people at the end of the asylum system. Section 4 provision under the IAA1999 will be abolished with a more limited form of s95A support under IA 2016. The two most concerning elements of this proposed provision of s95A support is that it must be applied for within the grace period after a person becomes ARE, which is 21 days and there is no right of appeal for refusals or discontinuations of support.

As seen in Chapter 2, LGBTQI+ people, especially those who are living openly as LGBTQI+, are less able to draw on informal communities for support. These changes, if brought into force, are likely to result in a rise of destitution and homelessness among people seeking asylum in the UK. This change will increase the likelihood that LGBTQI+ individuals are forced into seeking support in homonegative spaces. As seen in Chapters 2 and 3, seeking support in homonegative spaces creates limitations in terms of a person's ability to gather objective evidence for their SO asylum claim. This is because in mainstream asylum spaces interlocutors often had to keep queer subjectivities hidden and this also prevented them from making connections with other LGBTQI+ people, and accessing LGBTQI+ spaces, such as support organisations.

The re-emergence, and expansion of the policy direction of large sites to accommodate people in the asylum system, again, increases LGBTQI+ people's vulnerability. While there is extensive evidence of the risks for LGBTQI+ people within asylum accommodation, interlocutors' narratives demonstrate how the social experiences within these spaces again create barriers for LGBTQI+ people to evidence and present their asylum claim in the format expected by decision makers. As being placed in mainstream accommodation resulted in interlocutors hiding their queer subjectivity, to avoid discrimination, abuse and violence. At the time of these concluding remarks, a further three large sites for the use of accommodating people seeking asylum have been announced (Nevett, 2026). Again, this policy disproportionally impacts not only the safety of LGBTQI+ people. It was also apparent that the very hostile nature of the UK's asylum system delayed individuals from engaging with the formal asylum system. Given the political environment which has increased hostilities towards people since this research, how political and public hostilities impact the engagement with the formal asylum process warrants further exploration. There needs to be a comprehensive impact assessment of these policy developments for LGBTQI+ people and further scrutiny is required as further details of policy changes are put forward by the government.

In terms of continued engagement with religious communities, regardless of interlocutors' motivation, this was consistently shown to cast doubts on the authenticity of SO claimants stated sexuality. Chapter 3 illustrated the varied reasoning behind why interlocutors sought out religious communities and how informal religious communities provide a wide range of support and solidarity for people seeking asylum. Informal religious communities can be both supportive *and* homonegative. Interlocutors' experiences in support contexts were another reason why they chose to hide their sexuality in the UK. This reliance can prevent people from embodying the expected 'rainbow splash' (Akin, 2017), and queer visibility can lead to sudden withdrawal of support. Support located in informal religious communities is another space which places LGBTQI+ individuals in a catch-22 situation if claiming asylum on SO grounds. Maintaining links to CoO and religious communities limited interlocutors' ability to engage with LGBTQI+ communities and organisations and prevented them from starting relationships.

Chapter 4 sets out examples of the variety of ways religious experiences materialised within the SO asylum claim itself. The examples in this chapter, demonstrated how decision makers could not comprehend social factors and experiences which led to LGBTQI+ people maintaining connections with religious communities, especially if these spaces were homonegative. This highlights a need for greater comprehension by decision makers of the realities of LGBTQI+ people who seek asylum in the UK. This also needs to happen in conjunction with greater consideration of how deficiencies in formal asylum support force LGBTQI+ people to seek out help, that exposes them to risk.

Religious Experiences and Understanding of Queer Selves

In terms of enduring religiosity, Chapter 1 revealed how interlocutors all grew up within communities where religion was deeply embedded within the social fabric of their CoO. Religion and religious experience played a central role within their families and the wider community, and religious beliefs, teaching and rituals punctuated daily life. There is a need for greater understanding in asylum decision making of the experiences of LGBTQI+ people who come from contexts where religion is a central part of their social worlds.

Narrative vignettes of CoO experiences illustrated how institutionalised religion in CoO influenced individuals' understandings of their queer subjectivity and LGBTQI+ people more generally. Religious experiences were implicated in constitutions of negative understandings of queer self-hoods. In all instances, religious beliefs, scripture and teachings were drawn on to condemn those with queer subjectivity. A core insight from this research, its that while interlocutors experienced religiously inspired normative violence, religious responses were very effective for recovery from religiously inspired trauma. Therefore, there is a greater need for support spaces in the UK to provide for people who are both LGBTQI+ and maintain religious beliefs.

Prevalent among all interlocutors' narrative was how interlocutors employed a range of strategies to try to remain in CoO contexts despite living in predominantly homonegative social environments. These findings build on the scholarship that shines a light on the diversity of experience within queer lives in the context of religiously conservative countries and countries with high levels of homonegativity (Otu, 2022; Gaudio, 2009). The findings in Chapter 1 challenge stereotypical understanding that there is an impossibility of living queerly within conservative social contexts.

Interlocutors' CoO experiences highlight that there is a need, not only to expand considerations of persecution, but also to disengage from secular framings of queerness that discount the importance of religion for LGBTQI+ people. In CoO contexts, religion was not only a source of harm, but interlocutors drew on religious experience to try to 'cure' queer subjectivities; religious rituals were performed publicly to ensure sexual transgression was forgiven and allowed people to remain within CoO. It is not to argue that these practices are not harmful, but interlocutors did not always perceive them as being done to cause harm, seen in both Nofoto's and Yetunde's examples.

Scholarship has identified how considerations of persecution for sexual orientation asylum claims tend to focus on PSG to establish grounds of persecution for SO claimants. This has been criticised as too narrow and ignores the multifaceted and intersectional reasons why people may need to leave CoO contexts (Dustin and Held, 2018). As seen above, violence is not always motivated by the desire to harm LGBTQI+ people, but as seen in narratives, harm can be inflicted upon people to 'cure' them from queer desire, which can be seen as a sign of sickness or possession. The lens of religion highlights the more expansive causes of LGBTQI+ persecution that are outside of state or state-authorised violence, such as harms situated within families and communities or developed through social exclusion driven by society's social norms (Buxton and Ritholtz, 2026). Findings support the arguments of a need to widen consideration of persecution in SO asylum claims.

LGBTQI+ People and Religious Experiences in the UK

Seeking out support in religious communities was a central strategy for interlocutors in mitigating some of the impacts of enforced destitution and poverty caused by the asylum support system and process. People in the asylum process can wait years for a conclusion on their asylum claim, and therefore, informal sources of support are of great importance. This is during the in-betweenness of claims, where individuals have no access to any form of public funds, as seen in the experiences of Desire and Emenike. Again, due to hostile policy making, religious communities are often the only spaces of support for people who have no legal leave. However, religiosity and not destitution alleviation strategies were also seen to be one of the driving forces behind continued engagement with religion and religious communities. The assumption of religious abandonment ignores how important religious practice and engagement with religious communities remain for some sexually and gender diverse people. This is regardless of whether doctrinal teachings and/or the beliefs of other community members might be homonegative.

While there is evidence that LGBTQI+ people often need to hide their sexuality within informal support spaces, such as religious communities, interlocutors also made deliberate choices to seek the familiarity and comfort of religious communities over the formal asylum process. This was due to a fear of authorities and the consequences of making themselves visible within countries of asylum.

One of the most significant themes to emerge from this research was the importance of religious experience in enabling interlocutors to reconfigure religious beliefs. Interlocutors constructed lived and individualised beliefs, and while their religiosity was often still influenced by their institutional understandings of religion, interlocutors reinterpreted scripture, worship and practice to meet their own needs.

This in turn led them to reconceptualise both their queer subjectivity and religious beliefs that were at once affirming of both religious and queer subject positions. What was demonstrated by the narratives of interlocutors was how important religious communities or a religious authority figures were in helping them reconceptualise their understandings of previously held religious beliefs and interpretation of doctrine that viewed LGBTQI+ people negatively.

Significantly, narratives demonstrated the many diverse and complex ways interlocutors were simultaneously 'queer' and 'religious'. This was achieved through one or more, or a combination of the following: the community provided a different interpretation of theological understandings about queer subjectivities, the community or an individual created a space to discuss previous theological teachings (particularly theologically grounded negative framings of queer subjectivities), engagement with queer-affirming religious communities provided opportunities to re-engage in fellowship and communal worship and, finally, religious conversion or diversification.

Finally, continued state retrenchment of the provision of welfare towards those seeking asylum has led to a variety of third sector, community and individual responses towards people seeking asylum, with those who are religiously inspired often behind responses to assist and respond. Notably, religious communities and individuals not only provided material support, but compared to secular responses, provisions could be conceptualised as 'thick social solidarities' (Fiddian-Qasmiyeh et al., 2021). These ecounters provided interlocutors with not only material and financial security, but offered spiritual, emotional support and a community in which to belong.

Now more than ever, there is a greater need to build capacity in the support offered to LGBTQI+ people seeking asylum. State support for those seeking safety continues to make seeking safety in the UK as adverse as possible. Interlocutors' narratives highlight, the importance of understanding the complexity of religious responses to LGBTQI+ people seeking asylum. By doing so, this creates opportunities for support capacity to grow within religious communities in the UK.

There is a need for more human responses that not only offer practical support, but can provide warmth, welcome and healing from the emotional trauma of displacement. What was demonstrative in the responses provided within religious communities was their deep and long-lasting form of support, which was not reliant on funding conditions and in fact resisted hostile policies created by the state. This is especially the case for those who had received a refusal and have no legal leave to remain in the UK. These types of responses are needed now more than ever given the rapid development and proliferation of hostile legislation towards those seeking sanctuary in the UK and beyond. By bringing greater understanding of how the asylum process and social factors intersect and create increased barriers for LGBTQI+ people in making a successful claim for refugee asylum this research's aim is to build on efforts to create a more inclusive and fair asylum system for LGBTQI+ people seeking safety.

References

Abu-Lughod, L. 2015. *Do Muslim Women Need Saving?* London, England, Sage Publications Sage UK.

African Rainbow Family. 2024. *Key Issues: Access to Justice*. Available at: https://africanrainbowfamily.org/wp-content/uploads/2024/09/Access-to-Justice-for-LGBTIQ-People-Seeking-Asylum-and-Refugees-in-the-United-Kingdom-1.pdf (Accessed: 14/11/2025)

Ager, A. and Ager, J. 2015. *Faith, Secularism, and Humanitarian Engagement*, New York, Palgrave Macmillan.

Ager, A. and Ager, J. 2016. Religion, Forced Migration and Humanitarian Response. In B.J. Saunders, E. Fiddian-Qasmiyeh and S. Snyder (eds). *Intersections of Religion and Migration*. New York: Palgrave. pp 285–310.

Akachar, Soumia (2015). Stuck between Islamophobia and Homophobia: Applying Intersectionality to Understand the Position of Gay Muslim Identities in the Netherlands. *DiGeSt. Journal of Diversity and Gender Studies*, *2*(1–2), 173–187.

Akin, D. 2017. Queer asylum seekers: translating sexuality in Norway, *Journal of Ethnic and Migration Studies*, *43*(3), 458–474.

Alessi, E.J. and Kahn, S. 2017. A framework for clinical practice with sexual and gender minority asylum seekers, *Psychology of Sexual Orientation and Gender Diversity*, *4*(4), 383.

Alessi, E.J., Alexander, L., Lee, Y.G., Shan, L.F., Fletcher, C., Aziz, A., & Zadeh, L. 2025. How do legal aid cuts in England and Wales impact LGBTQ+ people seeking asylum? Perspectives from providers and directly affected people, *Sexuality Research and Social Policy*, *22*(2), 787–802.

Alessi, E.J., Greenfield, B., Kahn, S., Woolner, L. 2021. (Ir)Reconcilable identities: stories of religion and faith for sexual and gender minority refugees who fled from the Middle East, North Africa, and Asia to the European Union, *Psychology of Religion and Spirituality*, *13*(2), 175–183.

Alessi, E.J., Kahn, S., Greenfield, B., Leah Woolner, L., & Manning, D. 2020. A qualitative exploration of the integration experiences of LGBTQ refugees who fled from the Middle East, North Africa, and Central and South Asia to Austria and the Netherlands, *Sexuality Research & Social Policy*, *17*(1), 13–26.

All Party Parliamentary Group on Poverty and the All-Party Parliamentary Group on Migration (2024) *The Effects of UK Immigration, Asylum and Refugee Policy on Poverty: A Joint Inquiry by the APPG on Migration and the APPG on Poverty*. http://appgmigration.org.uk/the-effects-of-uk-immigration-asylum-and-refugee-policy-on-poverty-a-joint-inquiry-by-the-appg-on-migration-and-the-appg-on-poverty. (Accessed: 14//12/2025)

Allen, R. 2010. The bonding and bridging roles of religious institutions for refugees in a non-gateway context, *Ethnic and Racial Studies*, *33*(6), 1049–1068.

Allsopp, J., Sigona, N. and Phillimore, J. 2014. Poverty Among Refugees and Asylum Seekers in the UK: An Evidence and Policy Review, IRiS Working Paper Series (1), University of Birmingham. Available at: https://www.birmingham.ac.uk/documents/collegesocial-sciences/social-policy/iris/2014/working-paper-series/iris-wp-1-2014.pdf (Accessed: 10/11/2024).

Altman, D and Symons, J. 2016. *Queer Wars, The New Global Polarization over Gay Rights*. Cambridge, Malden: Polity Press

Alwakeel, R. and Bychawski, A. 2023. *Braverman Had No Evidence for 'fake gay asylum seekers' Claim*. Available at: https://www.opendemocracy.net/en/suella-braverman-fake-gay-asylum-seekers-home-office-rwanda-refugees/ [Accessed 01 2025].

Ammerman, N.T. 2013. *Sacred Stories, Spiritual Tribes: Finding Religion in Everyday Life*, New York: Oxford University Press.

Ammerman, N.T. 2016. Lived religion as an emerging field: an assessment of its contours and frontiers, *Nordic Journal of Religion and Society*, *29*(2), 83–99.

Asad, T. 1993. *Genealogies of religion: Discipline and reasons of power in Christianity and Islam*. London, Baltimore: Johns Hopkins University Press.

Ashe, F. and Mackle, D. 2024. *A Study of Conversion Practices in Northern Ireland*. Available at: https://www.rainbow-project.org/wp-content/uploads/2024/05/Conversion-Practices-Research-Report.pdf (Accessed: 23/03/2025)

Appeals Project (2026) *Overview of the changes to asylum support in the Immigration Act 2016*. Available at: https://www.asaproject.org/uploads/Overview_of_IA16_changes_to_asylum_support%2C_March_2026_clean.pdf (Accessed: 10/05/2026)

Avgeri, M. 2021. Assessing transgender and gender nonconforming asylum claims: towards a transgender studies framework for particular social group and persecution, *Frontiers in Human Dynamics*, *3*, https://doi.org/10.3389/fhumd.2021.653583.

Bachmann, C.L. 2016. *No Safe Refuge: Experiences of LGBT Asylum Seekers in Detention*. Available at: https://www.rainbowmigration.org.uk/publications/no-safe-refuge/ (Accessed: 2/11/2017)

Badgett, M.L. 2020. *The Economic Case for LGBT Equality: Why Fair and Equal Treatment Benefits Us All*, Boston, Massachusetts: Beacon Press.

Baker, C. 2016. The contagion of the sacred and the right to the city: modalities of belonging, becoming and participating amongst diasporic religious communities and the growth of the post-secular city, in A. Harris and J. Garnett (eds) *Rescripting Religion in the City*. Farnham and Burlington, VT: Ashgate. pp. 89–101.

Balaguera, M. 2023. Trans-asylum: sanctioning vulnerability and gender identity across the frontier, *Ethnic and Racial Studies*, *46*(9), 1791–1811.

Balogun, A. and Williams, R. 2024. *The Experience of Home Office Accommodation by BAME LGBTIQ+ People Seeking Asylum in the UK: A Case for Improvement*. Available at: https://africanrainbowfamily.org/wp-content/uploads/2024/01/ARF-Accommodation-Report-2023.pdf (Accessed: 28/11/2024).

Barnes, D.M. and Meyer, I.H. 2012. Religious affiliation, internalized homophobia, and mental health in lesbians, gay men, and bisexuals, *American Journal of Orthopsychiatry*, *82*(4), 505–515.

Bell, M. and Hansen, C., 2009. *Over not out: The housing and homelessness issues specific to lesbian, gay, bisexual and transgender asylum seekers*. Metropolitan Support Trust, Refugee Support.

Benedetti, C. 2006. Islamic and Christian inspired relief NGOs: between tactical collaboration and strategic diffidence? *Journal of International Development*, *18*(6), 849–859.

Bennett, C. 2014. Lesbians and United Kingdom asylum law: evidence and existence. In E. Arbel, C. Dauvergne and J. Millbank (eds) *Gender in Refugee Law: From the Margins to the Centre*. London: Routledge, pp. 138–156.

Berg, L. and Millbank, J. 2009. Constructing the personal narratives of lesbian, gay and bisexual asylum claimants, *Journal of Refugee Studies*, *22*(2), 195–223.

Berger, J. 2003. Religious nongovernmental organizations: an exploratory analysis, *Voluntas: International Journal of Voluntary and Nonprofit Organizations*, *14*(1), 15–39.

Berlant, L. and Warner, M. 1998. Sex in public, *Critical Inquiry*, *24*(2), 547–566.

Bjarnesen, J. and Turner, S. 2020. *Invisibility in African Displacements: From Structural Marginalization to Strategies of Avoidance*, London: Zed Books.

Blake (2021), Two Models of the Sanctuary City. *Migration and Society: Advances in Research*, 4 pp.19–30

Bloch, A. 2014. Living in fear: rejected asylum seekers living as irregular migrants in England, *Journal of Ethnic and Migration Studies*, *40*(10), 1507–1525.

Bloch, A., Sigona, N. and Zetter, R. 2009. *No Right to Dream: The Social and Economic Lives of Young Undocumented Migrants*. Available at: https://static.a-n.co.uk/wp-content/uploads/2017/08/No-right-to-dream-The-social-and-economic-lives-of-young-undocumented-migrants-in-Britain.pdf (Accessed 02/07/2023).

Bloch, A., Sigona, N. and Zetter, R. 2014. *Sans Papiers: The Social and Economic Lives of Young Undocumented Migrants*, London, Pluto Press.

Boellstorff, T. 2005. Between religion and desire: being Muslim and gay in Indonesia, *American Anthropologist*, *107*(4), 575–585.

Bonthuys, E. and Erlank, N., 2012. *Modes of (in) tolerance: South African Muslims and same-sex relationships*. Culture, Health & Sexuality, *14*(3), 269–282.

Bornstein, K. 1994. *Gender Outlaw*, New York, Vintage Books.

Boudou, B., Leaman, H. and Scholz, M.M. 2021. Sacred welcomes: how religious reasons, structures, and interactions shape refugee advocacy and settlement, *Migration and Society*, *4*(1), 99–109.

Bracke, S. 2012. From 'saving women' to 'saving gays': rescue narratives and their dis/continuities, *European Journal of Women's Studies*, *19*(2), 237–252.

British Red Cross and UNHCR (2022) *At risk: exploitation and the UK asylum system*. Available at: https://assets.redcross.org.uk/82b1e254-5524-0172-0612-9ce813c7824c/5d055b45-ae59-4cd3-a0bc-e4c2108dd51e/at-risk-exploitation-and-the-uk-asylum-system.pdf (Accessed: 02/04/2025)

Brown, G., Browne, K., Elmhirst R., & Simon, H. 2010. Sexualities in/of the Global South, *Geography Compass*, *4*(10), 1567–1579.

Butler, J. 1999. *Gender Trouble: Feminism and the Subversion of Identity*, New York, London, Routledge.

Butler, J. 2004a. *Precarious Life: The Powers of Mourning and Violence*, London, Verso.

Butler, J. 2004b. *Undoing Gender*, New York, London, Routledge.

Butler, J. 2016. *Frames of War: When Is Life Grievable?* Verso Books. London and New York.

Buxton, R. and Ritholtz, S. 2026. *The Way Out: Justice in the Queer Search for Refuge*, University of Oakland, California.

Cammett, M.C. and MacLean, L.M. 2011. Introduction: the political consequences of non-state social welfare in the Global South, *Studies in Comparative International Development*, *46*(1), 1–21.

Cartwright, s (2023) Napier Barracks: the inhumane reality an in-depth report of the experiences of men held in quasi-detention at Napier Barracks. JRS UK. Available at: https://www.jrsuk.net/wp-content/uploads/2023/03/JRS-UK-Report_Napier-Barracks-the-inhumane-reality_March-2023_WEB.pdf (Accessed: 13/03/2024)

Casey, L. (2016) *The Casey Review: A review into opportunity and integration*. London: Department for Communities and Local Government. https://www.gov.uk/government/publications/the-casey-review-a-review-into-opportunity-and-integration (Accessed: 21/05/2020).

Casey, L. 2016. The Casey review: a review into opportunity and integration. In *Government DfCaL*, London, Department for Communities and Local Government.

Chossière, F. 2022. Debunking the liberation narrative: rethinking queer migration and asylum to France. In *Queer and Trans African Mobilities: Migration, Asylum and Diaspora*, eds B. Camminga and J. Marnell, pp. 221–237, London, Bloomsbury.

Clare, M. 2015. *Refugees Don't Drink Wine, But Gay Men Should: Exploring the Intersections of Refugeehood, Sexuality and Nationality among Gay Syrian Refugees in Lebanon*.

Cloke, P., Williams, A. and Thomas, S. 2009. *FBOs and social exclusion in the United Kingdom. Faith-based organisations and social exclusion in European cities*. National Context Reports, pp. 283–342.

Cohen, J. 2001. Errors of recall and credibility: can omissions and discrepancies in successive statements reasonably be said to undermine credibility of testimony? *Medico-Legal Journal*, *69*(1), 25–34.

Committee HAS. 2025a. *The Home Office's Management of Asylum Accommodation*, London.

Committee HAS. 2025b. Oral evidence: asylum accommodation. In Ed. H.O Commons, London.

Connell, R. 2005. *Masculinities, Second edition*. Abingdon, Oxon: Routledge, Taylor & Francis Group. Available at: https://doi.org/10.4324/9781003116479.

Crawley, H., Hemmings, J. and Price, N. 2011. *Coping with Destitution: Survival and Livelihood Strategies of Refused Asylum Seekers Living in the UK*, Centre for Migration Policy Research Swansea.

Danisi, C., Dustin, M., Ferreira, N., et al. (2021). *Queering Asylum in Europe: Legal and Social Experiences of Seeking International Protection on grounds of Sexual Orientation and Gender Identity*, Springer Cham.

Darling, J. 2022. *Systems of Suffering: Dispersal and the Denial of Asylum*. London: Pluto Press.

DasGupta, D. 2019. The politics of transgender asylum and detention, *Human Geography*, *12*(3), 1–16.

Davis, M. 2024. Record number of asylum seekers claiming to be gay allowed to stay under refugee convention, *The Telegraph*. Available at: https://www.telegraph.co.uk/news/2024/11/16/asylum-seekers-claim-gay-rising-lie-cheat-system-boats/ (Accessed: 13/07/2025).

Decena, C. 2008. Tacit subjects, *GLQ*, *14*(2–3), 339–359.

Dhawan, N. 2013. The empire prays back: religion, secularity, and queer critique, *Boundary 2*, *40*(1), 191–222.

Diamond, L.M. 2008. *Sexual Fluidity, Understanding Women's Love and Desire*. Cambridge, Massachusetts: Harvard University Press.

Donnan, H. and Magowan, F. 2012. Sexual transgression, social order and self. In H. Donnan and F. Magowan (eds) *Transgressive Sex: Subversion and Control in Erotic Encounters*. New York: Berghahn Books, pp 1–21.

Douglas, M. 2023. Us and us: reflections of the wellbeing of church-based volunteers working with refugees and asylum-seekers, Edinburgh, Scotland, *Intervention Journal of Mental Health and Psychosocial Support in Conflict Affected Areas*, *21*(1), 76–79.

Dudhia, P. 2023. *See Us, Believe Us, Stand With Us: The Experiences of Lesbian and Bisexual Women Seeking Asylum in the UK*. Available at: https://www.refugee-women.co.uk/wp-content/uploads/2023/03/Women-for-Refugee-Women-See-Us-Believe-Us-Stand-With-Us.pdf (Accessed 7/08/2024).

Duffy Toft, M. 2012. Religion, terrorism, and civil wars. In T.S. Shah, A. Stepan and M. Duffy Toft (eds) *Rethinking Religion and World Affairs*. Oxford: Oxford University Press, pp 127–148.

Duggan, L. 2003. *The Twilight of Equality?: Neoliberalism, Cultural Politics, and the Attack on Democracy*, Boston, Massachusetts: Beacon Press.

Dustin, M. and Ferreira, N. 2021. Improving SOGI asylum adjudication: putting persecution ahead of identity, *Refugee Survey Quarterly*, *40*(3), 315–347.

Dustin, M. and Held, N. 2018. In or out? A queer intersectional approach to 'particular social group' membership and credibility in SOGI asylum claims in Germany and the UK, *GenIUS–Rivista di studi giuridici sull'orientamento sessuale e l'identità di genere*, *2018*(2), 74–87.

Dustin, M., 2018. Many rivers to cross: The recognition of LGBTQI asylum in the UK. *International Journal of Refugee Law*, *30*(1), pp.104–127.

Dustin, M. and Held, N. 2021. They sent me to the mountain': the role space, religion and support groups play for LGBTIQ+ asylum claimants. In Mole R.C.M (ed), *Queer Migration and Asylum in Europe*, London: UCL Press pp 184–215.

Dyck, J, Ferguson,S. Kobutetsi, F and Wasswa, M. 2019. *LGBT African Asylum Seeker Research Project Report*. Available at: https://mccnorthlondon.org.uk/wp-content/uploads/2019/09/LGBT-African-Asylum-Seeker-Research-Project-Report.pdf. (Accessed: 21/08/2026)

Eardley, N. and Davies, M. 2025. *Two military sites earmarked as asylum seeker accommodation*. BBC News, 28 October. Available at: https://www.bbc.co.uk/news/articles/cjr0lx7n0y3o (Accessed: 21/08/2026).

Edelman, L. 2004. *No Future: Queer Theory and the Death Drive*, Durham, London: Duke University Press.

El-Tayeb, F. 2012. 'Gays who cannot properly be gay': queer Muslims in the neoliberal European city, *European Journal of Women's Studies*, *19*(1), 79–95.

Epprecht, M. 2012. Religion and same-sex relationships in Africa. In, Ed. E.K. Bongmba (ed) *The Wiley-Blackwell Companion to African Religions*. Malden: Wiley-Blackwell, pp. 515–528.

Fajardo, K. 2008. Transportation: translating Filipino and Filipino American Tomboy masculinities through global migration and seafaring, *GLQ*, *14*(2–3), 403–424.

Farnell, R. 2009. 'Faiths, government and regeneration: a contested discourse. In Dinham, A., Furbey, R., & Lowndes, R., (eds.) *Faith in the Public Realm: Controversies, policies and practices*. Bristol: Policy Press. pp. 183–202.

Fassin, E. and Salcedo, M. 2015. Becoming gay? Immigration policies and the truth of sexual identity, *Archives of Sexual Behavior*, *44*(5), 1117–1125.

Fensham, C.J. 2021. Considering spiritual care for religiously involved lgbtqi migrants and refugees: a tentative map, *Religions (Basel, Switzerland)*, *12*(12), 1113.

Fenwick (2025) Asylum sites to be expanded as ministers bid to end hotel use. BBC News. 15 June 2025. https://www.bbc.co.uk/news/articles/cvg92lyr7yvo (Accessed 13/07/2025)

Ferreira, N. 2022. Utterly unbelievable: the discourse of 'fake' SOGI asylum claims as a form of epistemic injustice, *International Journal of Refugee Law*, *34*(3–4), 303–326.

Ferreira, N. 2023. Better late than never? SOGI asylum claims and 'Late Disclosure' through a Foucauldian lens, *UCLA Journal of International Law and Foreign Affairs*, *27*(1), 17–56.

Ferris, E. 2005. Faith based and secular humanitarian organisations, *International Review of the Red Cross*, *87*(858), 311–325.

Ferris, E. 2011. Faith and humanitarianism: it's complicated, *Journal of Refugee Studies*, *24*(3), 606–625.

Fiddian-Qasmiyeh, E. (2015) Engendering Understandings of Faith-Based Organisations: Intersections between religion and gender in development and humanitarian interventions, in A. Coles, L. Gray, and J. Momsen (eds.) *Routledge Handbook of Gender and Development*, London: Routledge. pp. 560–570.

Fiddian-Qasmiyeh, E. 2016. The faith-gender-Asylum nexus: an intersectionalist analysis of representations of the 'Refugee Crisis'. In L. Mavelli and E.K. Wilson (eds) *The Refugee Crisis and Religion: Secularism, Security and Hospitality in Question*. London: Rowman & Littlefield International, pp, 207–221.

Fiddian-Qasmiyeh, E. and Ager, A. 2013. *Local Faith Communities and the Promotion of Resilience in Humanitarian Situations: A Scoping Study*, Refugee Studies Centre Working Paper Series No. 90. https://www.rsc.ox.ac.uk/files/files-1/wp90-local-faith-communities-resilience-2013.pdf. (Accessed: 21/08/2026).

Fiddian-Qasmiyeh, E. and Pacitto, J. 2019. Southern-led faith-based responses to refugees: insights for the global north. In Eds B. Schewel and E.K. Wilson (eds) *Religion and European Society: A Primer*. London: Wiley Blackwell, pp. 195–214.

Fiddian-Qasmiyeh, E. and Qasmiyeh, Y.M. 2010. Muslim asylum-seekers and refugees: negotiating identity, politics and religion in the UK, *Journal of Refugee Studies*, *23*(3), 294–314.

Fiddian-Qasmiyeh, E., Rowlands, A. and Greatrick, A. 2021. *"Local Faith Community Responses to Displacement"* Refugee Hosts Project Recommendation for Research and Practice #4. Available at: https://refugeehosts.org/wp-content/uploads/2022/03/rh-brief-04.pdf (Accessed: 21/08/2026).

Fletcher, C. 2016. *How Do Refugees Interact with Faith-based Organizations to Help Them Sustain a Livelihood in the UK?* Unpublished Master's thesis. University College London.

Fletcher, C. 2024. Queerly Faithful: *The experiences of religion for those seeking asylum in the UK.* Unpublished Doctoral thesis (Ph.D), UCL (University College London).

Fletcher, C. 2024. Heteronormative accommodations: strategies of in/visibility for LGBTQI+ people in asylum accommodation, *Journal of Immigration, Asylum and Nationality Law*, *38*(1), 32–49.

Fox, (2024) – ox A (2024) *Asylum seekers 'traumatised' after hotel riot*. Available at: https://www.bbc.co.uk/news/articles/cvgxn0662x2o (accessed 06/03).

Francis, S. and Fenwick, J. 2025. *UK Will End Use of Asylum Hotels by 2029, Reeves Says.* BBC News. 15 June 2025. Available at: https://www.bbc.co.uk/news/articles/c8xgzprn1vjo [Accessed 08 January].

Gardner and Patel (2021). *We Are Here: Routes to Regularisation for the UK's Undocumented Population.* Joint Council for the Welfare of Immigrants. Available at: https://jcwi.org.uk/wp-content/uploads/2024/07/JCWI-We-Are-Here-2021-A4-web-ready-1.pdf (Accessed: 22/05/2023)

García Rodríguez, D. 2023. Critiquing Trends and Identifying Gaps in the Literature on LGBTQ Refugees and Asylum-Seekers, *Refugee Survey Quarterly*, *42*(4): 518–541, https://doi.org/10.1093/rsq/hdad018

García Rodriguez, D. 2024. *Gender, Sexuality and Islam in Contemporary Indonesia: Queer Muslims and Their Allies*, London, New York: Routledge.

García Rodriguez, D. 2025. You are a gay man, and you're also Christian – how is this possible? Homosecularism, religion and LGBTIQ+ asylum in the UK, *Ethnic and Racial Studies*, 1–19. https://doi.org/10.1080/01419870.2025.2484415

García Rodriguez, D. and Giametta, C. 2024. Queer asylum: between hostility and incredibility, *International Migration Journal*, *62*, 232–236.

Gaucher, M. and DeGagne, A. 2014. Guilty until proven prosecuted: the Canadian State's assessment of sexual minority refugee claimants and the invisibility of the non-Western sexual non-citizen, *Social Politics: International Studies in Gender, State & Society*, *23*(3), 459–481.

Gaudio, R.P. 2009. *Allah Made Us Sexual Outlaws in an Islamic African City*, Hoboken: John Wiley & Sons, Ltd.

Giametta, C. and Havkin, S., 2021. Mapping homo/transphobia: The valorization of the lgbt protection category in the refugee-granting system. *ACME: An International Journal for Critical Geographies*, *20*(1), pp.99–119.

Giametta, C. 2014. 'Rescued' subjects: the question of religiosity for non-heteronormative asylum seekers in the UK, *Sexualities*, *17*(5–6), 583–599.

Giametta, C. 2017. *The Sexual Politics of Asylum: Sexual Orientation and Gender Identity in the UK Asylum System*, Abingdon, New York Routledge.

Goss, R.E. 2002. *Queering Christ: Beyond Jesus Acted Up*, Cleveland, Ohio: Pilgrim.

Gower, M. (2023) *Asylum accommodation: hotels, vessels and large-scale sites.* Commons Library Research Briefing CBP 9831. London: House of Commons Library. 7 July.

https://researchbriefings.files.parliament.uk/documents/CBP-9831/CBP-9831.pdf (Accessed: 25/07/2025)

Gozdziak, E.M. and Shandy, D.J. 2002. Special issue: religion and forced migration, *Journal of Refugee Studies*, *15*(2), 129–246.

Greatrick, A. 2022. LGBTQ+ asylum and transformative accommodations between religion, faith and sexuality in the UK, *Ethnic and Racial Studies*, *46*(9), 1919–1939.

Griffiths, M. and Yeo, C., 2021. The UK's hostile environment: Deputising immigration control. *Critical Social Policy*, *41*(4), pp.521–544.

Habib, S. 2012. *Female Homosexuality in the Middle East: Histories and Representations*, New York, London: Routledge.

Habib, S., 2019. *We have always been here*. London: riverrun.

Hall, D.D. 1997. *Lived Religion in America: Toward a History of Practice*, Princeton: Princeton University Press.

Ham, J. and Gerard, A. 2014. Strategic in/visibility: does agency make sex workers invisible? *Criminology & Criminal Justice*, *14*(3), 298–313.

Harvey, L. 2023. LGBTQI+ *People's Experiences of Immigration Detention: A Pilot Study*. https://www.rainbowmigration.org.uk/wp-content/uploads/2023/02/LGBTQI-peoples-experiences-of-immigration-detention-Report.pdf (Accessed: 25/07/2025).

Held, N. 2015. Comfortable and safe spaces? *Gender, sexuality and 'race' in night-time leisure spaces, Emotion, Space and Society*, *14*, 33–42.

Held, N. 2016. What does a 'Genuine Lesbian' look like?: intersections of sexuality and 'Race' in Manchester's gay village and in the UK asylum system. In Y. Taylor, T. Reynolds, F. Stella, et al., (eds) *Sexuality, citizenship and belonging: trans-national and intersectional perspectives*. Routledge, London, pp. 131–148.

Held, N. 2023. "As queer refugees, we are out of category, we do not belong to one, or the other": LGBTIQ+ refugees' experiences in "ambivalent" queer spaces, *Ethnic and Racial Studies*, *46*(9), 1898–1918.

Herek, G. M. (1991). Stigma, prejudice, and violence against lesbians and gay men. In J. C. Gonsiorek & J. D. Weinrich (Eds.), *Homosexuality: Research implications for public policy* (pp. 60–80).

Herek, G.M., 2004. Beyond "homophobia": Thinking about sexual prejudice and stigma in the twenty-first century. *Sexuality research & social policy*, *1*(2), pp.6–24.

Henry, P. J., Nielson, M., & Napier, J. L. (2026). Religious-based homonegativity as a function of the endorsement of traditional gender norms. *Political Psychology*, *47*, pp. 1–26.

API Home Office (2016) *Sexual orientation in asylum claims*. Asylum Policy Instruction, Version 6.0. London: Home Office. Available at https://assets.publishing.service.gov.uk/media/5a804b17ed915d74e622d9dc/Sexual-orientation-in-asylum-claims-v6.pdf

Home Office. 2016. *Asylum Policy Instruction: Sexual Orientation in Asylum Claims*, London, Asset Publishing Service UK Government. Available at: https://www.gov.uk/government/publications/sexual-identity-issues-in-the-asylum-claim (Accessed: 21/08/2026).

House of Commons Committee of Public Accounts (2024) *Asylum Accommodation and UK-Rwanda partnership*. Thirty-Fourth Report of Session 2023–24. HC 639. London: House of Commons. Available at: https://committees.parliament.uk/publications/45116/documents/223695/default/

Home Office 2024. *Asylum claims on the basis of sexual orientation 2023*. Immigration system statistics, year ending June 2024. Available at: https://www.gov.uk/government/statistics/immigration-system-statistics-year-ending-june-2024/asylum-claims-on-the-basis-of-sexual-orientation-2023 (Accessed 03/02/2026).

Home Affairs Committee (2025) *The Home Office's management of asylum accommodation*. Fourth Report of Session 2024–26. HC 580. London: House of Commons. Available at: https://committees.parliament.uk/publications/49900/documents/297953/default/ (accessed 30/11/2025)

Home Office, 2025. *Restoring Order and Control: A statement on the government's asylum and returns policy*. Available at: https://www.gov.uk/government/publications/asylum-and-returns-policy-statement/restoring-order-and-control-a-statement-on-the-governments-asylum-and-returns-policy (Accessed 03/05/2026)

Home Affairs Committee (2025) *The Home Office's management of asylum accommodation*. Fourth Report of Session 2024–26. HC 580. London: House of Commons. Available at: https://committees.parliament.uk/publications/49900/documents/297953/default/ (accessed 30/11/2025)

Home Office 2025a. *Summary of latest statistics. Immigration system statistics, year ending March 2026*. https://www.gov.uk/government/statistics/immigration-system-statistics-year-ending-march-2025/summary-of-latest-statistics (Accessed: 01/12/2025).

Home Office, 2025b. *Restoring Order and Control: A statement on the government's asylum and returns policy*. Available at: https://www.gov.uk/government/publications/asylum-and-returns-policy-statement/restoring-order-and-control-a-statement-on-the-governments-asylum-and-returns-policy (Accessed 03/05/2026).

Home Office (2026a) *Immigration system statistics, year ending December 2025*. Available at: https://www.gov.uk/government/statistics/immigration-system-statistics-year-ending-december-2025 (accessed 12/3/2026)

Home Office (2026b) *Allocation of asylum accommodation policy* (v.16). Available at: https://www.gov.uk/government/publications/asylum-accommodation-requests-policy/allocation-of-asylum-accommodation-policy-accessible (Accessed: 09/09/2026)

Human Rights Watch 2023. "I Felt So Stuck" Inadequate Housing and Social Support for Families Seeking Asylum in the United Kingdom. Available at: https://www.hrw.org/report/2023/09/14/i-felt-so-stuck/inadequate-housing-and-social-support-families-seeking-asylum.

Human Dignity Trust (2026) *Map of Jurisdictions that Criminalise LGBT People*. Available at: https://www.humandignitytrust.org/lgbt-the-law/map-of-criminalisation/?type_filter=crim_sex_men (Accessed on: 24/06/2026)

Hutton, C. and Lukes, S. 2024. *Access to Advice on Asylum Support and Asylum Support Appeals*. Available at: https://www.asaproject.org/uploads/ASA0003_Access_to_Advice.pdf

Hynes, P. 2011. *The dispersal and social exclusion of asylum seekers: between liminality and belonging*, Bristol: Policy Press.

Independent Chief Inspector of Borders and Immigration (ICIBI) (2022) *An inspection of the initial processing of migrants arriving via small boats at Tug Haven and Western Jet Foil, December 2021 – January 2022*. London: Independent Chief Inspector of Borders and Immigration. Available at: https://www.gov.uk/government/publications/an-inspection-of-the-initial-processing-of-migrants-arriving-via-small-boats-at-tug-haven-and-western-jet-foil-december-2021-january-2022 (Accessed: 23/01/024)

Independent Chief Inspector of Borders and Immigration (ICIBI) (2024) *An inspection of asylum casework, June – October 2023*. London: Independent Chief Inspector of Borders and Immigration. Available at: https://assets.publishing.service.gov.uk/media/65e06d45f1cab36b60fc47ad/An_inspection_of_asylum_casework_June_to_October_2023.pdf (Accessed: 06/09/2025)

Immigration Act 2016 (c. 19). Available at: https://www.legislation.gov.uk/ukpga/2016/19/contents

Immigration and Asylum Act 1999. (1999) c. 33. London: The Stationery Office. Available at: https://www.legislation.gov.uk/ukpga/1999/33/contents (Accessed: 23/01/2024)

Jansen, S. 2013. Introduction: fleeing homophobia, asylum claims related to sexual orientation and gender identity in Europe. In ed. Spijkerboer, T., *Fleeing Homophobia: Sexual Orientation, Gender Identity and Asylum*, London: Routledge, pp 1–31.

Janssen, D.-J. and Scheepers, P. 2019. How religiosity shapes rejection of homosexuality across the globe, *Journal of Homosexuality*, *66*(14), 1974–2001.

Jeldtoft, N. 2011. Lived Islam: religious identity with 'non-organized' Muslim minorities, *Ethnic and Racial Studies*, *34*(7), 1134–1151.

Joint Committee on Human Rights (2007) *The Treatment of Asylum Seekers*. Tenth Report of Session 2006–07. Volume I. HL Paper 81-I, HC 60-I. London: The Stationery Office. Available at: https://publications.parliament.uk/pa/jt200607/jtselect/jtrights/81/81i.pdf (Accessed: 25/06/2026).

Jordan, S. and Morrissey, C. 2013. "On what grounds?" *LGBT asylum claims in Canada, Forced Migration Review, 42*, 13–15.

Jorgensen, N. 2025. *Asylum Accommodation in the UK*. https://migrationobservatory.ox.ac.uk/resources/briefings/asylum-accommodation-in-the-uk/ (Accessed: 03/02/2026)

Kahn, S., Alessi, E., Woolner, L., Kim, Hanna, K., & Christina, O., 2017. Promoting the wellbeing of lesbian, gay, bisexual and transgender forced migrants in Canada: providers' perspectives, *Culture Health & Sexuality*, *19*(10), 1165–1179.

Kaleidoscope Trust (2025) *Legal Battlegrounds: An Overview of Anti-LGBTQI+ Legislation*. Available at: https://kaleidoscopetrust.com/new-report-warns-of-accelerating-rollbacks-in-lgbti-rights/ (Accessed 21/08/2026)

Khan, A. 2020. Queer secularity, *Lambda Nordica*, *25*(1), 133–139.

Kilpatrick, S.D., Weaver, A.J., Mccullough, M.E., Puchalski, C., Larson, D.B., Hays, J.C., Farran, C.J. and Flannelly, K.J., 2005. A Review of Spiritual and Religious Measures in Nursing Research Journals: 1995–1999. *Journal of religion and health*, *44*(1), pp.55–66.

Kirkup, J. and Winnett, R. 2012. *Theresa May interview: 'We're going to give illegal migrants a really hostile reception'*, The Telegraph, 25 May. Available at: https://www.telegraph.co.uk/news/uknews/immigration/9291483/Theresa-May-interview-Were-going-to-give-illegal-migrants-a-really-hostile-reception.html (Accessed: 25/05/2024).

Kirk-Wade, E. (2026) *Asylum statistics*. Commons Library Research Briefing SN01403. London: House of Commons Library. Available at: https://researchbriefings.files.parliament.uk/documents/SN01403/SN01403.pdf (Accessed: 01/04/2026).

Kirmani, N. and Khan, A.A., 2008. Does faith matter: An examination of Islamic Relief's work with refugees and internally displaced persons. *Refugee Survey Quarterly*, *27*(2), pp.41–50.

Knibbe, K. and Spronk, R. 2022. Theorizing sexuality, religion, and secularity in postcolonial Europe, *New Diversities*, *24*(2), 2–12.

Knott, K., 2005. At home in the secular. *Journal of Comparative Religion*, *41*(2), pp.143–184.

Lant, B. 2017. Praxis community projects: a secular organization? Exploring the boundaries between religious and secular in migration support. In L. Mavelli and E.K. Wilson (eds) *The Refugee Crisis and Religion*. London New York: Rowman & Littlefield, pp 53–60.

Law Center NI, Migration Justice Project, and Rainbow Refugees NI (2024) "*We are getting hurt": Safe accommodation for LGBTQIA+ people seeking sanctuary in Northern Ireland*. Available at: https://www.lawcentreni.org/wp-content/uploads/2024/06/We-Are-Getting-Hurt-June-2024.pdf (Accessed -13/06/2025)

Lee, E.O.J., Reynolds, J. and Clark-Kazak, C. 2018. Tracing the coloniality of queer and trans migrations: resituating heterocisnormative violence in the global south and encounters with migrant visa ineligibility to Canada, *Refuge*, *34*(1), 60–74.

Lee, E.O.J. and Brotman, S., 2011. Identity, refugeeness, belonging: Experiences of sexual minority refugees in Canada. *Canadian Review of Sociology/Revue canadienne de sociologie*, *48*(3), pp.241–274.

Lenegan, S. 2024. *The Inadmissibility Process and the Three New Asylum Backlogs*. Available at: https://freemovement.org.uk/the-inadmissibility-process-and-the-three-new-asylum-backlogs/ [Accessed 2024].

Lewis, R. 2013. Deportable subjects: lesbians and political asylum, *Feminist Formations*, *25*(2), 174–194.

Lewis, R. 2023. Queering deportability: the racial and gendered politics of lesbian anti-deportation activism, *Sexualities*, *26*(7), 748–764.

LGBT Health and Wellbeing (2023) *Experiences of LGBTQ+ asylum seekers and refugees in Scotland: Housing, houselessness, hotel detention and impact*. Available at: https://www.lgbthealth.org.uk/wp-content/uploads/2023/07/Refugee-Report-Final-E-Copy.pdf (Accessed: 01/02/2024)

LGBT Health and Wellbeing (2025) *Written evidence submitted by LGBT Health and Wellbeing (AAC0094)* Available at: https://committees.parliament.uk/writtenevidence/136567/pdf/ (Accessed: 25/06/2026)

Lopes Heimer, R.d.V. (2019) "Homonationalist/Orientalist Negotiations: The UK Approach to Queer Asylum Claims," *Sexuality & Culture: An Interdisciplinary Quarterly*, *24*(1), pp. 174–196. Available at: https://doi.org/10.1007/s12119-019-09633-3.

Loul, B., Willot, J., & Robinson, S. (2014). Refugees' Encounters with christianity in everyday life. In Vincett, G., & Obinna, E., (eds.), *Christianity in the modern world: Changes and controversies*. Farnham/Burlington: Ashgate.

Luibhéid, E. 2008a. Queer/migration: an unruly body of scholarship, *GLQ*, *14*(2–3), 169–190.

Luibhéid, E. 2008b. Sexuality, migration, and the shifting line between legal and illegal status, *GLQ*, *14*(2–3), 289–315.

Luibhéid, E. 2014. Sexuality and international migration. In Buffington, R.M., Luibhéid, E., & Guy, D.J., (eds). *A Global History of Sexuality: The Modern Era*, West Sussex: Wiley Blackwell, pp. 119–150.

Lunn, J. 2009. The role of religion, spirituality and faith in development: a critical theory approach, *Third World Quarterly*, *30*(5), 937–951.

Macey, M. and Carling, A. 2011. *Ethnic, Racial and Religious Inequalities: The Perils of Subjectivity*, Basingstoke, New York: Palgrave Macmillan.

Mallett, R. and Hagen-Zanker, J. 2018. Forced migration trajectories: an analysis of journey-and decision-making among Eritrean and Syrian arrivals to Europe, *Migration and Development*, *7*(3), 341–351.

Manalansan, M.F. 2006. Queer intersections: sexuality and gender in migration studies, *International Migration Review*, *40*(1), 224–249.

Marfleet, P., 2007. Refugees and history: why we must address the past. *Refugee survey quarterly*, *26*(3), pp. 136–148.

Marfleet, P. 2011. Understanding 'Sanctuary': faith and traditions of asylum, *Journal of Refugee Studies*, *24*(3), 440–455.

Mayblin, L. 2017. *Asylum After Empire: Colonial Legacies in the Politics of Asylum Seeking*, London: Rowman & Littlefield International.

Mayblin, L. and James, P. 2018. Asylum and refugee support in the UK: civil society filling the gaps? *Journal of Ethnic and Migration Studies*, 1–20. https://doi.org/10.1080/1369183X.2018.1466695

Mayblin, L., Wake, M. and Kazemi, M. 2020. Necropolitics and the slow violence of the everyday: asylum seeker welfare in the postcolonial present, *Sociology*, *54*(1), 107–123.

Mayfield, W., 2001. The development of an internalized homonegativity inventory for gay men. *Journal of homosexuality*, *41*(2), pp.53–76.

McClure, P.K. 2017. Tinkering with technology and religion in the digital age: the effects of Internet use on religious belief, behavior, and belonging, *Journal for the Scientific Study of Religion*, *56*(3), 481–497.

McGuire, M.B. 2008. *Lived Religion: Faith and Practice in Everyday Life*, Oxford: Oxford University Press.

McGuirk, S. 2018. (In)credible subjects: NGOs, attorneys, and permissible LGBT asylum seeker identities, *Polar-Political and Legal Anthropology Review*, *41*, 4–18.

McGuirk, S. and Niedzwiecki, M. 2017. Loving God versus wrathful god: religion and LGBT forced migration. L. Mavelli and E.K. Wilson (eds). *The Refugee Crisis and Religion: Secularism, Security and Hospitality in Question*. London, New York: Rowman & Littlefield, pp. 1–22.

McKinney, C. J., Kennedy, S., Gower, M., and Sturge, G., & Tyler-Todd, J., (2025) *No recourse to public funds*. Commons Library Research Briefing CBP-9790. London: House of Commons Library. Available at: https://researchbriefings.files.parliament.uk/documents/CBP-9790/CBP-9790.pdf (Accessed:03/12/2025).

McKnight, P., Phillimore, J., River, D., et al. 2024. *Forced Migration and Sexual and Gender-based Violence in Queer Communities: UK Findings from the SEREDA Project*. Available at: https://www.birmingham.ac.uk/documents/college-social-sciences/social-policy/publications/queer-sereda-web.pdf (Accessed: 06/12/2025).

Middelkoop, L. 2013. Normativity and credibility of sexual orientation in asylum decision making. In T. Spijkerboer (ed) *Fleeing Homophobia*. Oxford: Routledge, pp. 154–175.

Millbank, J. 2002. Imagining otherness: refugee claims on the basis of sexuality in Canada and Australia, *Melbourne University Law Review*, *26*, 144.

Millbank, J. 2009. 'The ring of truth': a case study of credibility assessment in particular social group refugee determinations, *International Journal of Refugee Law*, *21*(1), 1–33.

Millbank, J., 2013. *Refugee status determination over the past 20 years*. In T, Spijkerboer (ed) *Fleeing Homophobia: Sexual Orientation, Gender Identity and Asylum*. London: Routledge, p.32–54

Mohammed, A., Nagarajan, C. and Aliyu, R. 2018. *She Called Me Woman: Nigeria's Queer Women Speak*, Abuja: Cassava Republic Press.

Mole, R (2021) Rethinking diaspora: Queer Poles, Brazilians and Russians in Berlin in R. Mole (ed.) *Queer Migration and Asylum in Europe*. UCL Press, pp. 57–77.

Moon, D. 2014. Beyond the dichotomy: six religious views of homosexuality, *Journal of Homosexuality*, *61*(9), 1215–1241.

Murray, D. 2011. Becoming queer here: integration and adaptation experiences of sexual minority refugees in Toronto, *Refuge*, *28*, 127.

Murray, D. 2014. Real queer: 'Authentic' LGBT refugee claimants and homonationalism in the Canadian refugee system, *Anthropologica*, *56*(1), 21–32.

Murray, D.A.B. 2016. Queer forms: producing documentation in sexual orientation refugee cases, *Anthropological Quarterly*, *89*(2), 465–484.

Muthien, B. 2007. Queerying borders: an Afrikan activist perspective, *Journal of Lesbian Studies*, *11*(3–4), 321–330.

National Audit Office (NAO) (2025b) *The Home Office's asylum accommodation contracts*. London: National Audit Office. Available at: https://www.nao.org.uk/wp-content/uploads/2025/05/home-offices-asylum-accommodation-contracts.pdf (Accessed: 12/06/2025)

National Audit Office (2025a) *An analysis of the asylum system: Home Office and cross-government*. HC 1517. London: House of Commons. Available at: https://www.nao.org.uk/wp-content/uploads/2025/12/an-analysis-of-the-asylum-system.pdf

NACCOM. 2023. *Refused? Experiences Following a Negative Asylum Decision*. Available at: https://naccom.org.uk/wp-content/uploads/2023/07/EMBARGOED-17.7.23-NACCOM-Refused-Experiences-following-a-negative-asylum-decision-FINAL.pdf (Accessed: 02/12/2025)

Nawyn, S.J. 2006. Faith, ethnicity, and culture in refugee resettlement, *American Behavioral Scientist*, *49*(11), 1509–1527.

Neitz, M. J., 2011 Lived Religion: Signposts of Where We Have Been and Where We Can Go from Here. In G. Giordan and W. H. Swatos Jr (eds) *Religion, Spirituality and Everyday Practice*. Dordrecht: Springer, pp.45–55.

Nynäs, P.E. and Yip, A.K.T.E. 2016. Re-framining the intersection between religion, gender and sexuality in everyday life. In P. Nynäs and A. Kam-Tuck Yip (eds) *Religion, Gender and Sexuality in Everyday Life*, London and New York: Routledge, pp. 1–16.

Otu, K.E. 2022. *Amphibious Subjects: Sasso and the Contested Politics of Queer Self-making in Neoliberal Ghana*, California: University of California Press.

Page, S.-J. and Yip, A.K.-T. 2020. Intersecting religion and sexuality: contributing to an unfinished conversation. In S-J, Page and A. K.T Yip (eds) *Intersecting Religion and Sexuality*. Leiden & Boston: Brill, pp. 1–22.

Parekh, S. 2020. Reframing the refugee crisis: from rescue to interconnection, *Ethics & Global Politics*, *13*(1), 21–32.

Peumans, W. 2014. Queer Muslim migrants in Belgium: a research note on same-sex sexualities and lived religion, *Sexualities*, *17*(5–6), 618–631.

Peumans, W. 2018. *Queer Muslims in Europe: Sexuality, Religion and Migration in Belgium*, London, New York: Bloomsbury Publishing.

Phillimore, Jenny and McCabe, Angus and Soteri-Proctor, Andri and Taylor, Rebecca (2010) *Understanding the distinctiveness of small scale, third sector activity: the role of local knowledge and networks in shaping below the radar actions*. Working Paper (33) University of Birmingham, Birmingham, UK.

Powell, A. 2020. Normative understandings: sexual identity, stereotypes, and asylum seeking. In C. Ashford and A. Maine (eds) *Research Handbook on Gender, Sexuality and the Law*. Cheltenham, UK, Northampton, MA: Edward Elgar Publishing, pp. 149–163.

Powell, A. (2024) The place where only gays go: constructions of queer space in the narratives of sexually diverse refugees. *Journal of Place Management and Development*, *17*(2), pp.171–185.

Powell, A. 2021. "Sexuality" through the kaleidoscope: sexual orientation, identity, and behaviour in asylum claims in the United Kingdom, *Laws*, *10*(4), 90.

Powell, A. 2023. The place where only gays go: constructions of queer space in the narratives of sexually diverse refugees, *Journal of Place Management and Development*. https://doi.org/10.1108/JPMD-11-2022-0108

Powell, A. and Rifath, R. 2023. Sexual diversity and the Nationality and Borders Act 2022, *Legal Studies*, *43*(4), 757–761.

Puar, J. 2013. Rethinking homonationalism, *International Journal of Middle East Studies*, *45*(2), 336–339.

Puar, J.K. 2007. *Terrorist Assemblages: Homonationalism in Queer Times*, Durham: Duke University Press.

Rainbow Migration R (2021) *Rainbow Migration's submission to the Women and Equalities Committee's Inquiry into equality and the UK asylum process*. Available at: https://www.rainbowmigration.org.uk/publications/rainbow-migrations-submission-to-the-women-and-equalities-committees-inquiry-into-equality-and-the-uk-asylum-process/ (Accessed 23/03/2022).

Rainbow Migration (2023) Risks to LGBTQI+ people in initial and contingency accommodation, December 2023. Available at: https://www.rainbowmigration.org.uk/wp-content/uploads/2024/01/Briefing-initial-and-contingency-accommodation.pdf (Accessed: 06/01/2024)

Rainbow Migration 2025. Written evidence from Rainbow Migration to the Home Affairs Select Committee inquiry into asylum accommodation (ASU0048). Available at: https://committees.parliament.uk/writtenevidence/114301/pdf/ (Accessed: 09/11/2025)

Ramachandran, C. 2024. The enforced destitution of asylum seekers in the UK, *Journal of Human Rights and Social Work*, *9*(1), 139–153.

Randall, A. 2015. Challenging the destitution policy: civil society organisations supporting destitute migrants. IRIS Working Paper Series 11. Available at: https://www.birmingham.ac.uk/documents/college-social-sciences/social-policy/iris/2015/working-paper-series/iris-wp-11-2015.pdf (Accessed: 21/08/2026)

Rehaag, S. 2009. Bisexuals need not apply: a comparative appraisal of refugee law and policy in Canada, the United States, and Australia, *The International Journal of Human Rights*, *13*(2–3), 415–436.

Rowlands, A. 2018. Temporality, dispossession and the search for the good: interpreting the book of Jeremiah with the Jesuit refugee service, *Political Theology: The Journal of Christian Socialism*, *19*(6), 517–536.

Rubin, G. 1984. Thinking Sex: Notes for a Radical Theory of the Politics of Sexuality. In H, Abelove, Barale, M.A, and Halperin, D. M, (eds) *The Lesbian and Gay Studies Reader*. New York, London: Routledge, pp 3–44.

Ryan-Flood, R. and Munt, S.R. 2021. Interview with Sally R Munt, sexualities journal, *Sexualities*, *24*(7), 957–971.

Saunders, B.J., Snyder, S. and Fiddian-Qasmiyeh, E. 2016. Introduction: articulating intersections at the global crossroads of religion and migration. In B.J. Saunders, E. Fiddian-Qasmiyeh and S. Snyder (eds) *Religion and Global Migrations*. Palgrave Macmillan, pp 1–46.

Savin-Williams, R.C. 2017. *Mostly Straight: Sexual Fluidity Among Men*, Cambridge, MA: Harvard University Press.

Scherer, B. 2017. Queerthinking religion: queering religious paradigms, *The Scholar and Feminist Online*, *14*(2).

Schlager, B. and Kundtz, D. 2007. *Ministry Among God's Queer Folk: LGBTQ Pastoral Care*, Cleveland: Pilgrim Press.

Shah, S. 2018. *The Making of a Gay Muslim: Religion, Sexuality and Identity in Malaysia and Britain*, London: Palgrave Macmillan.

Shah, S. 2020. Ethnicity, Gender and Class in the Experiences of Gay Muslims. In S.-J. Page and A.K.T. Yip (eds) *Intersecting Religion and Sexuality*. Leiden & Boston: Brill, pp. 23–44.

Shakhsari, S. 2014. The queer time of death: temporality, geopolitics, and refugee rights, *Sexualities*, *17*(8), 998–1015.

Shaw, A. and Verghese, N. 2022. *LGBTQI+ Refugees and Asylum Seekers: A Review of Research and Data Needs*. University of California, The Williams Institute. https://williamsinstitute.law.ucla.edu/wp-content/uploads/LGBTQI-Refugee-Review-Jul-2022.pdf (Accessed: 12/11/2025).

Shidlo, Ariel, (1994) 'Internalized homophobia: Conceptual and empirical issues in measurement' in Beverly A. Greene, and Gregory M. Herek, (eds.) *Lesbian and Gay Psychology: Theory, Research, and Clinical Applications*. Sage, pp. 176–205

Singer, S. 2021. How much of a lesbian are you? Experiences of LGBT asylum seekers in immigration detention in the UK. In M. Richard (eds) *Queer Migration and Asylum in Europe*, London: UCL Press, pp. 238–260.

Smellie, S., 2023. *Migration narratives in media and social media. The Case of the United Kingdom*. Available at: https://www.bridges-migration.eu/wp-content/uploads/2023/02/BRIDGES-Working-Papers-10_WP3-National-Report-UK.pdf (Accessed on 26/06/2026)

Snyder, S. 2011a. Encountering asylum seekers: an ethic of fear or faith? *Studies in Christian Ethics*, *24*(3), 350–366.

Snyder, S. 2011b. Un/settling angels: faith-based organizations and asylum-seeking in the UK, *Journal of Refugee Studies*, *24*(3), 565–585.

Snyder, S. 2012. *Asylum-Seeking, Migration and Church*, Surrey: Ashgate.

Spijkerboer, T.P. (2011). Fleeing homophobia. Asylum claims related to sexual orientation and gender identity in Europe. COC Nederland/Vrije Universiteit Amsterdam. Available at: https://research.vu.nl/ws/portalfiles/portal/2903587/Fleeing+Homophobia+report+EN.pdf

Squire, Vicki (2009) The Exclusionary Politics of Asylum. London: Palgrave Macmillan

Stanley, E. 2025. *Tolerating State Violence*, Taylor & Francis. Abingdon, Oxon, New York: Routledge.

Sullivan, N. 2003. *A Critical Introduction to Queer Theory*, New York: New York University Press.

Sveen, S., Anthun, K.S., Batt-Rawden, K.B., & Laila, T., 2022. Volunteering: a tool for social inclusion and promoting the well-being of refugees? A qualitative study, *Societies*, *13*(1), 12.

Swaminathan, R. and Mulvihill, T.M. 2017. *Critical Approaches to Questions in Qualitative Research*, New York: Routledge.

Tamale, S. 2011. Researching and theorising sexualities in Africa. In S. Tamale (ed) *African Sexualities: A Reader*. Oxford: Pambazuka Press, pp 11–36.

Tang, H. and Dempster, H. 2024. *Three Things to Know About LGBTQ+ Refugees This World Refugee Day*. Available at: https://www.cgdev.org/blog/three-things-know-about-lgbtq-refugees-world-refugee-day [Accessed 16 October 2025].

Taylor, D. 2023. Fears rise for LGBTQ asylum seekers over Home Office hotel room-sharing push. *The Guardian*. Available at: https://www.theguardian.com/uk-news/2023/dec/01/fears-mount-lgbtq-asylum-seekers-uk-ramp-up-hotel-room-sharing (Accessed: 04/11/2025).

Taylor, C. and Peter, T. 2011. "We Are Not Aliens, We're People, and We Have Rights." Canadian human rights discourse and high school climate for LGBTQ students, *The Canadian Review of Sociology*, *48*(3), 275–312.

Taylor, D. and Busby, M. 2019. Home office pays religious groups to help deport rough sleepers. *The Guardian*. Available at: https://www.theguardian.com/uk-news/2019/nov/05/home-office-pays-religious-groups-to-help-deport-rough-sleepers (Accessed 21/04/2022).

Thaut, L. C. (2009) The Role of Faith in Christian Faith-Based Humanitarian Agencies: Constructing the Taxonomy, *Voluntas: International Journal of Voluntary and Nonprofit Organisations*, 20 pp. 319–350.

The Asylum Seekers (Reception Conditions) Regulations 2005, SI 2005/7. Available at: https://www.legislation.gov.uk/uksi/2005/7/contents/made

Templeton, P. 2010–2019. *Global Religious Futures Project*. Available at: https://www.pewresearch.org/topic/religion/religious-demographics/pew-templeton-global-religious-futures-project/

Townsend, M. 2023. Shared rooms, rancid food, no clothes: new report lays bare shocking conditions of those seeking refuge in UK, *The Guardian*. Available at: https://www.theguardian.com/uk-news/2023/apr/22/shared-rooms-rancid-food-no-clothes-new-report-lays-bare-shocking-conditions-of-those-seeking-refuge-in-uk (Accessed: 21/08/2026).

Trust, H.D. 2025a. *Map of Countries that Criminalise LGBT People*. Available at: https://www.humandignitytrust.org/lgbt-the-law/map-of-criminalisation/ [Accessed 09 October].

Tschalaer, M. 2021. Victimhood and femininities in Black lesbian asylum cases in Germany, *Journal of Ethnic and Migration Studies*, *47*(15), 3531–3548.

UKLGIG. 2018. *Still falling short: The standard of Home Office decision-making in asylum claims based on sexual orientation and gender identity*. Available at: https://www.unhcr.org/publications/global-trends-2024 [Accessed 15 March 2019].

UK Lesbian & Gay Immigration Group (2010) *Failing the Grade: Home Office Initial Decisions on Lesbian and Gay Claims for Asylum*. London: UK Lesbian & Gay Immigration Group. Available at: https://www.rainbowmigration.org.uk/wp-content/uploads/2022/03/Falling-the-Grade-April-10_1.pdf (Accessed: 13/04/2023).

UNHCR. 2025. *Global Trends: Forced Displacement in 2024*. Available at: https://www.unhcr.org/publications/global-trends-2024 [Accessed 17 November 2025].

van Der Pijl, Y., Oude Breuil, B.C., Swetzer, L., Drymioti, M., & Goderie, M., 2018. "We Do Not Matter": transgender migrants/refugees in the Dutch asylum system, *Violence and Gender*, *5*(1), 1–11.

Walker-Said, C. 2022. Homophobia as public violence: politics, religion, identity and rights in the lives of lesbian, gay and bisexual asylum seekers from Cameroon. In B, Camminga and J, Marnell (eds) *Queer & Trans African mobilities: migration, asylum and diaspora*. London: Zed Books, 2022, pp, 115–132.

Walsh, P. W and Sumption, M (2024) *UK Policies to Deter People from Claiming Asylum*. Available at: https://migrationobservatory.ox.ac.uk/resources/commentaries/uk-policies-to-deter-people-from-claiming-asylum/ (Accessed: 21/08/2026)

Warner, M. 1993. *Fear of a Queer Planet: Queer Politics and Social Theory*, Minneapolis, London: University of Minnesota Press.

Weßels, Janna (2011) Sexual orientation in Refugee Status Determination Available at: https://www.rsc.ox.ac.uk/files/files-1/wp74-sexual-orientation-refugee-status-determination-2011.pdf

Wheeler, W. 2021. Conversion through destitution. In B. Meyer and P. van der Veer (eds) *Refugees and Religion: Ethnographic Studies of Global Trajectories*. London, New York, Ireland: Bloomsbury Academic, pp. 239–255.

Wheeler, W. 2024. *A Slow Violence: How Immigration Control Forces People in Greater Manchester into Destitution*. Available at: https://www.boaztrust.org.uk/pages/new-report-on-destitution-in-greater-manchester (Accessed: 21/08/2026)

Wilcox, M.M. 2009. *Queer Women and Religious Individualism*, Bloomington and Indianapolis: Indiana University Press.

Wilding, J. 2021. Beyond advice deserts: strategic ignorance and the lack of access to asylum legal advice, *Amicus Curiae*, *3*. Available at: https://doi.org/10.14296/ac.v3i3.5439 (Accessed: 21/08/2026).

Wilding, J. 2024. *Stemming the Tide: The Case for Demarketising the Legal Aid Sector*. Available at: https://ilpa.org.uk/stemming-the-tide-the-case-for-demarketising-the-legal-aid-sector/ [Accessed 2025].

Wilson, E.K. and Mavelli, L. 2017. The refugee crisis and religion: beyond conceptual and physical boundaries. In L Mavelli and E.K. Wilson (eds) *The Refugee Crisis and Religion: Secularism, Security and Hospitality in Question*. London, New York: Rowman & Littlefield, pp. 1–22.

Wimark, T. 2021. Housing policy with violent outcomes – the domestication of queer asylum seekers in a heteronormative society, *Journal of Ethnic and Migration Studies*, *47*(3), 703–722.

Yeo, C. 2022. *Welcome to Britain: Fixing Our Broken Immigration System*, London: Biteback Publishing.

Yip, A.K. 2016. Coming home from the wilderness: an overview of recent scholarly research on LGBTQI religiosity/spirituality in the West. In K. Browne, S. Munt and A.K.T. Yip (eds) *Queer Spiritual Spaces: Sexuality and Sacred Places*. London and New York: Routledge, pp. 51–66.

Yip, A.K.T. 2007. Sexual orientation discrimination in religious communities. In L. Badgett and J. Frank (eds) *Sexual Orientation Discrimination*. London, Routledge. Available at: https://doi.org/10.4324/9780203086650

Yip, A.K.-T. 2015. When religion meets sexuality: two tales of intersection. In P. Dickey Yong, H. Shipley and T.J. Trothen (eds) *Religion and Sexuality: Diversity and the Limits of Tolerance*. Vancover, Toronto: UBC Press, pp 119 – 137.

Yip, A.K. and Khalid, A. 2010. Looking for Allah: spiritual quests of queer Muslims. In K. Browne, S. Munt and A.K.T. Yip (eds) *Queer Spiritual Spaces: Sexuality and Sacred Places*. London and New York: Routledge, pp 81–109.

Yip, A.K.T. (2005) 'Queering religious texts: an exploration of British non-heterosexual Christians' and Muslims' strategy of constructing sexuality-affirming hermeneutics', *Sociology*, *39*(1): 47–65.

Young, P.D., Shipley, H. and Trothen, T.J. 2015. *Religion and Sexuality: Diversity and the Limits of Tolerance*, Vancouver: BC UBC Press.

Yuval-Davis, N., Wemyss, G. and Cassidy, K. 2019. *Bordering*, John Wiley & Sons. Cambridge: Polity Press.

Zaman, T. 2022. 'You Won't Find Religion Here': the (in)visibility of Muslim responses to situations of mass displacement, *The Muslim world (Hartford)*, *112*(1), 78–99.

Zeffman, H. and Francis, S. 2023. *Anti-gay Discrimination Not Qualification for Asylum, Says Suella Braverman*, BBC Politics. Available at: https://www.bbc.co.uk/news/uk-politics-66919416 (Accessed: 05/05/2024).

Zetter, R. 1991. Labelling refugees: forming and transforming a bureaucratic identity, *Journal of Refugee Studies*, *4*(1), 39–62.

Zetter, R. 2007. More labels, fewer refugees: remaking the refugee label in an era of globalization, *Journal of Refugee Studies*, *20*(2), 172–192.

Zetter, R., Griffiths, D. and Sigona, N. 2005. Social capital or social exclusion? The impact of asylum-seeker dispersal on UK refugee community organizations, *Community Development Journal*, *40*(2), 169–181.

www.ingramcontent.com/pod-product-compliance
Lightning Source LLC
LaVergne TN
LVHW020939031026
849429LV00029B/348